RUSSIAN LITERATURE
AND MODERN ENGLISH FICTION

GEMINI BOOKS
PATTERNS OF LITERARY CRITICISM

General Editors

MARSHALL McLUHAN
R. J. SCHOECK
ERNEST SIRLUCK

RUSSIAN LITERATURE AND MODERN ENGLISH FICTION

A Collection of Critical Essays

Edited and with an Introduction by
DONALD DAVIE

The University of Chicago Press
Chicago & London

Library of Congress Catalog Card Number: 65-18337

THE UNIVERSITY OF CHICAGO PRESS, CHICAGO & LONDON
The University of Toronto Press, Toronto 5, Canada

CONTENTS

CHEKHOV

GOGOL

INTRODUCTION

The first Russian novelist to make his mark with the reading public in Britain and America was Turgenev, the first translation of whose work appeared in 1855. This is not to be explained away by pointing out how Turgenev alone of the great Russian novelists visited England, and how during his long sojourns in France he was visited by English and American writers, notably the youthful Henry James. Nor is it enough to recognize how Turgenev, more than any other Russian writer, gratified and reassured Anglo-Saxon squeamishness by being "a realist" and yet for the most part steering clear of those forbidden subjects which, for many Victorian readers, ruled out of court French realists like Flaubert and, later, Zola. On the other hand, it is true that from the Crimean War through to about 1880 the British interest in Turgenev was not in any strict sense literary; when Turgenev was read in England at this time, it was for the information he could give about the state of the Russian peasantry or (a little later) about the psychology and activities of Russian terrorists and nihilists. In the United States, however, Turgenev's work was appreciated not only more warmly but also more keenly; and already in the 1870's, W. D. Howells was only the most prominent of several critics who pointed to Turgenev's novels as models of the sort of "realism" they were demanding of American writers. It was largely through Henry James that this current of opinion reached London, and the haughty refinement of James's temperament gave to the pro-Turgenev party a new flavor of fastidious exclusiveness which survived almost to the present day among admirers of Turgenev such as the late Charles Morgan.[1]

At the same time, Turgenev was the only Russian novelist who could be esteemed with any warmth by, for instance, the influential George Saintsbury, who scouted with weary urbanity the claims of any "realism" at all, and pinned his hopes for English fiction on the "romance" as practiced by Robert Louis Stevenson and Rider Haggard. Thus, from the 1880's onward,

[1] Charles Morgan, "Menander's Mirror," *Times Literary Supplement*, February 27, 1943. Reprinted in *Reflections in a Mirror* (London: Macmillan, 1944), pp. 165–73.

through a period when admirers of Turgenev felt themselves on the defensive in the face of the more sensational attractions of Dostoievsky and Tolstoy, there is an unlikely alliance between such fastidious and cosmopolitan minds as, on the one hand, Henry James and Joseph Conrad (who both refused to take Tolstoy or Dostoievsky seriously) and, on the other, readers of altogether coarser fiber who responded to Turgenev out of a taste which, in its self-conscious robustness, is defiantly insular. (It seems so even when, as in Saintsbury's case, it is backed up by wide and learned reading in the literatures of Western Europe.) It is in the person of George Moore that we see most clearly the alliance between lordly aestheticism in theory and the irresponsibility of the philistine.[2]

If Moore could say of Turgenev, "a sort of Jesus of Nazareth he was in art," Ford Madox Ford, almost as outrageously, declared (in *The Critical Attitude*, 1911), "Shakespeare, if he had taken time to think upon these matters, would have been as great an artist as Tourgenieff." Yet Ford was much more judicious and flexible than Moore, as well as more generous; and in the years before 1914, while he was editor of the *English Review*, he provided an invaluable link between the older writers, James and Conrad, and the young aspirants, first of the generation of Arnold Bennett and John Galsworthy (who both went through a phase of Turgenev-worship), and then of the later generation of Ezra Pound, D. H. Lawrence, and P. Wyndham Lewis. However, Ford and Conrad both believed that Turgenev, though immeasurably the finest of the Russian novelists, was wholly inimitable; and so Ford's influence, potent indeed on the finest talents, was to dissuade them very effectively from looking to any of the Russians for guidance in their own writing.

The first translation of Dostoievsky into English did not come until 1881: a version of *The House of the Dead* (*Zapiski iz Myertvogo Doma*), under the title *Buried Alive; Ten Years Penal in Siberia*. The book was presented as a piece of firsthand reportage. Dostoievsky, to evade censorship, had had

---

[2] Moore is not a straightforward case, for in *The Lake* he came as near as any novelist has done to writing in English a novel that is like Turgenev's. This has to do with its Irish theme, for there is a curious affinity between Turgenev and some Irish writers. Through Daniel Corkery, both Sean O'Faolain and Frank O'Connor learned to write on Turgenev's model.

to present the record of his Siberian experiences as if told to him by a third person, a fictitious character named Goryantchikoff. This device was lost on the sober English traveler who cited it among descriptions of Siberian life and thanked "Alexander Goryantchikoff" for his "life-like pictures."[3]

Dostoievsky's name was better known on the Continent, however. In 1885 rumors reached London of a German vogue for two novels called *Raskolnikov* and *Die Brüder Karamazov*, and even more important was a series of articles by E.-M. de Vogüé in the *Revue des Deux Mondes* for that year. These articles were incorporated in De Vogüé's *Le Roman Russe* of 1886, a book which was at once translated in America (Boston, 1886) but had to wait for a British translation until 1913. De Vogüé's book, enthusiastic, well-informed, and judicious, is a landmark, and the pages given to Dostoievsky are among the best. Some British readers, of course, knew De Vogüé's work in the French.

Meanwhile, an English version of *Crime and Punishment* had appeared. Robert Louis Stevenson, who read it in French, wrote in 1886 to a friend:

Raskolnikoff is easily the greatest book I have read in ten years; I am glad you took to it. Many find it dull: Henry James could not finish it: all I can say is, it nearly finished me. It was like having an illness.[4]

And Stevenson's *Markheim* is the best-authenticated example of an attempt to write a wholly Dostoievskyan novel in English. The English translation of *Crime and Punishment* got a good press, but for reasons that now seem irrelevant. Many reviewers were still naïvely looking in Dostoievsky, as they had in Turgenev, for factual information about Russian conditions; and whenever this was not the main focus of interest, controversy turned instead on whether Dostoievsky was a Russian Émile Zola. (De Vogüé had insisted that he was not, but Edmund Gosse still thought he was.)[5]

By 1900, the initial vogue for Dostoievsky was over, and

3 Henry Lansdell, *Through Siberia* (2d ed.; London: Sampson, Low & Co., 1882).

4 *The Letters of R. L. Stevenson*, ed. Sidney Colvin (4 vols.; London: Methuen, 1911), II, 274–75.

5 Edmund Gosse, *Questions at Issue* (London: Heinemann, 1893).

neither *The Possessed* nor *The Brothers Karamazov* had appeared in English. In 1908 the *Times Literary Supplement* could declare:

Before Gorki suddenly took the world by storm there were only three Russian writers whose books as well as their names were widely known beyond the frontiers of their own country—Tolstoi, Turgenev, and Dostoievski. There was a moment when the name of Dostoievski was the most popular of the three, and his celebrity overshadowed that of the others. The moment passed, however; the impression of commanding genius did not endure. . . .

This comfortable assurance that Dostoievsky had been tried and found wanting informs George Saintsbury's comments on him at this period. What reopened the case was Maurice Baring's *Landmarks in Russian Literature* (1910), a book of capital importance. Saintsbury had envisaged the enthusiast for Dostoievsky as similar to the first English Ibsenites, an intransigent modernist and iconoclast; but Baring was a scion of the British upper middle class, diplomat and classical scholar, author of witty and allusive *jeux d'esprit* as well as serious Shelleyan lyrics. And indeed it is hard to believe that the talented playboy of Dame Ethel Smyth's biography[6] should have commanded the moral fervor to write the chapter on Dostoievsky in *Landmarks of Russian Literature*. Much in Baring's attitude is derived from D. S. Merezhkovsky, whose reading of Dostoievsky had been available in English since 1902, though only as an appendix to his interpretation of Tolstoy; but Baring's discovery of "the Russian soul," of a spring of innate goodness and innocence in the untutored Russian mind, came in the first place from his own travels in Russia.[7] Gogol, Tolstoy, and Dostoievsky are in Baring's eyes counterparts of the Russian holy beggars who relinquished all worldly possessions to become "god-seekers"; and Dostoievsky is the greatest of the three because the most full of pity, attaining pity by self-sought humiliation, and seeking humiliation through self-sought sin. Baring is responsible for introducing some notions

[6] Dame Ethel Smyth, *Maurice Baring* (London: Heinemann, 1938).

[7] See "Moscow to Kharbin" in Baring's book of war-correspondent sketches, *With the Russians in Manchuria* (London: Methuen, 1905). And compare Stephen Graham's *With the Russian Pilgrims to Jerusalem* (London: Macmillan, 1913).

which are uncritical and have proved unhelpful. Such, for instance, is his notion of certain archetypal postures which the Russian personality automatically adopts. But the transparent sincerity of Baring's intentions, and even the very extravagance of his claims, removed Dostoievsky for ever from the niche of historical curiosity to which Saintsbury had wished to consign him.

Along with Constance Garnett's series of translations (1912–1920) came J. Middleton Murry's *Fyodor Dostoevsky* (1916), which retained the unmanageably perfervid tone of Maurice Baring (a tone which has never wholly disappeared from writing about Dostoievsky)[8] but emphasized the diabolical and Nietzschean elements in the writer, rather than the Christian. And although in recent years writing on Dostoievsky, as on other Russian authors, has more and more passed out of the hands of excited amateurs into those of professional Slavic scholars, the English-speaking public seems as far today as in the time of Maurice Baring from conceiving of Dostoievsky as an artist, working necessarily within conventions which may be determined, rather than as a prophet, a portent, or "a case." This may be why, throughout this period when Dostoievsky has been so often a subject of discussion in Britain and America, it is hard to find one British or American writer who, as literary artist, has learned from his art.

Oddly enough, though there is more excuse for this blurring of focus in Tolstoy's case (since Tolstoy wrote so many books which are overtly polemical or evangelizing), it has proved easier to isolate Tolstoy's art from his other preoccupations than in the case of Dostoievsky. All the same it has not been easy. If we except the translation of one early autobiographical work which was condemned in 1862 because it threatened the authority of a Victorian father on his own hearth,[9] and fifteen years later a translation of *The Cossacks* (New York, 1878), which got only slightly less condescending treatment from the reviewers, we find that Tolstoy was introduced to the English-speaking public (in that crucial decade of the 1880's when Dostoievsky similarly was first translated) by a

[8] Cf. J. C. Powys, *Dostoievsky* (London: John Lane, 1947), and Ivan Roe, *The Breath of Corruption* (London: Hutchinson, 1946).

[9] *Saturday Review*, March 29, 1862. See below in this volume, where the review is reprinted.

volume called *Christ's Christianity* (1885). This volume, which comprises the translations of two of Tolstoy's late confessional pamphlets, preceded in England any of the novels. And this is significant. The British public seems to have come to terms with Tolstoy quite easily to begin with, by seeing him as a Victorian sage and prophet, like Carlyle or Ruskin, and by regarding his novels only as the vehicle he chose to use for his evangelizing ends. The same assumption is present, in an only slightly more sophisticated guise, when we are invited to see in Tolstoy a conflict between the moralist and the artist, and to see in the notorious "conversion" of around 1880 the triumph of the moral zealot over the uncommitted artist. Neither D. H. Lawrence nor any of the English-speaking readers who approach Tolstoy in Lawrence's footsteps have taken account of what has been clear to Russian critics like Leontiev and Mirsky —the possibility of regarding the *volte-face* of 1880 as a radical change inside the artist, from one sort of art to another sort of *art*, and a matter of morality only to the extent that the choice of a form, for any serious artist, is necessarily the choice of one sort of moral vision rather than another. As Mirsky pointed out, Tolstoy's *Hajji Murad*, a very late work available in English though little known, is in most obvious respects a purer piece of literature, a tale told more exclusively just for the sake of the telling, than almost anything else Tolstoy wrote.

To mention *Hajji Murad* brings out one important way in which the English reception of Tolstoy necessarily differed from the reception of Turgenev or Dostoievsky. The English-speaking reader discovered Tolstoy, not when he was safely dead or even near to death, but when he had twenty unusually tumultuous and self-contradictory years yet to run—at a time when Tolstoy's own view of himself and his career was undergoing a drastic upheaval; when he was available at Yasnaya Polyana to be visited by variously earnest or impertinent travelers from Britain, the United States, and elsewhere; and in the period of the electric telegraph, which meant that he had to act out his private and domestic agonies under the glare of worldwide publicity.

It was in 1890, when W. T. Stead had secured from Tolstoy the right to serialize in his *Review of Reviews* the as yet unpublished *Kreutzer Sonata*, that Tolstoy began to act his private and intimate drama on this world-stage; and it was the publication of *The Kreutzer Sonata* (not in the *Review of Reviews,* for Stead was too shocked by the manuscript to print it, except fragmentarily) which brought about the first revulsion of feeling against the author of *What I Believe.* To be sure, even earlier there were doubtless those who sympathized with Maurice Thompson, when he wrote in the *Literary World* of Boston for July 23, 1887:

Tolstoi is a rich man who prefers to live in brutal vulgarity, a man who pretends to hate riches, but clings to all his cash; a heartless theorist, who pretends to believe that no evil should be forcibly resisted; who makes a pretence of shoe-making in order to attract attention to himself; who dresses like a clown for the same purpose, and who writes novels as dirty and obscene as the worst parts of Walt Whitman's 'Leaves of Grass.' . . .

But by and large the author of *Christ's Christianity* had with that book given such evidence of earnestly elevated purpose that readers of *War and Peace* (it appeared in three volumes, carelessly translated from the French, in 1886) felt safe in giving the novelist the benefit of any doubt. A reviewer in the *Guardian,* for instance, did not mean to dismiss or denigrate the novel when he found that "the whole is told with a sort of persistent weariness, an air of sarcastic unbelief in men and measures and causes, which seems to reflect the Nihilism of the author in every portion of his work."[10] This willingness to see "nihilism" in every aspect of Russian life and thought was characteristic of the period. But the "persistent weariness" and "air of sarcastic unbelief" come near to defining the tone of much of *War and Peace*—nearer, indeed, than any one was to come for nearly forty years. For in the interim we suffered, as we are suffering still, from interpretations which cannot afford to acknowledge this element in Tolstoy—from D. S. Merezhkovsky, for instance, whose brilliantly perceptive but one-sided view of Tolstoy is distorted by his determination to make Tolstoy and Dostoievsky antithetical; but still more from such critics as De Vogüé and Maurice Baring, who, weary and dissatisfied with the traditions of Western Europe, have in different ways and with more or less self-awareness looked in the Russians for some saving peasant wisdom of the Steppes.

[10] *Guardian,* February 16, 1886.

7

Whether Tolstoy was seen as the incarnation of such wisdom,[11] or as, compared with Dostoievsky, a partial and distorting channel for it, these assumptions obscured the extent to which Tolstoy the novelist is indeed a world-weary cosmopolitan, much influenced by the French rationalism of the Enlightenment. It was D. S. Mirsky, in his *History of Russian Literature* (1924) and his *Contemporary Russian Literature* (1926), who redressed this balance. Until this was done, neither novelists in English nor English-speaking readers could begin to distinguish the structural principles governing Tolstoy's novels and stories. They could see in them only what Henry James saw with distaste and Arnold Bennett, at one stage, saw with enthusiasm— something vast, capacious, cluttered with detail, undoubtedly lively, but all too untidily lifelike. And seen in that way, Tolstoy's fictions, whether they inspired enthusiasm or disgust, could not supply models for English or American novelists to follow.

It can be maintained that Russian writers have influenced writers of fiction in English, not in the sustained form of the novel, but in the short story. It is usual to cite Chekhov and Maupassant as the ancestors of the short story in modern English, and sometimes Gogol's name is invoked along with Chekhov's.[12] And it is difficult not to agree, when looking at the stories of Katherine Mansfield, that they would hardly be as they are if Chekhov's stories had never been translated.[13] As for Gogol, there is the special case of Vladimir Nabokov, a Russian émigré now writing in English. Nabokov has denied that his writing is specifically Gogolian, but his appreciative and brilliant book on Gogol[14] will reinforce the conviction of many readers that the cast of Nabokov's bizarre and ornate imagination is strikingly reminiscent of Gogol.

[11] Cf. the very title, *Leo Tolstoy: The Grand Mujik*, by G. H. Perris (London: T. Fisher Unwin, 1898).

[12] See, for instance, H. E. Bates, *The Modern Short Story: A Critical Survey* (London and New York: Nelson, 1941).

[13] Volumes of Chekhov's stories in translation appeared in 1903, 1908, and (three in one year) 1915. Constance Garnett's 13 volumes of the stories came out between 1916 and 1922. There are also two undated volumes of translations by A. E. Chamot.

[14] V. V. Nabokov, *Nikolai Gogol* (Norfolk, Conn.: New Directions, 1944). Unfortunately the book does not lend itself to being represented by excerpts; otherwise some of it would appear in this volume.

But in any case it would be absurd to deny that the Russian novelists have exerted a powerful influence on virtually every serious British and American prose writer in the twentieth century. This volume presents some evidence of this. For many reasons, however (some of them in the very nature of the case), this influence, excepting some freakish instances like Stevenson's *Markheim*, was never a *formal* influence. The truest way of regarding the history of Russian fiction in English translation, and the history of how English-speaking readers have reacted to Russian fiction, is as the story of a challenge presented to Anglo-American literary culture, and of the response made to that challenge. This story is unfinished: though the books about Russian authors are now more and more written by professors of slavic studies, there are still readers in Britain and America, mostly youthful, who experience the challenge and rise to it as best they can, much as R. L. Stevenson rose to the challenge of *Crime and Punishment*, or Henry James to the challenge of Turgenev's *On the Eve;* and some hundreds or thousands of miles away are Russian readers similarly discovering for the first time *Dombey and Son* and *David Copperfield*.

It would have been splendid if every piece reprinted in this book had been a little masterpiece in its own right, an example of how there is no method in literary criticism except the method that there is in a good poem or a good novel: that is to say, a laying-open of the self to experience without reservations, a total imaginative commitment. Some would claim that this is what we have in the pieces chosen from Thomas Mann and D. H. Lawrence. But my own view is that the only piece which deserves inclusion on these exalted grounds is Henry James's essay on Turgenev. Because of the quality of James's mind and the quality of the attention he gives to his subject, this essay requires less than any other in the book to be complemented and checked by further reading. At any rate this is true so long as the student wants to know the place of Turgenev's fiction in literature as a whole or in relation to other novels of Europe and America. For Turgenev's place in specifically *Russian* literature one must, of course, go to the work of minds which, though they are less distinguished, command specialized information such as James, who knew no Russian, could not have: for instance, to Avrahm Yarmolinsky's *Tur-*

genev. The Man, His Art, and His Age (1926, re-issued in 1960); to David Magarshack's *Turgenev. A Life* (1954); and Richard Freeborn's *Turgenev: The Novelist's Novelist* (1960). An important work which James could not have known is Turgenev's *Literary Reminiscences*, which was published in 1959 in a translation by David Magarshack, with an essay by Edmund Wilson. On the other hand, those who want to be guided further by Henry James toward a just appreciation of Turgenev will want to consult other writings by James on this subject, notably an early essay in which he gives an account of Turgenev in person as James knew him in Paris, and also "Daniel Deronda. A Conversation," in which James, seeking to do justice to one of his great British contemporaries, George Eliot, compares her work at certain points with Turgenev's. Some pages of Gilbert Phelps's *The Russian Novel in English Fiction* (1956) argue for reminiscences of specific novels by Turgenev in specific novels by James.

Ford Madox Ford was an intelligent and talented novelist and an influential critic. He is represented here, however, by something that is neither fiction nor criticism, but a memoir. And this memoir, "John Galsworthy," itself explains why I have had to go outside literary criticism for other pieces besides this one: the influence of Turgenev, as of the other Russian writers, was in England and America so far from being a *formal* influence, was something so much more diffused and pervasive, that only a capacious and casual form like the memoir can capture it. Ford's piece is much less casual than it seems; it is carefully written so as to give a casual effect. And this artistry in the writing is what made me choose it rather than, for instance, an excerpt from *The Craft of Fiction* (1921) by Percy Lubbock, or a chapter from Edward Garnett's pugnacious and historically important *Turgenev; A Study* (1917). This has meant treating of Turgenev's influence in England rather than in America; Turgenev's American influence has been admirably dealt with in R. A. Gettman's *Turgenev in England and America* (1941).

On Dostoievsky, a book which in some ways parallels Gettman's work on Turgenev, is Helen Muchnic's Smith College study of 1939, *Dostoievsky's English Reputation (1881–1936)*. The books written 40 or 50 years ago by excited amateurs such as J. Middleton Murry, who wrote of a Dostoievsky whom he knew only in English translation, have now only a curiosity value. This is true even of a writer as eminent and powerful as André Gide, whose *Dostoievsky* appeared in English translation in 1925, with an introduction by Arnold Bennett. Scholarly works, of which the first was É. H. Carr's *Dostoievsky* (1931), have superseded the pioneering works with a completeness that is not paralleled in the case of Tolstoy or other Russian authors. One main reason for this is the bulk of writing by Dostoievsky, and information about him, which has only recently been published for the first time, even in Russian. Because new material continues to appear, even such a scholarly work as E. J. Simmons' *Dostoievsky; The Making of a Novelist* (1940) cannot be regarded as definitive, or as much more than a thorough and dependable progress report. The one pioneering study influential in England which has more than just antiquarian interest is D. S. Merezhkovsky's essay on Dostoievsky, included in his *Tolstoi as Man and Artist*. Merezhkovsky (1865–1941) was a prolific writer who early achieved an international reputation with his historical novels (*Julian the Apostate*, or *Death of the Gods*, 1896; *Leonardo da Vinci*, 1901; *Peter and Alexis*, 1905; and others). These are not novels in any serious sense, but works of popularization; in their English versions they litter the shelves of secondhand bookstores, for Merezhkovsky has suffered the fate of most popularizers—his reputation died with the generation he wrote for. He is now a very unfashionable, indeed forgotten, writer; and so it is no more than just to represent in this collection his *Tolstoy and Dostoievsky*, for this was singled out by D. S. Mirsky as the one work by Merezhkovsky which deserves to be remembered.

D. S. Mirsky was a Russian émigré who worked and taught in London in the 1920's; he gradually became reconciled to the post-revolutionary regime in Russia, and in the 1930's returned to Moscow. There he was protected for a time by Maxim Gorky, but he vanished from sight at about the time of Gorky's death and his fate is unknown. Mirsky was the first, and is still the most brilliant, of all the professional and scholarly students of Russian literature in English-speaking countries. His *History of Russian Literature to the Death of Dostoievsky* (1924) and *Contemporary Russian Literature* (1926) are models of how literary history should be written: trenchant and incisive, yet catholic in taste; above all, magnificently ordered, with clarity and proportion. There is no history of English literature, whether in many volumes or few, which equals Mirsky's history of Russian literature as an ornament of the English language. Usefully conflated into one volume, in an abridgment by Francis J. Whitfield (*A History of Russian Literature* [1949]), Mirsky's work is the essential primer and reference book for those who study Russian literature in translation, as for those who study it in Russian. The essay by which he is represented here is a much less polished performance, and it takes a highly questionable minority view of its subject, Chekhov. But it has a hard-hitting urgency and verve which characterize Mirsky's writing. It should be supplemented by Ronald Hingley's *Chekhov; A Biographical and Critical Study* (1950), or David Magarshack's *Chekhov; A Life* (1952), as well as Magarshack's *Chekhov the Dramatist* (1952).

Tolstoy, from whatever direction we approach him, embarrasses us with riches. In each year that has passed since 1885, when Tolstoy's name first became known in England and America, distinguished people, social reformers, moralists, and theologians, no less than men of letters, have been trying to come to terms with Tolstoy, making up their minds about him and recording their opinions of him. Some of the most interesting of these occur incidentally, in their letters or records of their conversations. For instance, many of the most provocative and memorable of D. H. Lawrence's opinions about the Russian novelists are to be found in Lawrence's letters. The excerpts printed here show how Tolstoy came into Lawrence's mind continually, even when he was formally addressing himself to subjects as remote from Russia as Thomas Hardy or the Sicilian novelist, Giovanni Verga. Views exchanged in 1960, here reprinted from a British periodical, show how Lawrence's very personal interpretation of Tolstoy can be to some readers an aid, to others a stumbling-block, when they want to make up their minds about *Anna Karenina* in particular. Important landmarks in the assimilation of Tolstoy in the West are Romain Rolland's *Tolstoy*, translated into English by Bernard Miall in 1911; G. R. Noyes's *Tolstoy* (1919); Derrick Leon's *Tolstoy: His Life and Work* (1944); and E. J. Simmons' *Leo Tolstoy* (1946). Maxim Gorky's *Reminiscences of Tolstoy* first appeared in English in 1920. Detailed examinations of specific works by Tolstoy are hard to come by in English; *Tolstoy's "War and Peace." A Study* (1962), by R. F. Christian, stands almost alone.

Psychologists and psychoanalysts have investigated the personalities of Tolstoy and Dostoievsky in particular; Freud's essay "Dostoievsky and Parricide," which first appeared in German in 1928, is an especially important document. (It can be consulted in an English version in *The Realist*, Vol. I [1929], No. 4). Less satisfactory are books and articles which belong in a no-man's-land between literary criticism and depth-psychology, making disciplined use of neither. Gogol in particular has attracted attention of this dubious kind, and in English it is hard to find writings on this important author which are judicious and temperate, like Philip Rahv's essay printed here. V. V. Nabokov's *Gogol* (1947) is surely the most intelligent book on Gogol available in English; it is also highly idiosyncratic, and some think it wrongheaded. It may be supplemented by J. Lavrin's *Gogol* (1926).

NOTE: Transliteration of Russian names into English has yet to be successfully standardized. Accordingly, in preparing this volume, I have reproduced without emendation the Russian names as variously transliterated by different critics. Turgenev, for example, may appear as Tourguéneff, Turgénieff, or Tourguenieff.

The Resistance

I

Tolstoy's "Childhood and Youth"

"Whoever," says the translator of this work in the preface, "likes to come out into the fresh air of a fine day in spring, when all is fragrant, blooming, and promising, will enjoy reading this, the reflection of a youthful soul full of noble tendencies and earnest aspirations." Possibly it may be ignorance of Russian that makes the pleasure actually experienced fall short of the hopes held out, but certainly, so far as the translation goes, we much prefer the ordinary spring morning. Count Tolstoi does not come near it. Nor is it, as it appears to us, anything more than a figure of speech to say that this little volume reflects a youthful soul of noble tendencies and earnest aspirations. It is at the best a very thin narration of the early life of an affectionate and sensitive boy placed under such circumstances as must be very common in his class and country. To us in England it may be some little amusement to know how a Russian nobleman brings up his children, and this adds to the faint interest the book would otherwise excite. Count Tolstoi is also highly praised by the few Russians whose voices are heard in Western Europe, and we naturally wish to know what a creditable Russian is like. But the translator, although possessing a very fair command of the English language, knows very little of English tastes, or of the English standard of taste, when she announces to us that Count Tolstoi reveals himself to us as a poet and a philosopher. There is nothing to blame in the book. The incidents recorded are very trivial, and therefore, probably, true, and the whole production is insipid, unless we force an interest in it by reminding ourselves that it is improving to know how Russians write. But as a record of childhood it has its merits. It is not sickly or pretentious. Its merits are, however, mostly negative, and few compositions have less claim to philosophy. Perhaps, in the original, the lan-

From the *Saturday Review*, March 29, 1862. A review of *Childhood and Youth. A Tale*, by Count Nicola Tolstoi. (Translated from the Russian by Malwida von Meysenbug [London: Bell and Dalby, 1862].)

guage may be poetical, and there is an amiable tenderness of character shown in the childish history recorded, but that is the end of the poetry. The translator, as a matter of business, is quite right to try to make the public look through her spectacles at the book on which she has bestowed her labour. But not all the big sentiments that ever filled the biggest mind of a German translator can put poetry and philosophy in an original where they do not exist, and *Childhood and Youth* is at most a pleasing story of childhood, with the accidental advantage of teaching us a few foreign customs.

If a poet is to be poetical about his childhood at all, or a philosopher to philosophize about early affections, one would think it natural that the special subject to draw them out would be the tale of their first love. We take this instance, therefore, as a favourable one, and as calculated, if any, to produce on us the impression that we are gathering violets and primroses on a fine April morning. This is how the story is told. The author and his brother Woloda and his sister Lubotshka were playing together, and with them also played the heroine Katenka, aged thirteen. Lubotshka, during the game, tore away a leaf with a caterpillar on it, threw it with horror to the ground, lifted her hands, and "sprang aside as though afraid she would be splashed by it." Then the group examined the little beast on the ground, and began to torture it with the amiable ingenuity of childhood. Katenka tried to lift the caterpillar by means of another leaf, which she put in its way, and this brought on the crisis of the story. For the little girl, finding her clothes inclined to slip down, hoisted them up with her shoulder. Little Russians, however, are apparently cautioned against the process. "I remember that Mimi used to become angry at this manoeuvre, and to say it was a chambermaid's trick." Katenka, in spite of the warning, adopted the simple expedient, and thereby awoke young love in the breast of a poet.

Bending over the worm, Katenka now made this very movement, and, at the same instant, the wind lifted the handkerchief from her white neck. Her shoulder was just then close to my lips. I looked at it and kissed it. She did not turn round, and Woloda, without raising his head, said contemptuously,

"What tenderness!"

I felt the tears rushing to my eyes.

I could not turn my looks from Katenka. I had long been accustomed to her fresh, fair face, and had always loved her; but now I looked at her with increased attention and loved her still more dearly.

This is simple and natural. It is like the love of children—like their curiously sensitive and yet physical affection. If a man is to record at all how, when he was a little boy, he felt when looking at a caterpillar with a little girl, it is much better that he should tell us what really happened than that he should invent a faded counterpart of maturer love in order to make us think how forward he was. But at the same time nothing can be more bald than the manner in which the little incident is narrated. The odour of the fine spring morning we were promised does not seem to come particularly near it.

This is said to be a true history of Count Tolstoi's childhood, and the people introduced into it are real people. We are unable to say whether there is any disguise of names; but whether there is or not, it must be obvious to all Count Tolstoi's circle who is meant. As he is still a young man, most of those mentioned as companions of his childhood must be living. We are glad to find people in Russia are so patient, and can endure to hear plain unvarnished opinions on their physical and mental defects given to the world. We hope, for example, that the family of Prince Kornakoff is pleased with this May-morning effusion. In one part of the volume we meet with the following candid criticism:—"In the hall I found the Princess Kornakoff with a son and an almost incredible number of daughters. They had all the same face, just like the mother, and were very ugly; not one of them arrested my attention. Taking off their cloaks and boas, they talked at once with their voices, busying themselves, and laughing at something—probably that there were so many of them." These ladies must now peruse this flattering description of their young beauty with a lively wish that they had not met what then semed a harmless boy, but now proves to have been a poet and philosopher gushing as dewy May. The son does not come off much better. "Étienne was a boy of fifteen, tall, plump, with a meagre face, hollow bluish eyes, and for his age hideously large hands and feet. He was awkward, had a disagreeable and nervous voice, but seemed highly pleased with himself, and was, according to my ideas, just like what a boy would be who was habitually beaten with a rod." It is said that we should all be astonished if we could see ourselves as our friends see us, and now Étienne will have the pleasure of this surprise. No good-natured friend could be more candid. Nor is the account of Étienne's subsequent behaviour much more to his credit, although perhaps he did nothing more than every Russian boy is accustomed to do to his serfs. The most curious part of the narrative consists in the revelations it gives of the attitude assumed by Russians to their inferiors. It only needs a very little scratching for the Tartar to appear in this respect beneath the sham skin. At the same time the serfs are represented as venturing on a tone of familiarity mixed with cringing, which is not unlike the affectionate insolence of the model "nigger." Étienne had amused himself by making away with or losing Philip, the coachman's, whip, and so the footman was sent to ask where it was, and then the following dialogue ensued:—

"Your highness," said a footman, entering the hall, "Philip asks where you deigned to put the whip?"

"How, where I put it? I gave it to him."

"He says that you didn't."

"Well, I laid it on the lantern."

"Philip says you did not lay it on the lantern, and you had better say that you took it and tore it to pieces, and now Philip may answer for your pranks out of his own pocket," continued, in a more and more excited manner, the angry footman, who had the look of a serious and honest man, and seemed determined to sift the affair in defence of Philip.

From a feeling of delicacy I pretended not to remark anything, and turned aside, but the footmen present drew nearer and gazed with approbation at the old servant.

"Hem! well—I did tear it to pieces," replied Étienne, shrinking from farther explanation; "I shall pay him for the whip—that's ridiculous," added he, approaching me and drawing me towards the drawing-room.

"No, excuse me, sir, how will you pay for it? I know the manner in which you are wont to pay;—to Maria Walericana you have already owed twenty kopecks these eight months—to me also something for two years—to Peter—"

"Be silent! will you?" screamed the young prince, becoming pale with rage; "I shall tell all this."

"Tell all this, tell all this!" repeated the footman, "it is not fair, your highness," added he with a particular stress, whilst we entered the saloon, and he went with the ladies' wraps to the cloak-room.

"That's right," exclaimed some approving voice behind us in the hall.

This approving voice came from grandmamma, who thought it right to administer a sharp rebuke to the wayward young Étienne, and to do this effectually she freely availed herself of a secret art which she had at her command. "Grandmamma had a peculiar talent in employing, with a certain tone, in certain cases, the pronoun of the second person plural and singular, in such a manner as to express her opinion of people." This time, however, the engine of moral correction would not work. She let it off, but it did not hit. She addressed him with a "you" that, on principle, ought to have crushed him. "But Étienne was evidently not a boy of this sort of composition; he not only paid no attention to the reception of grandmamma, but none even to her person in general." It is the worst of those stupid strong boys with hollow bluish eyes and hideously large feet that they never know when they are sat upon.

Count Tolstoi seems to have been very fortunate in his mother, and her death was the great sorrow of his childhood. He relates, with his usual honesty, what passed in his mind at the time, and is easily able, with the experience of later life, to detect the insincerity which mingles so largely even with the sincerest grief of the young, and from which no grief is, perhaps, wholly exempt. That is, no grief, or scarcely any, is what in imagination we picture grief to be. It is liable to be distracted. Passing events demand a passing attention, and if a theory denies this, and an attempt is made to have a grief that is wholly absorbing, there is doubtless what may be called insincerity. There are, however, traits in the character of others which it is better not to analyse; and it appears to us by no means desirable that sons should publish to the world the short-comings they may perceive in the demeanor or conduct of their parents on solemn occasions. Count Tolstoi tells us that his father was, in his opinion, too theatrical on the occasion of his mother's funeral. The bereaved husband did all that was proper, and that Russian customs enjoined; but he rather overdid it. "Papa stood at the head of the coffin—he was white like snow, and only with an effort kept back his tears; his tall figure, in a black dress-coat, the pale expressive face, and, as usual, the graceful assured manners when he made the sign of the cross, inclined himself, touching the floor with his hand, took the candle from the hands of the priest, or went to the coffin— all was exceedingly effective: but I don't know why, I did not like in him the being capable of showing himself effective at this moment." In another passage he expresses himself more fully about his father, and tells us that, in spite of his being a model of deportment, he was addicted to many very serious weaknesses. We do not like this. It makes no difference whether a writer is a Russian, or a German, or an Englishman—whether he is or is not like a spring morning, or what may be his noble tendencies. He is not, we think, justified in telling his family history in this way, and in probing the failings of parents in order that he may have the satisfaction of sketching his own childhood. It is no excuse to say that, unless he puts in the dark shades, the picture cannot be truthful. There is no reason why he should draw the picture at all. The world can get on very well without criticisms written by a son on the behaviour of his father at his mother's funeral. It would destroy all family confidence if we were all of us liable to be sacrificed in this way to the exigencies of literary art; and if this is the style in which sons who are like spring mornings write, most fathers would devoutly wish their own offspring should be like autumn evenings.

II

GEORGE SAINTSBURY

Turgenev, Dostoievsky, and Tolstoy

The present writer has no hesitation in ranking Tourguenieff
as the greatest novelist of Russia, and almost her only one fit
to take a seat in the cabinet council of European novelists of
the nineteenth century. That he has been eclipsed by Dostoieffsky and Tolstoi, even by the mere grime-novel of Maxim
Gorky, does not matter at all. The passion for strange local
colour, for topsy-turvy sentiment, for extravagant Naturalism,
—together with some even less respectable forms of the sheer
silliness which seems, in the late nineteenth century, to have
succeeded the somewhat narrow wisdom of the eighteenth and
the extensive wiseacreishness of the earlier nineteenth itself,—
sufficiently account for this. But he has the qualities of the
artist in all but the very highest degree; and he applies them
to matter of quite sufficient interest. Take, for instance, what
is perhaps his capital work *Nov* (*Terres Vierges* or *Virgin Soil*).
The amateur of local colour, of local manners, must be a
glutton indeed if he is not satisfied with the amount of it here,
or in *Smoke*. But instead of this local stuff remaining crude
and undigested, as it does in so many books of the last half
century, it has undergone the universalising touch—the touch
which, if not quite Shakespearian, is of the family of Shakespeare.

Mark how completely Negdanoff, the Russian Hamlet, is
"succeeded," as wine-merchants say of a vintage; how the
artist has exactly hit off the mean between too little and too
much. Characters like Machourina and Marianne are much
more really explanatory of that singular Russian specialty, the
revolutionary girl, than, say, Mary Paulovna in Tolstoi's *Resurrection*, precisely because they are less photographic. And so

From *The Later Nineteenth Century* (London, 1907), Volume XII of
Periods of European Literature, edited by George Saintsbury. Reprinted
by permission of William Blackwood & Sons, Ltd.

of the minor characters, among whom "Fomouschka and Fimouschka" are simply triumphs. The way they turn the tables on their modern visitors is humorous to the sublime; in fact, enough in itself to disgust all those in whom the sense of humour is dead or dormant,—a sad but numerous band. In certain points—humour, perfect projection of character, and perhaps also a certain neglect of plot as plot—Tourguenieff reminds one of Thackeray, of course with numerous accompanying differences. His style is highly praised by those who can judge. Even Mérimée, a most competent and a very severe critic, could find no fault with Tourguenieff's writing, except that it occasionally abused the abundant but rather disorderly resources of the language. And the same infrequent but accomplished censor notes, as a specially Shakespearian touch in Tourguenieff, his extraction of "the soul of goodness in things evil," which is all the more remarkable in that Mérimée was not exactly a belauder of the sentimental. "Le soin que ces messieurs mettent à signaler les vilains côtés du monde où nous vivons" is most undoubtedly the main fault of Russian literature. Certainly Tourguenieff does not sin by undue optimism, but from this unhallowed *soin* he is free.

That the two remarkable writers to whom we now come are not free from it is clear enough to all; that their slavery is a cause of their popularity is clear enough to some. It is fair to say that neither of the two appears to have taken the least pleasure in these studies of the repulsive, but to have been driven to them by some curious overmastery of impulse. The lesser of them—Feodor Mikailovitch Dostoieffsky—was born, like Tourguenieff, in 1818, and, like him, published his first work (*Poor People*) in 1846. The very title speaks the tone and subject; but the author brought upon himself opportunities for even closer study of human misery. He engaged in some of the plots of the stormy period of '48, was arrested, tried, and condemned to twelve years' labour in the Siberian mines—seven of which he actually served, though he was released in 1856. He wrote a definite account of his experiences as prisoner soon afterwards; but the chief fruit of them was his famous masterpiece of *Crime and Punishment* (1868). He did a good many other things, and died in 1881, having latterly turned to a sort of Old-Russian patriotism, very excusably intolerant of the introduction of those Western ideas which have certainly done Russia very little good hitherto, and which in at least many cases appear to be totally unsuited to her. Dostoieffsky's general characteristics are somewhat narrow strength and depth, occupying themselves by preference on subjects unhappy, squalid, and altogether unbeautiful, but by no means rejoicing in moral grime. It will, therefore, necessarily appeal very differently to different temperaments. Those who follow the fashion will like it (or think, or say, that they like it), because it is eccentric from the older kinds of art; some may like it sympathetically, or dislike it from want of sympathy; while yet others may regard it as a curious "sport" of nature affected by time and circumstance, interesting in a way, certainly not horrible or disgusting, but unattractive, and "such as one could have done without."

The foremost instance of the necessity of dealing here with living persons is undoubtedly Count Leo Tolstoi. Actively as he is of the present in some ways, his age makes him a writer of the last generation; and he is also . . . the fourth of the quartette who have dominated European literature for the last quarter of a century.* About his biography we shall say little or nothing here, only noting that most of those who write about him (including himself) say a very great deal, and that there is something tell-tale in the fact. Hardly anybody can require to be told that Count Tolstoi, who was born in 1828, belongs to a family of unusual distinction in many ways. He was himself heir to large estates; fought in the Crimean war; wrote tales and sketches (partly autobiographical) very early; became a prominent novelist on a larger scale; went through (about 1878) a process of "conversion" to undogmatic and revolutionary religion, but to revolutionary politics of a non-resistance kind; and has since written freely in support of his convictions, both in and out of the novel form. The singularity of his career, the eccentricity of his principles, and the qualities of the works in which, first more or less covertly, then openly and deliberately, he has set them forth, have obtained him European—indeed, world-wide—notoriety; and he has, through his writings, probably influenced more writers and more readers than any other author except the three so often referred to in his company.

* These four, according to Saintsbury, are Ibsen, Zola, Nietzsche, and Tolstoy.—Editor's Note.

In the case of these (except as far as regards Nietzsche's unhappy affliction) it was not necessary to say anything about the men. It is one of the first important points about Count Tolstoi that, in his case, the man is much more prominent than the writer. One cannot say that his personality "obtrudes itself," because there is something offensive and ungentlemanly in the idea of obtrusion. Now, except on religious questions (where everybody except the very elect loses his balance, and where nobody is the elect to anybody but himself) it would be impossible for Count Tolstoi to be offensive. It is curious that he, leveller and, as it were, New Fifth Monarchy man as he is, is one of the finest and most absolute gentlemen in literature. This comes out in the most curious fashion when one compares him with his companions. For it would be impossible to perceive from the works of Ibsen and of Zola that they even knew what the word gentleman means; while, though Nietzsche certainly did, or could have done so, he chose to select for his admiration the Renaissance or Caesar-Borgian variety of gentleman—a variety which, on the whole, one prefers to leave in museums. It is needless to say that this gentlemanhood, though birth and breeding may have assisted its development, has nothing necessarily or exclusively to do with them. The Count is a gentleman as Lamb was and as Byron was not; just as he is a gentleman as Shelley was and as Hazlitt was not.

But he is a gentleman of most eccentric differences, and these differences show themselves in all his work. On the less strictly literary part of it we must not dwell long, but must say a little—the chief texts being *What Is Art?* and still more the invaluable collection of *Essays and Letters*, presenting comments on all sorts of things, contemporary and otherwise, during the last twenty years.[1] Here you may find explained with almost invariable *epieikeia*—the exceptions are, as just hinted, in religious parts, where the Count exposes himself a little to Lamb's rapier-question to Southey, "You never spoke disrespectfully of what *you* thought sacred, but how about what others think?"—how Count Tolstoi is of those who for-

[1] Translated by Aylmer Maude (London, 1903). Not much need be said as to his recent lucubrations on Shakespeare. They contain much to amuse, and nothing to surprise or shock.

bid to marry and command to abstain from meats; how he
mentions with ingenuous wonder that "many English men and
women, *for some reason or other*, are specially proud of using
a great deal of soap and pouring a large quantity of water over
themselves"; how he ejaculates in derisive horror, "Christianity (or virtue in general) *and beefsteaks!*"; how he is certain
that all bad things occur because people will imagine (*et
toi-même, M. le Comte?*) that "they know what is necessary
for mankind and the world"; how angry he is with Nietzsche
(who, you see, thought different things necessary for the
world); how prostitutes and madmen *all* smoke; what hard
things (in both senses hard, for they are hard to answer) he
has to say of science; how horrified he is at corporal punishment (one of the infallible marks of the crank); how, in the
original strict Godwinian, and therefore amiable, sense he is
an anarchist—quite certain that everything will go on charm-
ingly without any government, law, police at all. It is perhaps
not ill to read these things and so "focus" the author—find his
range—before reading the novels. For, though what are generally taken as the greatest of these were written before the
conversion, the drift of them is quite clear. And the most remarkable thing in the volume—the *Afterword to "The Kreutzer Sonata"*—contains, like most afterwords and postscripts,
the gist of the matter.

Count Tolstoi's work is extensive. As he says in his peculiar
way, "I write books, and therefore know all the evil they produce"; and the present writer is not acquainted with the whole
of it, even so far as it has been translated. But the early Cossack
stories, the two great novels of *War and Peace* and *Anna
Karenina, Ivan Ilyitch* and some other short stories, *The Kreutzer Sonata* itself and the long recent novel of *Resurrection*,
should give fair texts for judgment on those points that can
be judged from translation. One thing strikes us in all, as it
struck even a critic so favourably disposed as the late Mr.
Matthew Arnold,—that the novels are hardly works of art at
all. It is, however, pleaded for them that they are "pieces of
life"; and so perhaps they are, but in a strangely unlicked and
unfinished condition. One constantly finds touches, not of talent so much as of genius. But these touches are hardly ever
worked even into complete studies; while the studies, complete
or incomplete, are still less often worked into pictures. It is

almost startlingly exemplary and symptomatic, for instance, to find, in the early, vivid, but emphatically local studies of the Cossacks, that the best of all Olyenin's moods and manners is a study of Incompleteness itself. The greatest and most powerful thing, in the writer's humble judgment, that Tolstoi has ever done,—*Ivan Ilyitch*, that terrible and wonderful picture of the *affres* of death and the preliminary gloom of hopeless disease,—however marvellously observed and imagined, *has* to be incomplete, and so escapes the fault found elsewhere.

Again, Count Tolstoi owes nothing to deliberate Impressionism, yet he is the head malefactor of the Impression itself. Even Mr. Arnold himself gently complained of the irrelevances of *Anna Karenina*, and these are multiplied ten times in *Resurrection*. Yet more, there is in him, and in fact in most of the authors of these younger literatures . . . a singular particularist parochialism. They are so constantly absorbed in special things that they cannot bring them *sub specie aeternitatis*. They do not see, as their literary elders, by no merit of their own, have been brought to see, that things are merely parts of life,—that you must rise and "find the whole"; while of course in books like *Resurrection*, the purpose, the *tendenz*, entirely blinds them to proportion, art, and everything else. They seem—at least this greatest of them seems—to be constantly duped by single observations or sets of observations, just as they are by individual writers: not merely, in Tolstoi's case, serious if faulty thinkers like Herbert Spencer and Karl Marx, but mere blatant quacks like Henry George. So that the great war scenes of *War and Peace*, the sketches of society and the autobiographical study of Levine in *Anna Karenina*, the "crimes and punishments" of *Resurrection*, leave us—all of them, if not all of us—with a sense of the half-digested, the crude.

This crudity comes no doubt from more causes than one; but one of the causes from which it comes is very noteworthy. Soon after *The Kreutzer Sonata* became known among us, an English critic admiringly observed that when you compared *Tom Jones* with it you saw "what a simple toy-like structure had served Fielding for a human world." It was rather unlucky for this critic that Count Tolstoi very shortly afterwards explained, in the remarkable paper referred to above, to what the complexity of *The Kreutzer Sonata* was due. It was due (*habemus confitentem*) to the existence of a large number of

crotchets and fads, most, if not all, of which Fielding undoubtedly would not have admitted to his simple, toy-like
structure. And these crotchets group themselves round a central one—the doctrine that marriage, and love itself, are bad
things *per se*. There is no need, if there were room, to discuss
this crotchet here. But it cannot be improper to say, at the
end of a survey of European literature, that almost all the great
things in that, and in all literature most probably,—that an
enormous proportion of these things to a mathematical certainty,—have been dictated, directly or indirectly, by the inspiration of Love—physical Love in the end, though sublimated
more or less now and then. The man who denies himself this
inspiration is in effect a member of the sect, in Russia itself,
of whom most tolerably well-informed people must think
when they read some of Count Tolstoi's writings. He con-
demns himself to sterility and impotence.

This particular craze, though it had not developed itself explicitly at the time of the writing of *Anna Karenina*, explains
why the heroine of that book and the book itself, interesting
as they seem to be to some people, are almost absolutely uninteresting to others. Anna has no more real love for Wronsky
than for her husband; and her false love is infinitely less interesting than that of Emma Bovary, with whom Mr. Arnold
very rashly compares her, to her and her creator's advantage.
But we must not digress into particulars. The point is that a
man who sets his face, as Tolstoi does, against both Love and
War (though he had really utilised the latter in *War and
Peace*, and had tried to utilise the former in *Anna Karenina*),
deprives himself of the two great reagents, solvents, harmon-
ising and unifying *catholica* of his art. There remains Death,
and he has, as we saw, got a wonderful success out of that;
but even in days that like to deal with gloom and grime, Death
is not a card that you can play very often. He may by sheer
tours de force—and again in a time which likes *tours de force*—
utilise exceptional and minor motives to some extent. But he
cuts himself off from the real and principal things. Add to this
that Tolstoi, though not exactly destitute of humour,—he has
a few quaint and interesting touches of it,—possesses it in
nothing like the abounding and universal supply which makes
it almost a sufficient solvent or *menstruum* of itself. Add once
more that in him—as in all his three compeers—we never get

rid of the passing hour: and it will be of little need or use to say more. Ladies who are not prepared to wear their garments for a day and then to cast them to the winds or the waiting-maids, have a well-grounded objection to things that "date themselves"—that are *merely* fashionable. In literature nothing that is merely fit to be cast to the winds, and the readers in circulating libraries, is of any value at all; and here too the fact of "dating itself" too much is a serious drawback to any work. That there is much in Count Tolstoi which is not merely fashionable may be and has been freely granted. But there is a great deal too much that is. "What does it matter to me," Prince Prosperity will say, "that this was the way they crotcheted then? Art is long, and the crotchet, thank Heaven! is short. Give me Art and give me Nature, which is long likewise." Now, the Prince will not find very much art in the Count, and the nature which he *will* find is too often unnatural.

III

GEORGE MOORE

Turgenev and Tolstoy

One morning, while thinking of Tourguéneff, my thoughts were interrupted by the galloping of a horse. A runaway, I cried; and for no traceable reason, fell to wondering if the cab were bringing me a Russian visitor. Sir, a gentleman wishes to see you. What is his name? I can't pronounce it, sir; it's a foreign name; but it ends in off. And while my visitor was leaving his hat and coat in the ante-room I waited, asking myself who this friend of Tourguéneff's might be. I'm afraid my servant's pronunciation of Russian names is defective; I did not catch—He mentioned his name, and I knew him to be one of Tolstoy's critics, and one of Tourguéneff's translators. I've come, he said, to ask if you will give me an interview, and if you will tell me what you think of—Tourguéneff? I interrupted. No; to ask you to tell me what you think of Tolstoy's latest declaration regarding art and the objects of art, he replied. Would your purpose not be equally well suited if I were to tell you what I thought of Tourguéneff's article on Don Quixote and Hamlet? All you say would be interesting, no doubt, he answered, on that or any other subject, but you see I am collecting the opinions of writers, painters and musicians regarding Tolstoy's latest declarations. You have read the book, *What is Art?*

Of the book I knew nothing but the name, but I continued to talk about Tolstoy, hoping all the while that the conversation would turn on Tourguéneff. A literary conversation cannot dispense with him, and, having known Tourguéneff, my visitor would doubtless tell me, sooner or later, about the packet of love letters that had been discovered lately—love letters addressed to Madame Viardot. But it was hard to lead

From *Avowals* by George Moore (London, 1919). Chapters V and VI. Reprinted by permission of Field Roscoe & Company.

him away from Tolstoy. He would not be enticed away. He began again and again!

Tolstoy's argument is, that if a man infects another with a feeling that he has experienced, he has produced a work of art. And he concludes, no doubt, I chimed in, that the best art is the art that communicates the best ideas, the best ideas being, of course, Tolstoy's ideas. My visitor protested, but I would not hear any further explanation. If you'll allow me, I'd prefer to speak of Tolstoy's novels. Do you admire them? he asked, and on my telling him that I did, he begged me to say why I admired them, and within three minutes my conversation was indistinguishable from what one reads in the newspapers. I'm afraid you've heard all I'm saying before? And his manner signified that he had. I daresay you have, I continued, for I'm not saying what I really think. I admire Tolstoy; but if I only dared—I beg of you, he interrupted. Well, I continued, Gautier used to boast that the visible world was visible to him, but to no one was it ever so visible as it is to Tolstoy. His eyesight exceeds all eyesight before or since. At this point I paused, and my visitor and I sat looking at each other, myself very much abashed. Pray go on, said he, for I am wondering if your conclusion will be the same as Tourguéneff's. He once spoke to me in much the same way. Now you frighten me, and I can say no more until you tell me what Tourguéneff said. I will not tell you what Tourguéneff said until you conclude. What is your conclusion? That Tolstoy is not a great psychologist, I answered tremblingly, for when he comes to speak of the soul he is no longer certain; he doesn't know. But I'm saying something that no one will agree with, that no one has ever said. You're repeating what Tourguéneff said, my visitor answered. He used nearly the same words in speaking of Tolstoy. Is that so? Is that really so? You've no idea what a pleasure it is to me to hear that on the subject of Tolstoy's genius Tourguéneff and I—would you mind repeating what you have just said? Is it really true that—?

He assured me that it was true, and in the course of conversation I learnt much about the love letters and the suppressions that were made in them; a passage was deleted in which Tourguéneff expressed a wish he were the carpet under her feet, for Madame Viardot was afraid that it might lead readers to think she had been Tourguéneff's mistress. But of course she was, and to her very great honour, I cried. Why else should we be talking about her? Tell me more, my visitor, and my visitor told me he had made all the suppressions she asked, but had deposited the complete manuscript in the Bibliothèque Nationale. I obtained her consent to the publication only by assuring her that if she did not give it, the story of her friendship with Tourguéneff would be lost for ever for her grandchildren would certainly oppose the publication. She wished for the honour of his bed, but would like the *i*'s to remain undotted. Just so, my visitor answered, and the conflict in her mind was plain in her face. I could have gone on talking for hours about her, but my interviewer pressed me for information regarding Tolstoy's popularity in England, and it seemed shameful that my part of the conversation should be limited to such matters as that it was the late Mr. Vizetelly who had introduced Tolstoy to the English public, and that the translation he had issued was a revised version of an American translation. We talked of the difficulties of translation, and I learnt that Tourguéneff had always been fortunate in the matter of translation. His *Liza* had been excellently well done into English by Mr. R. S. Ralston, and from a copy that Tourguéneff had specially revised for the purpose, and then, catching enthusiasm from the theme, I told him that it was not the poverty of the translation that stood between Tourguéneff and popular appreciation in England but the noble simplicity of his stories. However deep the water may be, I said, the public cries: It is but a shallow if the water be clear. We must stir up the mud to deceive the public. I told him that Mr. Vizetelly also published *Crime and Punishment*, and we fell to criticising the critics. The critics were awed by the length of the Russian novel. *Crime and Punishment* is no longer than any modern English novel, and *War and Peace* is the longest novel ever written if we except *Les Misérables*. But the larger part of *Les Misérables* is history. True that there is some history in *War and Peace*, but Napoleon's battles are not so plainly extraneous, so independent of the characters in the novel, as Victor Hugo's rhetorical descriptions of Waterloo.

The conversation paused, and fearing that my visitor would leave me, I began to argue that Tolstoy's realism and ethics were the cause of his popularity. A popular novel is a compound of amusement and admonition, and the most popular are those in which clowning is sandwiched with preaching; a sudden somersault or a crude exhortation will draw a crowd. But few care to listen to the poet. Verlaine and Tourguéneff only gathered few disciples during the term of their natural lives, but henceforth they will find disciples in every generation; in a hundred years many more will have listened to them than ever listened to the clown or the preacher. In time the greater writer is read by the greater number. Beautiful rhythms acquire more subtle enchantments as the years go by, whereas the coarser rhythms of the preacher and the clown interest only a single generation—not always even so long; the preacher and the clown often live to see their followers leave them, attracted by new doctrines and new somersaults. So did I talk. In the presence of an interviewer we remember all our aphorisms and serve them up again to convince him of our great wit and wisdom; and an answer I once made the late Mr. Henley was brought in cleverly as a sort of Parthian shaft. Mr. Henley had once said to me: Tolstoy could wear Tourguéneff on his watch-chain, and I answered: The trinket on the watch-chain is often more valuable than the chain. But my visitor was not brought to bay as I expected he would be, and I allowed him to leave, promising, however, to meet him in Paris. Meanwhile I would read *What is Art?* He had said he would not be sending his copy to the printer before the end of the month, and immediately after I heard the sound of galloping hooves and began to think that perhaps my visitor had come in a droshky; and so real was the belief that I did not dare to look out of the window lest I should be disappointed.

The fire was burning brightly, and there were many things to think about: the delicious flattery that my thoughts had once moved along the same plane as Tourguéneff's, the love letters, and then Tolstoy himself, who, after all, was worth while thinking about. And now or never was the time come to say vital things about Tolstoy, things worthy of myself, things surpassing anything Henley could have said, and so I fell to thinking, saying to myself: in the nineties we were all cowed by the spell of realism, external realism, myself less than Henley, for in me there had always been misgivings, even Tourguéneff's praise of Tolstoy failing to convince me. And I pondered that, however deep the spell he casts upon us, the sensation he communicates is a harsh one, even ugly. His breath is a blast from the north but Tourguéneff breathes like the south wind always; even on his death-bed he could write to Tolstoy:

Dearest Lyof Nikolaievitch,—It is long since I wrote to you. I have been in bed, and it is my death-bed. I cannot get well; that is no longer to be thought of. I write to you expressly to assure you how happy I have been to be your contemporary, and to present to you a last, a most urgent request. Dear friend, come back to literary work! This gift came to you whence all gifts come to us. Ah! how happy should I be if I could think that you would listen to my request. My friend, great writer of our land of Russia, grant me this request.

The letter is extraordinary—even in this somewhat frigid, somewhat partial translation—the French translation contains more lines than this one, but I cannot lay hands on it at this moment, but I remember that Tourguéneff says, in a last sentence, that he can write no more. The letter was unfinished, but it betrayed, it is true, a hope that in health he would not have indulged in, that Tolstoy might change his destiny, which, notwithstanding many marvellous gifts, was clearly set in the direction of morals and doctrinal inquiry. For knowing human life to be a sordid story, he knocked at a Jewish door; or shall I say, at a Syrian Greek door, whereas Tourguéneff's more sensuous temperament allowed him to see life beautiful: and whosoever would do this must stint himself of everything but exhibition, for though the artist may teach, it must be indirectly; only with beautiful images and ideas may he draw men's minds from baser things. For man is made of many needs, I murmured to myself, and one of these is beauty, but Tolstoy looks upon art as a means whereby we communicate our ideas. My visitor admitted that Tolstoy repudiates beauty. But it is impossible to write the simplest sentence without some rudimentary sense of rhythm. Rhythm is beauty. His ugly temperament intervenes between him and his intelligence. That is it, I said, throwing myself back in my arm-chair in my low-ceilinged room so that I might meditate better. The beauty, I said, that I recognize in *War and Peace* is the vast architecture, the number of characters all going hither and thither, each on an errand big or little, the multiplicity of events, all perfectly controlled by one central purpose. *War and Peace* may be compared to the canvases of Tintoretto and Veronese, I muttered, and a moment after, the accidental phrase—his temperament is an ugly one—led me to consider *War and Peace* from a different point of view, and I said to myself: No comparison between Tolstoy and the great pagans of the sixteenth century is valid, for their temperaments were not ugly as their palettes tell us, but if we forget the design of *War and Peace*, and consider Tolstoy's palette, we find upon it very little else but black and white. It is true that Rembrandt's portrait of his wife, the one that hangs in the Louvre, is but bitumen and white faintly tinted with bitumen, a little rose madder showing in the cheeks. But no comparison between Rembrandt's palette and Tolstoy's is possible. There is nothing on the Russian's but a thin grey, and it might be truer to compare his designs to Kaulbach's than to Tintoretto's. But to be just we will admit without equivocation that his drawing is far in advance of Kaulbach's; it is that, but, all the same, it lacks what is known in the studios as quality; the quality of the original should transpire in the translation to some extent, and if we have to think of him as a painter I must think of him as a designer of vast cartoons moral as Kaulbach's, with, say, here and there such a well-observed piece of drawing as we meet with in Sir John Millais in his Pre-Raphaelite days. In these early days Millais was always beautiful. I am afraid these comparisons are not very happy, and yet—

However, the first two volumes are filled with pictures—that is to say, scenes taken from life, if I may be permitted to use an expressive colloquialism; and in reading them the reader must be a very casual reader indeed if he fail to ask himself if it were Tolstoy's intention to transcribe the whole of life. His intention seems certainly to have been to include all the different scenes that come to pass in civilised life, and no doubt he ran them over in his mind, for a scene of ladies in a drawing-room taking tea is followed by a scene in a ballroom with ladies dancing, and this is followed by a scene in a barrack-room with a quarrel among the officers. Scene after scene! the first volume of *War and Peace* reminding us of a picture gallery of second-rate Dutch pictures, for there are sledging, skating and hunting scenes, and every scene is described by an eye that sees clearly, and after some twenty or thirty scenes executed in the dry and angular manner of Meissonier we begin to long for chapters in which there are no pictures. We turn the pages; but alas, there are more pictures, and curiosity taking the place of the pleasure of art, we ask ourselves how it was that Tolstoy forgot to include a description of a yacht race. The book is long, but even if it were three times as long many scenes would remain unrecorded, and we can imagine Tolstoy waking up in the middle of the night regretting that he had not included a yacht race, and another night awaking, screaming: I forgot High Mass, and sinking back on his pillow trying to find consolation in the thought that he had described many religious ceremonies, with the same minuteness as a traveller would the religious rites of a newly discovered people. For no writer ever tried harder to compete with Nature than Tolstoy. Yet he was a clever man, and must have known that he would be defeated in the end; but he is one of those men to whom everything is plain and explicit except the obvious, and *War and Peace* is so plainly the work of a man with a bee in his bonnet that, despite the talent manifested in every description, we cannot help comparing him to a swimmer in a canal challenging a train going by to a race. The reader is at first interested and then amused, but before the end of the second volume he wearies of the absurd competition and lays down the book, and will never take it up again unless mayhap somebody tells him of the scene in which Prince Andrei lies wounded on the battle-field, looking at the stars. That is how it came to pass that I picked up the book, and while seeking out the scene of Prince Andrei's death I read the whole of the battle of Borodino, marvelling greatly at the ceaseless invention with which Tolstoy takes Pierre from one regiment to another, from tent to tent, showing us what is happening at every part of the immense battle, explaining the different plans of the Russian generals. Now the battle of Borodino is as interesting as a newspaper, as casual life is, but Prince Andrei's death is external life, and we do not come upon life again in any but external aspects till Pierre is taken prisoner and forced to follow the French army from Moscow. He meets a peasant philosopher on the way who has a little pink puppy (the puppy generally runs on three legs), and it is during the retreat from Moscow that we begin to understand that the hero of the book is Destiny. For everybody in the book sets out to do something, and everybody does something, but no one does what he set out to do; and we marvelled greatly how Tolstoy could have described all the things he described in the first volume without once communicating the idea that must have been at the back of his mind. He gathers up his threads in the fourth volume very neatly: Natasha abandons her sensuous, frivolous girlhood, and becomes extraordinarily interested in her babies, even in their disgusting little ailments; we assist at the sinking into old age of the generation we knew in middle age in the first volume; we catch sight of the young people whom we knew in the first volume dropping into middle age, and though some years have gone by since I read the book, I still remember Natasha's brother standing on the balcony watching the small rain that the thirsting oats are drinking up greedily, thinking that he must be, after all, no more than a commonplace man who married an ugly princess.

Pierre too has lost some of his illusions, but not all: he still goes up to St. Petersburg to attend spiritualistic *séances*, but now he is only faintly interested in spiritual things, and for this knowledge of himself and that life will know no further change for him, we must look upon Pierre as Tolstoy's one creation, if he be a creation. But what do we mean by a creation? Let the word pass; for what we have to decide is if Pierre be an entity in the sense that Bazaroff, or Insarov, or the would-be Nihilist in *Virgin Soil* are entities; if his foolish humanity can be compared with Bazaroff's pessimism; and if Natasha's interest in her children's ailments expresses life as intensely as Rudin's in the story that bears his name, or Helen's courage in *On the Eve*.

When we see the volumes of *War and Peace* on the table, they seem to us as long as life itself, and we go on reading them as we go on living, and we remember them but very little. As soon as we lay the books aside Tolstoy's characters begin to recede, and distance reveals the barrenness of the ways that we walked in, but the very contrary seems to me to be true about Tourguéneff. It is true that the very size of his books prevents us from believing them to be great books; they seem merely pretty stories, somewhat slight, and it is not until long after-

wards that their beauty appears, distance lifting Liza, Lavret-
sky and Helen out of the circumstances in which Tourguéneff
places them. And not for many years after do we begin to
recognise them as typical of all that the heart ponders and
remembers; the difference between the men is immense. Tolstoy is lord over what is actual and passing; he can tell better
than anybody how the snipe rise out of the marsh, and the feelings of a young man as he looks at a young girl and desires her,
but his mind rarely reaches a clear conception of a human soul
as a distinct entity; his knowledge of the soul, except in the
case of Pierre, is relative and episodic. And the house he built
reminds one somewhat of a palatial hotel where everything is
supplied except beauty. All kinds of different people are met
with in the passages. There is a central hall with dinner-parties
going up the staircase; the building is lit with electric light;
there are bands and winter gardens. Tolstoy's book is terribly
nineteenth century, but Tourguéneff's *House of Gentlefolk* is
much older; as soon as it comes into view we feel that it is part
of the landscape, so long has it stood there. It seems as if it had
always been inhabited by the same people; generations of the
same family must have lived in it, and these have given the
house its character. It contains but a dozen or fifteen rooms,
twenty at most, but every room bears the trace of him or her
who lived in it. A watercolour drawing of an old-time mill tells
the story of somebody gone; a collection of shells tells another
story; the furniture was not all brought together at one time;
the house breathes the story of the four or five people who sit
in its rooms and walk in its garden. There is no sense of home
in Tolstoy; he is mainly engaged in telling the stories of the
visitors who go up and down the staircase and gather to hear
the band in the winter gardens. The country house has its own
story; the hotel furnishes no commanding story, only episodes.

Helen, in *On the Eve*, goes out to life with both hands open
to grasp it; but what she grasps are the hands of a consumptive
man. I do not know, and no one will ever know, if Tourguéneff intended to contrast Liza, who shrinks from life, daring
hardly a glance, with Helen, who grasps life so eagerly and
passionately that life extinguishes in her grasp. A writer is not
conscious of the whole of his idea, some part of it exists only in
his subconsciousness; but Tourguéneff was a subtle thinker, and
though the idea is only indicated, and will not be perceived by

the casual reader, yet it is difficult to feel sure he was not aware of it. If he were not aware of it, Insarov was consumptive merely because Tourguéneff wished a tragic end to his love story—an unpinning of plot that few will deem consistent with Tourguéneff's genius; and if the alternative be accepted, it will be allowed that no writer has woven so delicate a thread into his woof of story, not since the Greeks certainly. And our thoughts striking at random we are tempted to think that *On the Eve* is a last effort of Greek genius risen after centuries in the Crimea. Did not whisper once reach me that Tourguéneff came from the Crimea, once a Greek colony?

It has been admitted, it is true with some reservations, that *War and Peace* reminds us of the great canvases of Tintoretto and Veronese, but let it not be forgotten that the minds of the great Venetian artists were unburdened with any idea but beauty, and that we followed Napoleon's army from Moscow to the frontiers of Russia, learning the great plains of Russia as from a map, a wonderful vision, or, shall we say, a seeing but with no story in it, for no one has suffered in his heart and no one has dreamed, which brings us to an important point, that Tolstoy was not a natural tale-teller. He might have been, or anything else in literature had he chosen, so extraordinary were his gifts. But his object was to rid himself of all sense of beauty, to crush it out of his heart; his whole life was a long preaching against beauty; beauty was the original sin and he hated it with the hatred of the ancient Jew. He reviled it, he spurned it, he spat upon it. He cried from the steppes: let it be burned up like stubble. A veritable Jeremiah of the steppes whose hatred of beauty can only be explained by the supposition of some recrudescence of the Jew in him. A mere fancy this suggestion is, but no better proof of any sort can I put forward in support of it but his art. Art, like the microscope, reveals many things that the naked eye does not see, and Tolstoy's art is as cosmopolitan as the art of the modern Jew. If we consider it we notice at once that it lacks original form, recalling in many ways English and French fiction. The composition of *Anna Karenina* seems to be derived from the English novel, and its realism suggests a French source; just as we have a family divided into four parts in *Vanity Fair*, we have a family divided into four parts in *Anna Karenina*, and the different threads are picked up in the fourth volume in much the same way, and the descriptive writing in this novel and in the novel that preceded it, *War and Peace*, recalls the realism of Flaubert. *Madame Bovary* was published in '57. *War and Peace* was published in '60. Most of it must have been written in '57, which destroys any theory that can be put forward of Tolstoy's indebtedness to the Frenchman. All the same there is much that recalls Flaubert, and though we prefer Tolstoy's writings to Flaubert, it would seem to us, if we did not know the dates, that Tolstoy had gotten a hint from Flaubert. But to set aside the possibility of this we must perforce fall back upon Balzac as having suggested the realism of both Tolstoy and Flaubert, a suggestion that does not seem to me very valid, but I cannot put forward anything better today, and am perplexed by the numerous and implicated sources of Tolstoy's art. The nearest thing to truth that can be said about it is that it arose in the middle of the nineteenth century in Western Europe, and represents in art the scientific ideas of Taine, Herbert Spencer and Darwin. With this difference, however, that Tolstoy was unwilling to believe that when he wrote *War and Peace* man's origin was merely the survival of the fittest. He was, however, impressed by the notion that if you would understand the insect, you must understand the leaf upon which the insect lives. It was out of such scientific beliefs that the elaborate descriptions of *Madame Bovary* arose, and it is hard for me to believe that they were not shared by Tolstoy, for how else can we account for the fact that his realism so often reminds us of a lady dressed in the French fashion for 1870 going out for a walk on the steppes? We can, however, regard *War and Peace* with kinder eyes, discovering in it the realism of children—the realism of the early Italian painters who stop at the wayside to tease a beetle, to investigate a bush. We may do this, for it would not surprise me at least if some part of its realism is a folk inheritance; it would be strange if the element of folk did not exist in the work of a *muzhik* who had read Western literature and science; and it may be that incidentally we are on the trail of a new idea, that art is always rising out of folk-lore—the romantic spirit, and that classic art is a shedding of the folk-lore element, for whereas Flaubert described Madame Bovary's house because she lived there always, Tolstoy described an inn through which some travellers pass, telling, among many other things, the number of freckles on the nose of the servant girl who brings in the samovar. Yes; his realism is as irrelevant as that of the painter Pinturicchio, who introduced quails picking grain about the embowered throne of the virgin surrounded by saints and angels.

Argument as to what is romantic and what is classical art has filled the reviews for a century or more, without the difficulty showing any signs of clearing up. But it has come to seem to me that if we were to substitute the words folk and culture for the words romantic and classical we should be in the straight way towards apprehending what is really meant by the words classical and romantic. Art begins in the irresponsible imaginations of the people, like a spring in a mountain waste; the spring rises amid rocks, trickles and forms a rivulet, swells into a stream, and after many wanderings, perhaps after a brief sojourn in artificial ponds and basins, it returns to the earth whence it came. And if this be the natural history of art, Homer is art emerging out of folk, and Sophocles is art at the extreme point of culture—the point at which art must begin to decay. In Shakespeare we find culture and folk side by side; and sometimes, as in *Hamlet*, we assist at the shearing away of the folk element from the tale. *As You Like It* is folk in substance; the various dukes and the forest denizens are pure folk; but the writing is culture. To pass from literature to painting, we stop before Pinturicchio, who seems to us a very tale-teller among people emerging from the religious gloom of the Middle Ages; we might almost call him the pavement artist of an artistic period; we find him in the midst of religious processions, in narrow Gothic streets, always delightfully spontaneous, telling tales of saints and miracles, and always heedless of culture—that is to say, of proportions and anatomies. Culture enters in the person of Botticelli; he represents it in its first stage and Raphael represents it in its last, just before art began to slip into decadence.

Perhaps better than literature or painting, architecture will enable me to show how art is always rising out of folk and descending into culture. The Irish Romanesque chapels are examples of pure folk, and the Gothic cathedrals are examples of pure culture, but while the architecture of Chartres is pure culture, the sculpture on its walls is folk. The argument might be prolonged almost indefinitely, but it is germane to the explanation of Tolstoy's realism, that while in Italy, art progressed gradually from folk into culture—we note every change, its beautiful progression from Pinturicchio to Michelangelo, how it paused, how Raphael marked the pause, and how it declined from Raphael to the Carracci, whereas in Russia, owing, perhaps, to the rapid transmission of ideas by means of newspapers and railways, we find art, folk and culture in the same parcel—Tourguéneff a Greek lost in a trance of beauty, and Tolstoy a Tartar hungering for the desert, reminding us in one speaking photograph of a Hebrew prophet. Looking at it we hear the harsh admonition: I stand on the brink of the grave, and can have no interest in telling you lies. Repent, even if there be no God; repent, even if the kingdom of heaven be illusory; renounce the kingdom of earth, for it is worthless.

Turgenev and His Followers in England

IV

HENRY JAMES

Ivan Turgénieff (1818–1883)

There is perhaps no novelist of alien race who more naturally than Ivan Turgénieff inherits a niche in a Library for English readers; and this not because of any advance or concession that in his peculiar artistic independence he ever made, or could dream of making, such readers, but because it was one of the effects of his peculiar genius to give him, even in his lifetime, a special place in the regard of foreign publics. His position is in this respect singular; for it is his Russian savor that as much as anything has helped generally to domesticate him.

Born in 1818, at Orel in the heart of Russia, and dying in 1883, at Bougival near Paris, he had spent in Germany and France the latter half of his life; and had incurred in his own country in some degree the reprobation that is apt to attach to the absent—the penalty they pay for such extension or such beguilement as they may have happened to find over the border. He belonged to the class of large rural proprietors of land and of serfs; and with his ample patrimony, offered one of the few examples of literary labor achieved in high independence of the question of gain—a character that he shares with his illustrious contemporary Tolstoy, who is of a type in other respects so different. It may give us an idea of his primary situation to imagine some large Virginian or Carolinian slaveholder, during the first half of the century, inclining to 'Northern' views; and becoming (though not predominantly under pressure of these, but rather by the operation of an exquisite genius) the great American novelist—one of the great novelists of the world. Born under a social and political order sternly repressive, all Turgénieff's deep instincts, all his moral passion, placed him on the liberal side; with the consequence

From *Library of the World's Best Literature*, edited by Charles Dudley Warner (New York: International Society). Copyright 1897 by R. S. Peale and J. A. Hill.

that early in life, after a period spent at a German university, he found himself, through the accident of a trifling public utterance, under such suspicion in high places as to be sentenced to a term of tempered exile—confinement to his own estate. It was partly under these circumstances perhaps that he gathered material for the work from the appearance of which his reputation dates—*A Sportsman's Sketches*, published in two volumes in 1852. This admirable collection of impressions of homely country life, as the old state of servitude had made it, is often spoken of as having borne to the great decree of Alexander II the relation borne by Mrs. Beecher Stowe's famous novel to the emancipation of the Southern slaves. Incontestably, at any rate, Turgénieff's rustic studies sounded, like *Uncle Tom's Cabin*, a particular hour: with the difference, however, of not having at the time produced an agitation—of having rather presented the case with an art too insidious for instant recognition, an art that stirred the depths more than the surface.

The author was designated promptly enough, at any rate, for such influence as might best be exercised at a distance: he travelled, he lived abroad; early in the sixties he was settled in Germany; he acquired property at Baden-Baden, and spent there the last years of the prosperous period—in the history of the place—of which the Franco-Prussian War was to mark the violent term. He cast in his lot after that event mainly with the victims of the lost cause; setting up a fresh home in Paris—near which city he had, on the Seine, a charming alternate residence —and passing in it, and in the country, save for brief revisitations, the remainder of his days. His friendships, his attachments, in the world of art and of letters, were numerous and distinguished; he never married; he produced, as the years went on, without precipitation or frequency; and these were the years during which his reputation gradually established itself as, according to the phrase, European—a phrase denoting in this case, perhaps, a public more alert in the United States even than elsewhere.

Tolstoy, his junior by ten years, had meanwhile come to fruition; though, as in fact happened, it was not till after Turgénieff's death that the greater fame of *War and Peace* and of *Anna Karénina* began to be blown about the world. One of the last acts of the elder writer, performed on his deathbed, was to address to the other (from whom for a considerable term he had been estranged by circumstances needless to reproduce) an appeal to return to the exercise of the genius that Tolstoy had already so lamentably, so monstrously forsworn. 'I am on my death-bed; there is no possibility of my recovery. I write you expressly to tell you how happy I have been to be your contemporary, and to utter my last, my urgent prayer. Come back, my friend, to your literary labors. That gift came to you from the source from which all comes to us. Ah, how happy I should be could I think you would listen to my entreaty! My friend, great writer of our Russian land, respond to it, obey it!' These words, among the most touching surely ever addressed by one great spirit to another, throw an indirect light—perhaps I may even say a direct one—upon the nature and quality of Turgénieff's artistic temperament; so much so that I regret being without opportunity, in this place, to gather such aid for a portrait of him as might be supplied by following out the unlikeness between the pair. It would be too easy to say that Tolstoy was, from the Russian point of view, for home consumption, and Turgénieff for foreign: *War and Peace* has probably had more readers in Europe and America than *A House of Gentlefolk* or *On the Eve* or *Smoke*—a circumstance less detrimental than it may appear to my claim of our having, in the Western world, supremely adopted the author of the latter works. Turgénieff is in a peculiar degree what I may call the novelists' novelist—an artistic influence extraordinarily valuable and ineradicably established. The perusal of Tolstoy—a wonderful mass of life—is an immense event, a kind of spendid accident, for each of us: his name represents nevertheless no such eternal spell of method, no such quiet irresistibility of presentation, as shines, close to us and lighting our possible steps, in that of his precursor. Tolstoy is a reflector as vast as a natural lake; a monster harnessed to his great subject—all human life!—as an elephant might be harnessed, for purposes of traction, not to a carriage, but to a coach-house. His own case is prodigious, but his example for others dire: disciples not elephantine he can only mislead and betray.

One by one, for thirty years, with a firm, deliberate hand, with intervals and patiences and waits, Turgénieff pricked in his sharp outlines. His great external mark is probably his concision: an ideal he never threw over—it shines most perhaps even when he is least brief—and that he often applied with a rare felicity. He has masterpieces of a few pages; his perfect things are sometimes his least prolonged. He abounds in short tales, episodes clipped as by the scissors of Atropos; but for a direct translation of the whole we have still to wait—depending meanwhile upon the French and German versions, which have been, instead of the original text (thanks to the paucity among us of readers of Russian), the source of several published in English. For the novels and *A Sportsman's Sketches* we depend upon the nine volumes (1897) of Mrs. Garnett. We touch here upon the remarkable side, to our vision, of the writer's fortune—the anomaly of his having constrained to intimacy even those who are shut out from the enjoyment of his medium, for whom that question is positively prevented from existing. Putting aside extrinsic intimations, it is impossible to read him without the conviction of his being, in the vividness of his own tongue, of the strong type of those made to bring home to us the happy truth of the unity, in a generous talent, of material and form—of their being inevitable faces of the same medal; the type of those, in a word, whose example deals death to the perpetual clumsy assumption that subject and style are—aesthetically speaking, or in the living work—different and separable things. We are conscious, reading him in a language not his own, of not being reached by his personal tone, his individual accent.

It is a testimony therefore to the intensity of his presence, that so much of his particular charm does reach us; that the mask turned to us has, even without his expression, still so much beauty. It is the beauty (since we must try to formulate) of the finest presentation of the familiar. His vision is of the world of character and feeling, the world of the relations life throws up at every hour and on every spot; he deals little, on the whole, in the miracles of chance—the hours and spots over the edge of time and space; his air is that of the great central region of passion and motive, of the usual, the inevitable, the intimate—the intimate for weal or woe. No theme that he ever chooses but strikes us as full; yet with all have we the sense that their animation comes from within, and is not pinned to their backs like the pricking objects used of old in the horse-races of the Roman carnival, to make the animals run. Without a patch of 'plot' to draw blood, the story he mainly tells us, the situation he mainly gives, runs as if for dear life. His first book was practically full evidence of what, if we have to specify, is finest in him—the effect, for the commonest truth, of an exquisite envelope of poetry. In this medium of feeling—full, as it were, of all the echoes and shocks of the universal danger and need—everything in him goes on; the sense of fate and folly and pity and wonder and beauty. The tenderness, the humor, the variety of *A Sportsman's Sketches* revealed on the spot an observer with a rare imagination. These faculties had attached themselves, together, to small things and to great: to the misery, the simplicity, the piety, the patience, of the unemancipated peasant; to all the natural wonderful life of earth and air and winter and summer and field and forest; to queer apparitions of country neighbors, of strange local eccentrics; to old-world practices and superstitions; to secrets gathered and types disinterred and impressions absorbed in the long, close contacts with man and nature involved in the passionate pursuit of game. Magnificent in stature and original vigor, Turgénieff, with his love of the chase, or rather perhaps of the inspiration he found in it, would have been the model of the mighty hunter, had not such an image been a little at variance with his natural mildness, the softness that often accompanies the sense of an extraordinary reach of limb and play of muscle. He was in person the model rather of the strong man at rest: massive and towering, with the voice of innocence and the smile almost of childhood. What seemed still more of a contradiction to so much of him, however, was that his work was all delicacy and fancy, penetration and compression.

If I add, in their order of succession, *Rudin, Fathers and Children, Spring Floods,* and *Virgin Soil,* to the three novels I have (also in their relation of time) named above, I shall have indicated the larger blocks of the compact monument, with a base resting deep and interstices well filled, into which that work disposes itself. The list of his minor productions is too long to draw out: I can only mention, as a few of the most striking—*A Correspondence, The Wayside Inn, The Brigadier, The Dog, The Jew, Visions, Mumu, Three Meetings, A First Love, The Forsaken, Assia, The Journal of a Superfluous Man, The Story of Lieutenant Yergunov, A King Lear of the Steppe.* The first place among his novels would be difficult to assign: general opinion probably hesitates between *A House of Gentle-*

folk and *Fathers and Children.* My own predilection is great for the exquisite *On the Eve;* though I admit that in such a company it draws no supremacy from being exquisite. What is less contestable is that *Virgin Soil*—published shortly before his death, and the longest of his fictions—has, although full of beauty, a minor perfection.

Character, character expressed and exposed, is in all these things what we inveterately find. Turgénieff's sense of it was the great light that artistically guided him; the simplest account of him is to say that the mere play of it constitutes in every case his sufficient drama. No one has had a closer vision, or a hand at once more ironic and more tender, for the individual figure. He sees it with its minutest signs and tricks—all its heredity of idiosyncrasies, all its particulars of weakness and strength, of ugliness and beauty, of oddity and charm; and yet it is of his essence that he sees it in the general flood of life, steeped in its relations and contacts, struggling or submerged, a hurried particle in the stream. This gives him, with his quiet method, his extraordinary breadth; dissociates his rare power to particularize from dryness or hardness, from any peril of caricature. He understands so much that we almost wonder he can express anything; and his expression is indeed wholly in absolute projection, in illustration, in giving of everything the unexplained and irresponsible specimen. He is of a spirit so human that we almost wonder at his control of his matter; of a pity so deep and so general that we almost wonder at his curiosity. The element of poetry in him is constant, and yet reality stares through it without the loss of a wrinkle. No one has more of that sign of the born novelist which resides in a respect unconditioned for the freedom and vitality, the absoluteness when summoned, of the creatures he invokes; or is more superior to the strange and second-rate policy of explaining or presenting them by reprobation or apology—of taking the short cuts and anticipating the emotions and judgments about them that should be left, at the best, to the perhaps not most intelligent reader. And yet his system, as it may summarily be called, of the mere particularized report, has a lucidity beyond the virtue of the cruder moralist.

If character, as I say, is what he gives us at every turn, I should speedily add that he offers it not in the least as a synonym, in our Western sense, of resolution and prosperity. It wears the form of the almost helpless detachment of the short-sighted individual soul; and the perfection of his exhibition of it is in truth too often but the intensity of what, for success, it just does not produce. What works in him most is the question of the will; and the most constant induction he suggests, bears upon the sad figure that principle seems mainly to make among his countrymen. He had seen—he suggests to us—its collapse in a thousand quarters; and the most general tragedy, to his view, is that of its desperate adventures and disasters, its inevitable abdication and defeat. But if the men, for the most part, let it go, it takes refuge in the other sex; many of the representatives of which, in his pages, are supremely strong—in wonderful addition, in various cases, to being otherwise admirable. This is true of such a number—the younger women, the girls, the 'heroines' in especial—that they form in themselves, on the ground of moral beauty, of the finest distinction of soul, one of the most striking groups the modern novel has given us. They are heroines to the letter, and of a heroism obscure and undecorated: it is almost they alone who have the energy to determine and to act. Elena, Lisa, Tatyana, Gemma, Marianna—we can write their names and call up their images, but I lack space to take them in turn. It is by a succession of the finest and tenderest touches that they live; and this, in all Turgénieff's work, is the process by which he persuades and succeeds.

It was his own view of his main danger that he sacrificed too much to detail; was wanting in composition, in the gift that conduces to unity of impression. But no novelist is closer and more cumulative; in none does distinction spring from a quality of truth more independent of everything but the subject, but the idea itself. This idea, this subject, moreover—a spark kindled by the innermost friction of things—is always as interesting as an unopened telegram. The genial freedom—with its exquisite delicacy—of his approach to this 'innermost' world, the world of our finer consciousness, has in short a side that I can only describe and commemorate as nobly disinterested; a side that makes too many of his rivals appear to hold us in comparison by violent means, and introduce us in comparison to vulgar things.

V

FORD MADOX FORD

John Galsworthy

I must have asked myself a hundred times in my life: If there had been no Turgenev what would have become of Galsworthy? . . . Or, though that is the way the question has always put itself to me, it might be truer to the thought I want to express to say: What would Galsworthy have become?

I might have asked the same question about Henry James, for the influence of Turgenev on James must have been enormous, but I did not know James before he had come across Turgenev, whereas I did know Galsworthy whilst he was still himself and still astonishingly young. And I remember distinctly the alarm that came over me when Galsworthy one morning mentioned Turgenev for the first time at breakfast. It was both the nature of the mention of the beautiful Russian genius and Galsworthy's emotion of the moment that alarmed me. I had known him for a long time as a charming man-about-town of a certain doggedness in political argument. Indeed, I don't know how long I hadn't known him; to find out exactly I should have to do more delving in thought into my own past than I care to do. But I knew that he was passing through a period of great emotional stress, and as I had a great affection for him I was concerned to find him expressing more emotion over an anecdote than I had ever known him to show.

The anecdote was this: Turgenev had a peasant girl for mistress. One day he was going to St. Petersburg and he asked the girl what he should bring her back from town. She begged him to bring her back some cakes of scented soap. He asked her why she wanted scented soap and she answered, "So that it

From *Mightier than the Sword* by Ford Madox Ford (London: George Allen & Unwin, 1938). Published in the United States as *Portraits from Life* (Boston: Houghton Mifflin, 1937). Reprinted by permission of Allen & Unwin and Miss Janice Biala.

may be proper for you to kiss my hand as you do those of the great ladies, your friends."

I never liked the anecdote much, myself. But Galsworthy, telling it in the sunlit breakfast room of my cottage at Winchelsea, found it so touching that he appeared to be illuminated, and really had tears in his eyes. I daresay the reflection of the sunlight from the tablecloth may have had something to do with the effect of illumination, but it comes back to me as if, still, I saw him in a sort of aura that emanated from his features. And from that day he was never quite the same. . . . The morning is also made memorable for me by the ghost of the odour of a very strong embrocation that hung about us both. He was, at the moment, suffering from severe sciatica, and I had spent the last half-hour of the night before and the first half-hour of that morning in rubbing him in his bed with that fluid which consisted of turpentine, mustard, and white of egg. And suddenly I had of him a conception of a sort of frailty, as if he needed protection from the hard truths of the world. It was a conception that remained to me till the very end . . . till the last time but one when I came upon him accidentally watching one of his own plays in New York, all alone and, seemingly, very perturbed. I don't know by what.

The disease from which he suffered was pity . . . or not so much pity as an insupportable anger at the sufferings of the weak or the impoverished in a harsh world. It was as if some portion of his mind had been flayed and bled at every touch. It entered into his spirit at about the date of which I am speaking and remained with him all his life. And, for me at least, it robbed his later work of interest, since the novelist must be pitiless at least when he is at work.

And it filled me with disappointment. I think I must have been the first person really to take Galsworthy seriously as a writer. For most other people who knew him then—except of course for the lady who subsequently became Mrs. Galsworthy —he was still an amiable, rather purposeless man-about-town, with a liking for racing, with some skill with the shotgun, a proper connoisseurship in cricket. But I had already recognised in him a certain queerness, a certain pixylike perversity . . . and a certain, slight, authentic gift. So that I had expected him, if he persevered, to provide for us another—a possibly sunnier kind, of Trollope, and I very much did not want him to become overserious or emotional.

And suddenly there was Turgenev—the most dangerous of all writers for his disciples—Turgenev and emotionalism appearing in the mentality of that sunny being with the touch of genius. . . .

I am always being hammered by my associates for saying that Galsworthy had a touch of genius as a novelist. And indeed I was hammered by Galsworthy himself for telling him that that was what he had. He was himself obstinately of the opinion that if ever a writer was constructed it was he. And in the process of getting himself made he submitted to an incredible amount of buffetings by advisers. It used to seem almost a miracle that he could find his way about his own works whilst he was writing them, so frequently was he counselled by one person and another to change all the salient passages of his books. Certainly the Galsworthy who emerged from all that was someone immensely changed, hardened, and, except for his plays in which his native gift was more allowed to have its way, he was dulled. . . . To that I shall return. Let me for the moment try to finish getting in my original Galsworthy.

During the earlier years of our acquaintance I had gathered the impression from Conrad, who knew him as a pleasant idler long before I did, that his rather slight figure and blond head contained a frame and a brain of iron. Conrad, with characteristic generosity when speaking of a dear friend, used to declare that Galsworthy held the mile record at Oxford. At times it would even be the world record. But it was certainly the Oxford one. And, on my first meeting with him—though not my first sight, for I had seen him at a club—he had elected, rather than to ride in my dog-cart, to trot beside me the two miles from Sandling Junction to the Pent. He said he needed exercise, but as the road was uphill it had seemed a stiffish way to take it. So I had accepted Conrad's account of his friend's exploits without demur and, as it wasn't the kind of thing that Englishmen would talk about, there was in my mind no question of his being a mile record-holder at the time I rubbed him in Winchelsea.

Actually he had rather distinguished himself at Harrow at cricket and on the cinder track. If I had known that, I should have considered his first literary efforts more seriously. Because for a man to go through the terrific grind of preparing himself when comparatively mature for the effort of taking a mile record would be the worst training imaginable for a literary life, whereas for an adolescent to distinguish himself at Harrow would merely mean that he was a stocky fellow.

These slight shades of English ruling-class life at that date are difficult to convey, but they are worth dwelling upon. To excel in those days in anything even in private was regarded as extremely dangerous. To excel to the point of anything like publicity would be to write yourself down a bounder, and if you incurred the slightest suspicion of that it was all over with you. It was nice to have a Blue—for cricket or rowing. It would even help you at the Bar afterwards if you wanted to be a practising barrister. . . . But then in the boat there were eight of you and in the cricket team eleven, so you did not stand out. And I am certain that, just as my friend Marwood, who was one of the finest mathematicians of his day—just as he purposely made a slip in his final examination at Cambridge so as to be second and not Senior Wrangler—so Galsworthy, if there had been any danger of making a record at Oxford, would have stumbled before reaching the tape.

Later, indeed, I happened to ask him some question about running—it was at the time of the first Olympic Games in Athens—and said innocently:

"You hold the mile record at Oxford, don't you?"

He really jumped a couple of feet away from me—we were walking in the Park—and exclaimed:

"Good gracious, no! Oh goodness gracious, no! I did a little running at Harrow. But at Oxford I never did anything but loaf about the High. . . ." As a matter of fact, he declared, the very little running he had done at the school on the hill had injured his heart so he could not have done anything in that line at Oxford. And, as a matter of fact, too, he had, he said, not done anything in any line at all. He had just scrambled through his examination for the Bar. That was all.

He had duly eaten his dinners at the Middle Temple and, like every other gentleman's son of those days, had been called to the Bar. That is to say that if one was at all "born," one had, till about then, gone either to the Bar or into the Army. Or if one were born and a very younger son one went into the Church. But at the time Galsworthy was called to the Bar, the

Army was already showing signs of becoming a rather serious affair, and with the fall in the value of agricultural tithes, the Church had become a not very lucrative profession. So he had donned a wig and gown for a ceremonial attendance on the Courts, as being the proper thing for a gentleman's son who had no ambitions and intended to loaf through life. He had, I understood, appeared once or twice in cases, representing, as a junior counsel, the important firm of which his father was the chief partner, and, during the voyage on the *Torrens*, of which ship Conrad was the chief mate, he had rather desultorily studied naval law.

And there he was, an athlete with a mildly damaged heart, a barrister with no desire for briefs, the perfect man-about-town . . . and for me a very incomprehensible figure. Conrad said that he was as hard as iron under a soft exterior and tenacious as a bulldog in spite of a carefully feigned pococurantism. On and off I saw a good deal of him, but his talk was mostly of the Eton and Harrow cricket match, the sires and dams of racehorses, very desultorily of tariff reform, the woes of Ireland, the behaviour of the Boers. Occasionally he would talk a little about some concert or other, his sister, Mrs. Reynolds, being melomane, and occasionally he would talk about pictures, his sister, Mrs. Sauter, being married to an artist. When it was a question of books, I did the talking and he would listen with an interest that I took to be merely polite.

We both at that time inhabited an august, sedate hilltop in the royal borough of Kensington called Campden Hill, he on the one side and I on the other of a concreted open space given up to tennis courts—it was really the cover of a waterworks reservoir. And on days when I was not expecting Conrad, who was in lodgings not far off, I would breakfast with Jack in his sunlit, converted stable.

At any rate that is how it comes back to me—the doors and windows always open, the sunlight streaming in on the hissing silver teakettle, the bubbling silver entrée dishes, the red tiles of the floor, the bright rugs, the bright screens. And we would talk until it was time for me to go back along the waterworks wall and take up the interminable job of writing, in my dining-room, patchwork passages into *Romance*, when Conrad was not writing *Nostromo* up in my study. And Galsworthy would be going to ride in the Park. . . .

And then, suddenly, they all went . . . Pop! As if someone had cut the key string of a net, they all unravelled and disappeared—those tranquillities.

It began with that Turgenev anecdote. I had been right to be alarmed. I had by then known for some time that Galsworthy occasionally wrote a short story, rather desultorily as young ladies paint landscapes in water-colours. Then one day with a rather ironic, dubious expression, Conrad told me that "poor Jack" wanted me to read some of his stuff . . . and I rather liked some of it. Even at that he seemed too shy to talk about his writing, so I had made a few remarks as to *progression d'effet*, the *mot juste*, and the like. And I had imagined that he had dropped his writing. But immediately after the Turgenev anecdote I opened inadvertently a letter addressed to him in care of myself. It was the morning after he had gone back to Town. Then I knew immediately after the reading of merely three amazing words and the signature that poor Jack had his troubles of the heart.

It gives the measure of the passion that I have for not knowing anything about the private lives of my friends—particularly if they are writers—that, as I have somewhere related, I should have gone to extremes of trouble over the forwarding of that letter. I desperately did not want Galsworthy to know that I knew. It seemed to me that that must inevitably take the bloom off the pleasure that I had in our gentle and unexciting conversations. I knew then at once that the emotion he had shown over the Turgenev anecdote was a sign that he was suffering a great deal over his hidden affair of the heart. I knew from the signature that it was one that could not run smoothly. If he had been an ordinary layman I should have stuck the letter up, inscribed it "Opened by mistake," and forwarded it to its owner. But Galsworthy was by now more than an ordinary stockbroker or politician. He had come alive. And I took a great deal of trouble to get that letter to him without any indications of its having been opened.[1]

[1] I told this story of the letter recently, as a case of conscience, in one of my books, suppressing of course Galsworthy's name. Now, however, that his official biographer has told the whole story of the fortunate love affair of the author of *The Man of Property*, there seems to be no reason for further concealment.

Galsworthy gave no signs of thinking that the letter had been tampered with, and for a little time it looked as if everything was as it always had been. We breakfasted and talked about the weather and the crops; we went together to concerts that his sister, Mrs. Reynolds, was organizing; we discussed the alterations that his sister, Mrs. Sauter, suggested in the story he was writing . . . which was, I think, then the *Villa Rubein*, a book for which I had and still have a great affection. Then gradually the change came.

He began to talk of Turgenev as the emancipator of the serfs in Russia; about the reform of the poor laws; about the reform of the incidence of the income tax on the poorer classes. And above all, of course, about the reform of the marriage laws, and perhaps still more about the re-estimation of marriage as an institution. He uttered one day the sentiment that where there is no love, there is no duty.

Then one evening he knocked on my door in a really pitiable state of distress. I was giving a rather large dinner, one of the motives of which was to introduce Galsworthy himself to the more formidable critics and men of letters of the London day. His book was then near publication and Conrad and I had conspired to do that amount of log-rolling. And suddenly there was Galsworthy at seven-thirty saying that he could not come to that dinner. He said that if I knew what was happening I should not want him to come to dinner; that all my guests would think the same. Mysterious things were happening to him; he would probably never again be invited to dinner by anyone. I should know all about it to-morrow; then I should see how right he was.

It was no use saying that if he had been hammered on the stock exchange or neglected to pay his racing debts it would make no difference to my desire to have him at that dinner. He said: No, no! It would be unthinkable. It would be an offence to myself such as he would never pardon if it had been offered to him—It was the first time I had come up against his immense, his formidable, obstinacy.

He wrote to me next day to say that he had that afternoon been served with papers as co-respondent in a divorce case. Of course my guests would have hated meeting him! And he wanted to know if it would make any difference in our friendship.

Times of course have changed, but I think that even then the ordinary man would have taken the matter less tragically. Galsworthy, however, insisted on considering that his social career and more particularly that of his future wife was at an end, and that for the rest of their lives they would be cut off at least from the public society of decent people. He was, of course, quite wrong. Even at that date London society took the view, that, for a decent man and woman, passing through the divorce courts was a sufficient ordeal to atone for most irregularities. Once they were through, they had taken their punishment and decent society does not approve of two punishments being exacted for one misdemeanour. . . . But at the time it was no good putting that view to Galsworthy. He was in many ways singularly old-fashioned and strait-laced.

But more than anything he was sensitive to the sorrow of other people. He was that even before he had thus got, as it were, religion, and the long excruciation of waiting years for the opportunity of happiness had made him sensitive beyond belief. The anticipation of possible future grief for his wife rendered him at the time almost out of his normal mind, and the emotion was rendered all the stronger by the thought of the suffering that, for years before that, she had had to endure . . . with, as it were, Soames Forsyte. I really thought that, at about the time when he had just received those divorce papers, he might have gone mad. . . . And that note of agonized suffering at the thought of oppression or cruelty became at once the main note of his character and of his public activities. It led him, in his novels, into exaggerations or slight strainings of the humanitarian note which distinguished every page of his writings of that date and, as we shall see, it influenced the very framework of his novels themselves. And his very exaggerations tended to negate the truths of the morals that he meant to enforce.

So you had the once-famous controversy of the rabbit. . . . At the end of the description of a battue in *The Country House,* having rendered, with all the spirit of Tolstoi after his conversion, the massacre of game that had taken place, in order to get the full drama out of the stupidity and cruelty that obviously distinguish those barbaric slaughters of harmless beings, he found it desirable to emphasize the note and to describe how "one poor little rabbit" crept out into the open to die. Now, two sentences of the description of the slaughter of deer in the *St. Julien l'Hospitalier* of Flaubert, utterly dispassionate and without comment as they are, might well suffice to put you off the shooting of all game whatever ... certainly off the massacre of driven game. But wounded rabbits do not ever die in the open ... of choice. Even domestic animals, if you let them alone while they are dying, will creep under a bush if a bush is to be found ... or else under a low piece of furniture. ... And we ourselves seldom like to die under the sky, preferring to turn our faces to some wall.

So someone noted this exaggeration of poor Jack's. And controversy broke out, in the sporting journals, in men's clubs, in bar parlours, in country-houses. The more scientific readers of the journals wrote to say that, wherever rabbits die, they never die in their burrows. Their companions would force them out to die where they could. Hardened rabbit-hunters for the pot, warren-breeders, gamekeepers, wrote or declared in inn corners that that was all nonsense. Again and again when digging out rabbits they had found dead ones among the living. The scientists declared that this only occurred when the dying rabbit was too large and heavy to be forced out of his lair. The living rabbits would then, in order to avoid living with the putrefying body, have to abandon that home and dig a new one. ... But one and all declared that Galsworthy did not know what he was talking about. So the book lost a good deal of influence with its readers. It would be unfair to say that it had been written with the sole object of stopping the practice of shooting driven game. But that had been one of its purposes. And he gave the upholders of game-preserving and intensive shooting the chance to say that damaging thing.

For Galsworthy knew perfectly well what he was talking about. But his Tolstoian reaction against his former life had made him forget what, in his subconsciousness, he must have known to be the truth. At any rate, before his regeneration, he had spent nearly all his autumns shooting driven grouse, pheasants, and partridges. Many of his earlier letters contain expressions of exhilaration at the thought that the game season was opening again. But his revulsion from the life of the man-about-town was at that date very thorough, and the emotion of shuddering at every one of his former habits penetrated to every fibre of his being. He was determined, if he could, to bring about a change of heart in human society.

There was at this time raging in literary and artistic society in London such a clash of views as lately distinguished New York. Reformers of all types declared that no work of art could be real art if it were not also a work of propaganda for the Left. And nearly all serious English novelists were finally driven to take that view. The novel became a vehicle for every kind of "ism"; a small but noisy minority backed Imperialism and bank-holiday patriotism, but the serious novel as a whole interested itself almost solely in sociological questions.

As against that, as I have already adumbrated, a still smaller but sufficiently formidable band of foreign writers had at the time settled mostly in the South of England. The most important of them were the writers I have here treated of, and the other body of writers for the once immensely famous *Yellow Book*. That organ had been founded by Henry Harland, the author of *The Cardinal's Snuffbox*, an American who had come to London by way of Paris, and its supporters were all either foreigners or had had foreign, mostly Parisian, trainings. It was the day when England, and America too, rustled all over its literary quarters with the names of Flaubert, Maupassant, and, above all, Turgenev. That camp proclaimed that a work of art must be a passionless rendering of life as it appears to the artist. It must be coloured by no exaggerations, whether they tend to exalt either the Right or Left in politics. The public function of the work of art in short was, after it had given pleasure, to present such an epitome of life that the reader could get from it sufficient knowledge to let him decide how to model both his private and his public lives. Thus Flaubert wrote that if France had read his *Éducation Sentimentale*, she would have been spared the disasters of the Franco-Prussian War. He meant, not that France would have learned from him how to choose a better rifle than the *chassepot*, but that if France had learned from that book how to question her accepted ideas she would have had a set of citizens capable of studying public questions with realism. Then she could have taken earlier precautions against the Prussians. . . . The business, then, of the artist was to study the works of his predecessors . . . the works that had given pleasure. In that way he would learn how to give pleasure in his turn. And, rendering the life of his day as he saw it and without preconceptions, his world would at least be enlightened as to the conditions in which it lived. It might even, then, improve itself.

Those at any rate were the two schools of opposed literary thought that divided the world when Galsworthy came on the artistic scene. In addition, the Conrad-James-Crane school, to which I belonged, believed that you could learn nothing technically from Turgenev. There are, that is to say, certain writers—Shakespeare is among them—who have not really "methods" . . . who write, as it were, solely from their temperaments. Such writers are exceedingly dangerous to the learner. He can learn nothing technically from them and he is extremely likely to fall into an imitation of their mannerisms and into trying to assume their temperaments. Galsworthy says in a letter that Mr. Marrot prints[2] that he did not consider himself a born writer, but one who had made himself by the labours of the eleven years that preceded the writing of his *Man of Property*. At that I have already hinted. He said it again and again at many different stages of his life. He repeated it even in the draft of the speech in thanks for the receipt of the Nobel Prize, which death prevented his delivering. And if he said it at that moment of his apotheosis he must have believed it to be true. It was not true, of course.

It might have been true to say that he was not a born novelist and, from my particular angle, it might be true to say that he never was a novelist at all. But writing is not all novel-writing, and there were departments of the art of projecting things on paper in which he really excelled and was conscious that he excelled. It is true that a writer must be born a writer. But it is true, too, that a born writer can be made over . . . to his detriment; and I do not think that any real writer can have ever been so made over as the unfortunate young Galsworthy. I must have written him reams and reams of letters about his early work. Mr. Marrot prints one that takes up some four whole small-print pages of his book. And sometimes Galsworthy took my advice and sometimes he stood out against it

[2] *Life and Letters of John Galsworthy*, by H. V. Marrot. The author kindly lent me advance sheets of the work when I had reached this stage of this article.

with the grim obstinacy that was his chief characteristic. For myself I should have found such a letter intolerable if it had been addressed to me, but Galsworthy was always ready for more . . . and ready for more from almost anybody who would address advice to him. His chief advisers in those early days were Conrad, Mr. Edward Garnett, who was adviser to Fisher Unwin, the publisher; and his sisters, Mrs. Sauter and Mrs. Reynolds . . . and the lady who was to become Mrs. Galsworthy, and myself. And I think I can say that it was the last-mentioned two who had the earliest and most complete belief that he had genius.

I do not believe that any of the others, at any rate at that time, had at all that feeling. The sisters had towards him a nervous maternal attitude such as was natural in sisters with a brother who wanted to do anything as wayward as "write." For, if he would be merely normal, he would be assured of a perfectly comfortable position as a man-about-town and a member of the best clubs. Conrad never really liked Galsworthy's writing. He had for him, I should say, a real personal affection and appeared radiantly pleased when Jack came to visit him. But, I suppose just because of that personal affection, he was not ready to accord that pleasant boy any share of talent. It did not seem that anyone so pleasant could have the sort of grim persistence that Conrad considered to be indispensable for a writer. He wrote him of course letters full of an appreciation of his work that he expressed in terms of superlatives. But at the same time in private he always spoke of "poor Jack" with sighs; and as Mr. Marrot brings out, he wrote to his own private correspondents letters expressing no sort of opinion at all of Galsworthy's gifts. As against that he gave himself a very great deal of trouble to place Galsworthy's work.

And later, when Jack was beginning to succeed, Conrad's indignation at the younger man's dogged humanitarianism went beyond bounds. He used to say that, as a writer, Galsworthy took a sadic pleasure in rendering the cruelties that the world inflicted on the weak and the unfortunate . . . and that he would be upset if those wrongs were righted because then he would have so much the less to write about. That of course was not true.

But as I have said, Galsworthy had about him a pixylike

quality that rendered him very difficult to understand. I don't mean to say that I understood him altogether. There were about him too many irreconcilabilities; there was the impressive surface softness and a subcutaneous quality, as if of corundum. His benevolences were unparalleled; no man can ever have given a greater share of his income or a greater proportion of his time and worried thought to the unfortunate of every type. This appears sufficiently in Mr. Marrot's book, but if Mr. Marrot had a great deal exaggerated that note he would still have been well within the bounds of the truth. I know this because of the constant stream of miserable people which came almost straight from Galsworthy's doorstep in Addison Road to the offices of the *English Review*. Nearly all of them Galsworthy would have already relieved. Or rather he would have relieved all of them. But occasionally he would telephone to me to say that if So and So should come to me he did not consider him to be a proper person to receive relief from the fund that at that time I administered for the help of literary men in distress. . . . And it is to be remembered that the cases that I knew of were merely those of writers . . . there must have been more than as many more again who were laymen that he helped. Mr. Marrot says that Galsworthy lived on half his income, devoting the rest of it to public charities or causes; but more than half the sum that he set aside for his own use must in addition have gone to private cases. For those private charities were to him his life.

I think that, even more than his writing or his public honours, they were his life. . . . But suddenly there would come out an incomprehensible touch of hardness, as if some unfortunate had incurred his displeasure, or as if some public cause had all of a sudden appeared to have undesirable aspects. These things would be irreconcilable. He would at one time declare that the very fact that a man was no good was the reason that he should be helped, untiringly. Because it is poor, weak things that must be helped. Men with backbone can always in the end help themselves. And then, suddenly, of the most dreadful case of totally undeserved misfortune that I have ever come across he said, shutting his jaw tight, that the fellow was no good and had better not be helped any more . . . and that after he had been helping the man for a long time.

Of course it is given to no man to be consistent. But in Galsworthy it was something more than inconsistency: it was two distinct psychologies working side by side in the same being. That was why I have said that he seemed to be like a pixy . . . as if he were one of those good, serene, and beautiful immortals that had not human souls and yet occupied themselves with human affairs.

It was something of that quality that I felt myself to discern in his earliest work. Conrad, in writing compliments to Galsworthy, said about one of his stories that enthusiastic as he was, my admiration was much the greater. And my emotion was much more of a keen delight in a natural phenomenon—as if a new bird had suddenly sung—than of pleasure in a technical, literary achievement. It was the pixylike quality of his temperament that had called it forth. It was a quality that I hadn't found anywhere else in the world . . . and that I do not think you will still find anywhere else.

And that, in the end, is the justification of the artist in words —that he should be and express something that has never yet been, or been expressed. To me it became apparent gradually that Galsworthy was probably never meant to be a novelist. Or it would be more just to say that thoughts of the world of injustice pressed too strongly on him to let him continue to be a novelist. That was why, at Winchelsea, I was alarmed at his rendering of the Turgenev anecdote. . . . I can assure you that I felt a genuine pleasure and impatience at the thought of coming across a person with the aspects for me of an authentic genius . . . and if I perceived a threat to the prospect of the fruits of that genius growing eventually ripe beneath the sun, I was proportionately dismayed. And I thought I perceived that threat. I foresaw for a moment his preoccupation with the unhappinesses of lovers and the helpless poor . . . and that preoccupation leading him to become not a dispassionate artist but an impassioned, an aching, reformer.

The premonition was too true. *Villa Rubein* was a novel of a sunlit quality. But its successor, *The Island Pharisees*, was already a satire, and *The Man of Property*, which came next, was an attempt to cast discredit on the marriage laws of the day. And after that, in his novels, he was the reformer almost to the end.

And unfortunately his temporal success as novelist obscured

his much greater artistic achievement with the drama. His novels suffered from his dogged determination to find ironic antitheses. His one "effect" as a novelist was to present a group of conventionally virtuous, kindly people sitting about and saying the nicest things about all sorts of persons. . . . A divorced woman is thrown over their garden hedge and breaks her collar bone, and all the kindly people run away and do not so much as offer her a cup of tea. And that goes on for ever, the situation being always forced to bring in that or some similar effect. Mr. Marrot quotes a really amazing correspondence between Mr. Garnett and Galsworthy about the end of *The Man of Property*. It raged for months. Galsworthy was determined that his Bosinney—who was the last person in the world to do it—should commit suicide in order, really, to prove that the propertied middle classes were very cruel people . . . with of course the aim of shaming those classes into becoming really kinder. Mr. Garnett, all reformer as he too was, is shocked at the idea that Bosinney—who, I repeat, was the last person in the world to commit suicide—should be forced to take his own life so as to show the effects of the cruelty of the middle classes. What Bosinney would have done—and what the situation demands—would have been to run away with Irene and live in inconspicuous bliss in Capri ever after. But no, says Galsworthy, that would not prove that the middle classes are always cruel and victorious over the unfortunate. . . . And the argument seems to go on for ever, each party maintaining exactly the same ground. In the end poor Bosinney has to be run over by a bus, the reader being left uncertain whether it is the result of an accident or a suicide . . . and there seeming to be no moral lesson at all.

But the same dogged determination to present antitheses which produced an effect of monotony in the later novels was exactly suited to the theatre. There effects are of necessity more fugitive and need to be harsher—more cruel. And the keen pleasure that, at the play, the mind feels at appreciating how, unerringly, Galsworthy picks up every crumb of interest and squeezes the last drop of drama out of a situation . . . that pleasure is the greatest humanity can get from a work of art. It is the greatest because pleasures, shared as they are in the playhouse, are contagious and can be unbounded. And it is one of the most legitimate of man's pleasures.

John Galsworthy

When you came away from the first performance of *The Silver Box* you knew that something new had come into the world . . . a new temperament, a new point of view, a new and extraordinarily dramatic technique. And the conviction was strengthened by each new play. For myself I preferred *Joy* to all the others because it was more a matter of dramatic discussion than of situations, and because it had some of the lightness that had distinguished the *Villa Rubein* of our youths. But the characteristic of building up antitheses which, monotonous as it becomes in the novel, is always legitimate and exciting in the swifter moving play, that characteristic distinguished as much his handling of situation as of staged controversy. And finally that conviction came to be shared by the large, unthinking public, the plays began to run for periods of years in both London and New York, and Galsworthy moved from triumph to deserved triumph. No other modern dramatist had anything approaching Galsworthy's loftiness of mind, his compassion, his poetry, his occasional sunlight or the instinctive knowledge of what you can do on the stage. And by himself he lifted the modern stage to a plane to which until his time it had seemed impossible that it could attain.

And so he made towards supreme honours a tranquil course that suggested that of a white-sailed ship progressing inevitably across a halcyon sea. You would have said that he had every blessing that kings and peoples and Providence had to bestow. Having refused a knighthood he was awarded the highest honour that the King had at his disposal—that of the Order of Merit. He presided in Paris at the dinner of the international P.E.N. Club, which is the highest honour that the members of his craft could find for him; and, in the end, the Nobel Prize Committee honoured itself by selecting him for one of its laureates. It seemed, all this, appropriate and inevitable, for, in honouring him, the world honoured one of its noblest philanthropists.

The last time I saw him was in Paris when he gave his presidential address to his beloved P.E.N. And singularly, as he emerged above the shadow of all those hard French writers, there re-emerged at any rate for me the sense of his frailty . . . of his being something that must be shielded from the harder earnestnesses of the world. I don't know that he was conscious on that last public triumph of the really bad nature of the hard men who surrounded him. The world had moved onward since the days when he had read Maupassant and Turgenev for what he could learn of them. Both those writers were what he called dissolvents and the Paris *littérateurs* now wanted above all constructive writing and would have agreed with him if he had said—as he did in one of the last letters that he wrote—that Tolstoi was a greater writer than Turgenev.

But, there, he said nothing of the sort. He seemed to float, above all those potential assassins, like a white swan above a gloomy mere, radiating bright sunlight . . . and with his gentle, modest French words he made statements that ran hissing through Paris as if he had drawn a whip across all those listening faces.

For the French writer of to-day, Maupassant is the Nihilist Enemy—an enemy almost as hated as the last M. Anatole France.

And Turgenev is an alien ugly duckling who once disgusted the paving-stones of Paris with his foreign footsteps. Nothing indeed so infuriates the French of to-day as to say that Turgenev was really a French writer. . . . And there, enthroned and smiling, poor Galsworthy told that audience that shivered like tigers in a circus cage that, if he had trained himself to have any art, and if that training had landed him where he was, that art had been that of French writers.

A sort of buzzing of pleasurable anticipation went all round that ferocious assembly. The author of *Fort comme la Paix* looked at the author of *Nuits Ensoleillées* and thought: "Aha, my friend, this is going to be a bitter moment for you. When I consider the *dédicace* of the ignoble volume that this barbarian chieftain presented yesterday to me . . . when I consider the fulsome, but nevertheless deserved, praise that he wrote on that fly-leaf, I don't have to doubt whom he is going to claim as his Master. . . ." And the author of *Nuits Ensoleillées* looked back at the author of the other classic and thought exactly the same thing—with the necessary change in the identity of the author. And every French author present looked at every other French author and thought thoughts similar. And when the applause subsided poor Jack went on:

Yes, he repeated, all the art he had had he had had of the French. If he stood where he was, if he was honoured as he was, it was because all his life long he had studied the works, he had been guided by the examples of . . . Guy de Maupassant and of him who though a foreigner by birth was yet more French in heart than any Frenchman—Ivan Turgenev!

I have never seen an audience so confounded. If an invisible force had snatched large, juicy joints of meat from the very jaws of a hundred Bengal tigers the effect would have been the same. They simply could not believe their ears. . . . As for me, I was so overwhelmed with confusion that I ran out of that place and plunged, my cheeks still crimson, into the salon of the author of *Vasco*, who was preparing to give a tea-party at the end of the Île St. Louis. And the news had got there before me. It was in the salon of every author of the Île, of the Rue Guynemer, of the Rues Madame, Jacob, Tombe Issoire, and Notre-Dame des Champs, before the triumphant Galsworthy had finished his next sentence. . . . For that was the real triumph of his radiant personality, that not one of the fierce beasts quivering under his lash so much as raised a protest. No other man in the world could have brought that off!

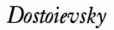

Dostoievsky

VI

D. S. MEREZHKOVSKY

Dostoievsky and Tolstoy

D. S. Merezhkovsky (1865–1941) very early achieved reputation
as a poet, but is now remembered only for his many historical
romances, beginning with *The Death of the Gods* (*Julian the Apostate*, 1896), which were early translated into English and are still
easy to come by in secondhand bookstalls. His permanent place in
Russian literary history, however, is as a publicist and theorist, most
representative and influential between 1893 and 1905. D. S. Mirsky,
in *A History of Russian Literature,* declared Merezhkovsky's *Tolstoy and Dostoievsky* (first published in a periodical in 1901) to be
his most important work and "the most intelligent and readable thing
he ever wrote." Mirsky observes that "his interpretation of the personalities of Tolstoy and Dostoievsky dominated Russian literature
for many years." The book appeared in translation in London in
1902 as *Tolstoi as Man and Artist, with an Essay on Dostoievski.*

If in the literature of all ages and nations we wished to find
the artist most contrary to Tolstoi we should have to point to
Dostoievski. I say contrary, but not remote, not alien; for often
they come in contact, like extremes that meet.

The "heroes" of Tolstoi . . . are not so much heroes as victims. In them the human individuality, without being perfected
to the full, is swallowed up in the elements. And as there is not
a single heroic will ruling over all, so there is not one uniting
tragic action: there are only separate tragic *nodi* and situations
—the separate waves which rise and fall in purposeless motion,
not guided by a current within, but only by external forces.
The fabric of the work, like the fabric of humanity itself,
apparently begins nowhere and ends nowhere.

With Dostoievski there is throughout a human personality
carried to the extremes of individuality, drawing and developing from the dark animal roots to the last radiant summits of
spirituality. Throughout there is the conflict of heroic will

From *Tolstoi as Man and Artist* by D. S. Merezhkovsky (London: Constable, 1902), Chapter XIV. Reprinted by permission of the publisher.

with the element of moral duty and conscience, as in Raskolnikov; with that of passion, refined, deliberate, as in Svidrigailov and Versilov; in conflict with the will of the people, the State, the polity, as in Peter Verkhovenski, Stavrogine, and Shatov; and lastly in conflict with metaphysical and religious mystery, as in Ivan Karamazov, Prince Myshkine, and Kirillov. Passing through the furnace of these conflicts, the fire of enflaming passions and still more enflaming will, the kernel of human individuality, the inward *ego*, remains undissolved and is laid bare. "I am bound to display self-will," says Kirillov in *The Daemons*,* to whom suicide, which seems the limit to self-abnegation, is in fact the highest pitch of the assertion of his personality, the limit of "self-will." All Dostoievski's heroes might say the same. For the last time they oppose themselves to the elements that are swallowing them up, and still assert their *ego*, their individuality and self-will, when their end is at hand. In this sense even the Christian resignation of the Idiot, of Alesha, and old Zosima is an insuperable resistance to evil forces about them; submission to God's will, but not to man's, that is the inversion of "self-will." The martyr dying for his belief, his truth, his God, is also a "hero": he asserts his inward liberty against outward tyranny, and so of course "displays self-will."

In accordance with the predominance of heroic struggle the principal works of Dostoievski are in reality not novels nor epics, but tragedies.

Peace and War and *Anna Karénina*, on the other hand, are really novels, original epics. Here . . . the artistic centre of gravity is not in the dialogue between the characters, but in the telling of the story; not in what they say, but in what is said of them; not in what we hear with our ears, but in what we see with our eyes.

With Dostoievski, on the contrary, the narrative portion is secondary and subservient to the construction of the whole work. And this is apparent at the first glance; the story, written always in one and the same hasty, sometimes clearly neglected language, is now wearisomely drawn out and involved, heaped with details; now too concise and compact. The story is not quite a text, but, as it were, small writing in brackets, notes on

* I.e., *The Devils*, or *The Possessed*.—EDITOR'S NOTE.

the drama, explaining the time and place of the action, the events that have gone before, the surroundings and exterior of the characters: it is the setting up of the scenery, the indispensable theatrical paraphernalia—when the characters come on and begin to speak, then at length the piece begins. In Dostoievski's dialogue is concentrated all the artistic power of his delineation: it is in the dialogue that all is revealed and unrevealed. There is not in all contemporary literature a writer equal to him for mastery of dialogue.

Levine uses just the same language as Pierre Bezukhov or Prince Andrei, Vronski or Pozdnyshev: Anna Karénina the same phrases as Dolly, Kitty, or Natasha. If we did not know who was talking, we should not be able to distinguish one person from another by the language, the sound of the voice, as it were, with our eyes shut. True, there is in Tolstoi a difference between the language of the common folk and the gentry, but this is not external or personal, but merely internal and according to class. In its essence the language of all the characters in Tolstoi is the same, or all but the same: it is colloquial parlance, as it were the sound of the voice of Leo himself, whether in gentleman's or peasant's dress. And merely for this reason we overlook the fact that in his works it is not what the characters *say* that matters, *but how they are silent*, or else groan, howl, roar, yell, or grunt: it is not their human words that matter, but their half-animal, inarticulate sounds, or ejaculations—as in Prince Andrei's delirium "i titi-titi-titi," or the "bleating of Vronski" over the dead horse, or the sobbing of Anatole over his own amputated leg. The repetition of the same vowels, a-o-u, seems sufficient to express the most complex, terrible, heartrending, mental and bodily emotions.

In Dostoievski it is impossible not to recognize the personage speaking, at once, at the first words uttered. In the scarcely Russian, strange, involved talk of the Nihilist Kirillov we feel something superior, grating, unpleasant, prophetic, and yet painful, strained, and recalling attacks of epilepsy—and so too in the simple, truly national speech of "holy" Prince Myshkine. When Fedor Karamazov, suddenly getting quite animated and ingurgitating, addresses his sons thus: "Heigh, you, children, bairns, little sucking pigs, for me—all my life through—there were no such thing as touch-me-nots. Even old maids, in them sometimes you would make valuable discoveries if you only made them open their eyes. A beggar woman, and a touch-me-not: it is necessary at the first go off to astonish—that is the way to deal with them. You must astonish 'em to ecstasy, to compunction, to shame that such a gentleman has fallen in love with such a slut as she." We see the heart of the old man, but also his fat, shaking, Adam's apple, and his moist, thin lips; the tiny, shamelessly piercing eyes, and his whole savage figure—the figure of an old Roman of the times of the decadence. When we learn that on a packet of money, sealed and tied with ribbon, there was also written in his own hand "for my angel Grushenka, if she wishes to come," and that three days later he added "and the little darling," he suddenly stands before us wholly as if alive. We could not explain how, or why, but we feel that in this belated "and the little darling" we have caught some subtle, sensual wrinkle on his face, which makes us feel physically uncomfortable, like the contact of a revolting insect, a huge spider, or daddy-long-legs. It is only a word, but it holds flesh and blood. It is of course imaginary, but it is almost impossible to believe it is *merely* imaginary. It is just that last little touch which makes the portrait too life-like, as if the painter, going beyond the bounds of his art, had created a portrait which is ever on the point of stirring and coming out of the frame like a spectre or a ghost.

In this way Dostoievski has no need to describe the appearance of his characters, for by their peculiar form of language and tones of voices they themselves depict, not only their thoughts and feelings, but their faces and bodies.

With Tolstoi the movements and gestures of the outward bodily frame, revealing the inward shapes of mind, often make profoundly significant the most paltry words of his heroes. Not less distinctness in the physical appearance does Dostoievski achieve by the contrary process: from the internal he arrives at the external, from the mental at the physical, from the rational and human we guess at the instinctive and animal. With Tolstoi we hear because we see, with the other we see because we hear. Not merely the mastery of dialogue, but other characteristics of his method bring Dostoievski near to the current of great tragic art. At times it seems as if he only did not write tragedy because the outward form of epic narration, that of the novel, was by chance the prevailing one in the literature of his day, and also because there was no tragic stage worthy of him, and what is more, no spectators worthy of him. Tragedy is, of course, composed only by the creative powers of artist and audience: it is necessary that the public, too, should have the tragic faculty in order that tragedy may really be engendered.

Involuntarily and naturally Dostoievski becomes subject to that inevitable law of the stage which the new drama has so thoughtlessly abrogated, under the influence of Shakespeare, and by so doing undermined at the root the tragic action. It is the law of the three unities, time, place, and action, which gives, in my opinion, such incomparable power, as against anything in modern poesy, to the creations of the Greek drama.

In the works of Tolstoi there always, sooner or later, comes a moment when the reader finally forgets the main action of the story and the fate of the principal characters. How Prince Andrei dies, or how Nicolai Rostov courses hares, how Kitty bears children, or Levine does his mowing, are to us so important and interesting that we lose sight of Napoleon and Alexander I, Anna, and Vronski. It is even more interesting, more important to us at that moment whether Rostov runs down his hare than whether Napoleon wins the battle of Borodino. In any case we feel no impatience, we are in no hurry to learn the ultimate fate of these persons. We are ready to wait, and have our attention distracted as much as the author likes. We no longer see the shore, and have ceased to think of the destination of our voyage. As in every true epic there is nothing unimportant: everything is equally important, equally leading. In every drop there is the same salt taste, the same chemical composition of water as in the whole sea. Every atom of life moves according to the same laws as worlds and constellations.

Raskolnikov kills an old woman to prove to himself that he is already "on the wrong side of good and evil," that he is not "a shuddering being," but a "lord of creation." But Raskolnikov in Dostoievski's conception is fated to learn that he is wrong, that he has killed, not "a principle," but an old woman, has not "gone beyond," but merely wished to do so. And when he realizes this he is bound to turn faint, to get frightened, to get out in the square and, falling on his knees, to confess before the crowd. And it is precisely to this extreme point, to this one last moment in the action of the story, that everything is directed, gathers itself up and gravitates; to this tragic catastrophe everything tends, as towards a cataract the course of a river long confined by rocks.

Here there cannot, should not be, and really is not, anything collateral or extraneous, arresting or diverting the attention from the main action. The events follow one another ever more and more rapidly, chase one another ever more unrestrainedly, crowd together, are heaped on each other, but in reality subordinated to the main single object, and are crammed in the greatest possible number into the least possible space of time. If Dostoievski has any rivals they are not of the present day, but in ancient literature the creators of Orestes and Oedipus: I mean in this art of gradual tension, accumulation, increase, and alarming concentration of dramatic action.

"How well I remember the hapless day," Podrostok* cries wonderingly; "it always seems as if all these surprises and unforeseen mishaps conspired together and were showered all at once on my head from some cornucopia." "It was a day of surprises," remarks the narrator of *The Daemons*, "a day of untying of old knots and tying of new, sharp elucidations, and still worse confusions. In a word, it was a day when astounding events happened together." And so it is in all his stories—everywhere that infernal "cornucopia," from which are poured on the heads of the heroes unexpected tragedies. When we finish the first part of *The Idiot*—fifteen chapters, ten printed quires—so many events have taken place, so many situations have been placed before us, in which are entangled the threads of the most varied human destinies, and passions and consciences have been laid bare, that it would seem that long years had passed since the beginning of the story: in reality it is only a day, twelve hours from morning to evening. The boundless picture of the world's history which is enfolded in *The Brothers Karamazov* is condensed, if we do not count the intervals between the acts, into a few days. But even in one day, in one hour, and that almost on one and the same spot—between a certain seat in the Pavlovski Park and the Terminus, between Garden Street and Haymarket Square—the heroes of Dostoievski pass through experiences which ordinary mortals do not taste in a lifetime.

Raskolnikov is standing on the staircase, outside the door of

*I.e., *A Raw Youth*.—EDITOR'S NOTE.

the old female usurer. "He looked round for the last time, pulled himself together, drew himself up, and once more tried the axe on the lock. 'Shall I not wait a little longer, till my heart ceases to throb?' But his heart did not cease. On the contrary, as if to spite him, it beat harder and harder. *And he scarcely felt the presence of the rest of his body.*"

To all the heroes of Dostoievski there comes the moment when they cease "to feel their bodies." They are not beings without flesh and blood, not ghosts. We know well what sort of body they *had*, when they still felt its presence. But the highest ascent, the greatest tension of mental existence, the most burning passions—not of the heart and the emotions, but of the mind, the will, and the conscience—give them this divorce from the body, a sort of supernatural lightness, wingedness, and spiritualization of the flesh. They have the very "spiritual, ethereal bodies," of which St. Paul spoke. These are the men who are not suffocated by flesh and blood, or the Tolstoyan "human bubble." It seems as if, at times, they were bodily invisible, only their intense souls could be seen.

"We look at you and say, 'She has the face of a kind sister,'" says the Idiot, describing the beauty of a certain woman. It is curious to compare these instantaneous, supersensual descriptions of Dostoievski with those of Tolstoi—for instance, the figure of Anna Karénina, so full of deep-seated sensuality; the living souls of Dostoievski with the overgrown beef of Tolstoi. All Dostoievski's heroes live, thanks to his higher spirituality, an incredibly rapid, tenfold accelerated life: with all of them, as with Raskolnikov, "the heart beats harder and harder and harder." They do not walk like ordinary mortals, but fly; and in the intoxication of this flight fly into the abyss.

In the agitation of the waves we feel the increasing nearness of the whirlpool.

At times in Greek tragedy, just before the catastrophe, there suddenly sounds in our ears an unexpectedly joyous chant of the chorus in praise of Dionysus, god of wine and blood, of mirth and terror. And in this chant the whole tragedy that is in progress and almost completed, all the fateful and mysterious that there is in human life, is presented to us as the careless sport of the spectator god. This mirth in terror, this tragical play, is like the play of the rainbow, kindling in the foam of some cataract above a gulf.

Dostoievski is nearest of all to us, to the most inward and deeply-seated principles of Greek tragedy. We find him depicting catastrophes with something of this terrible gaiety of the chorus.

Tolstoi's "still heat" before thunder is here broken, into what roaring of thunder, what lightning of terror! It is no longer, as in Tolstoi, difficult to breathe; in that dragging, deathly heaviness which weighs down the heart in everyday life. All expands and expands. At times, even in Dostoievski's work, we lose our breath from the rapidity of the movement, the whirl of events, the flight into space. And what reviving freshness, what freedom there is in this breath of the storm! The most petty, paltry, and commonplace features of human life here become splendid under the lightning.

We may say of the Muse of Tolstoi what Pierre Bezukhov once said of Natasha. "Is she clever?" asked Princess Maria. Pierre hesitated. "I think not," he said at last, "or rather, she is. *She does not condescend to be clever.* No, she is resourceful, but no more."

The resourcefulness of Tolstoi's Muse lies precisely in this, that she, as it were, "does not condescend to be clever," that with her you sometimes forget the existence of the human mind.

As for Dostoievski's Muse, we may doubt any other qualities of hers we please, only not her intelligence. He remarks in one place that an author ought to have *a sting;* "this sting," he proceeds to explain, "is the rapier point of deep feeling." I consider that no Russian writer, except Pushkin, was such a master of "the mental rapier of feeling" as Dostoievski himself.

In contradistinction with the favourite heroes of Tolstoi, who are not so much intelligent as "philosophising," the principal heroes of Dostoievski—Raskolnikov, Versilov, Stavrogine, Prince Myshkine, and Ivan Karamazov—are clever men first and foremost. Indeed it would seem that, taken on the whole, they are the cleverest, most rational, cultured, and cosmopolitan of Russians, and are European because they "in the highest degree belong to Russia."

We are accustomed to think that the more abstract thought is, the more cold and dispassionate it is. It is not so; or at least, it is not so with us. From the heroes of Dostoievski we may see how abstract thought may be passionate, how metaphysical theories and deductions are rooted, not only in cold reason, but in the heart, emotions and will.

There are thoughts which pour oil on the fire of the passions and inflame man's flesh and blood more powerfully than the most unrestrained licence. There is a logic of the passions, but there are also passions in logic. And these are essentially *our* new passions, peculiar to us and alien to the men of former civilizations.

Raskolnikov "sharpened his casuistry like a razor." But with this razor of abstractions he cuts himself almost fatally. His transgression is the fruit, as the public prosecutor Porphyry puts it, "of a heart outraged theoretically." The same may be said of all the heroes of Dostoievski: their passions, their misdeeds, committed or merely "resolved on by conscience," are the natural outcome of their dialectic. Icy, razor-sharp, this does not extinguish, but kindle and inflame. In it there is fire and ice at once. They feel deeply because they think deeply; they suffer endlessly because they are endlessly deliberate; they dare to will because they have dared to think. And the further, apparently, it is from life—the more abstract, the more fiery is their thought, the deeper it enters into their lives. O strange young Russia!

And the most abstract thought is, at the same time, the most passionate: the burning thought of God. "All my life God has tortured me!" owns the Nihilist Kirillov. And all Dostoievski's heroes are "God-tortured." Not the life of the body, its end and beginning, death and birth, as with Tolstoi, but the life of the spirit, the denial or affirmation of God, are with Dostoievski the ever-boiling source of all human passions and sufferings. The torrent of the most real, the most "living" life, falling only from these very highest summits of metaphysics and religion, acquires for him that strength of flow, that turbulence of action and striving, which carries him to his tragical catastrophes.

The great poets of the past ages, in depicting the passions of the heart, left out of consideration the passions of the mind, as if they thought them a subject out of the reach of the painter's delineation. If Faust and Hamlet are nearest to us of all heroes, because they think more than any, yet they feel less, they act less, precisely because they think more. The tragedy of both men lies in the contradiction which they cannot solve, between the *passionate heart and passionless thought.* But is not a tragedy of *thinking* passion or passionate *thought* possible? The future belongs to this tragedy and no other. And Dostoievski was one of the first to make an approach to it.

He has overcome the superstitious timidity, common to modern artists, of feeling in presence of the mind. He has recognized and showed us the connexion there is between the tragedy of our hearts and that of our reason, our philosophical and religious consciousness. This, in his eyes, is pre-eminently the Russian tragedy of to-day. He has observed that cultivated Russians have only to come together—be it in fashionable drawing-rooms like the hearers of Prince Myshkine, or in dirty little inns, like Podrostok with Versilov, in order to begin to dispute about the most abstract of subjects—the future of European civilization, the immortality of the soul, the existence of God. In reality it is not only men of culture, but the whole Russian people (witness, for instance, the history of our dissenters), from the Judaizers of the fifteenth century to the present day Skoptsy and Dukhobortsy, who are absorbed in these thoughts. "All men philosophize, all make inquiries about belief on the roads and in the places of commerce," complained even the holy Joseph Volotski. And it is just by reason of this innate philosophical and religious animation (so Dostoievski thought) that Russians are, "in the highest degree, Europeans" —I mean the Europeans of the future. This insatiable religious thirst is the presage that Russia will share, and perhaps lead, the universal civilization of the future.

As in our bodily impressionability something is altered after reading Tolstoi, so after reading Dostoievski something is changed in our spiritual impressionability. It is impossible to forget, to either reject or accept him with impunity. His reasonings penetrate not only into the mind, but into the heart and will. They are momentous events which must have consequences. We remember them some time or other, and perhaps precisely at the most decisive impassioned crises of our lives. "Once touch the heart," he says himself, "and the wound remains." Or, as the Apostle Paul puts it, he "is quick and powerful, sharper than any two-edged sword, piercing even to the dividing asunder of soul and spirit, of joints and marrow."

There are simple-minded readers, with the effeminate, sickly sentimentality of our day, to whom Dostoievski will always seem "cruel," merely "a cruel genius." In what intolerable, what incredible situations he places his heroes! What experiments does he not play with them: through what depths of moral degeneracy and spiritual trials (contrast the bodily trials of Ivan Ilyich) does he not lead them, to crime, suicide, even idiocy! Does he not give expression in the humiliating situations in which he places human souls to that same cynical malice which Tolstoi finds expression for by terrible and humiliating physical conditions? Does it not sometimes seem as if he tortures his "dear victims" without object, in order to enjoy? Yes, of a truth he is one who delights in torture, a grand Inquisitor, "a cruel genius."

And is all this suffering natural, possible, real? Does it occur? Where has it been seen? And even if it occurs, what have we sane-thinking people to do with these rare among the rare, exceptional among the exceptional cases, these moral and mental monstrosities, deformities, and abortions, fancies of fever and delirium?

Here is the main objection to Dostoievski, one that all can understand, unnaturalness, unusualness, apparent artificiality, the absence of what is called "healthy realism." "They call me a psychologist," he says himself; "it is not true, I am only a *realist in the highest sense of the word*, i.e. I depict all the soul's depths." This is what Turgeniev meant in objecting to Dostoievski's "psychological mole-runs."

But he is a searcher into human nature; also at times "a realist in the highest sense of the word"—the realist of a new kind of experimental realism. In making scientific researches he surrounds in his machines and contrivances the phenomena of Nature with artificial and exceptional conditions. He observes how, under the influence of those conditions, the phenomenon undergoes changes. We might say that the essence of all scientific research consists precisely in deliberately "artificialising" the surrounding conditions. Thus the chemist, increasing the pressure of atmospheres to a degree impossible in the conditions of nature as known to us, gradually densifies the air and changes it from gaseous to liquid. May we not call unreal, unnatural, supernatural, nay miraculous, that transparent liquid, dark blue as the clearest sky, evaporating, boiling and yet cold, inconceivably colder than ice? There is no such thing as liquid air, at least in terrestrial nature as it comes within our scrutiny. It seems a miracle. We do not find it; yet it exists.

But is anything of the sort done by Dostoievski in his experiments with human souls? He also places them in extraordinary and artificial conditions, not knowing himself, but waiting to see, what will become of them. In order that unforeseen aspects, the powers hidden "in the depths of man's soul," may be revealed, he needs a degree of pressure of the moral atmosphere rarely met with to-day. He submits his characters either to the rarefied icy air of abstract dialectics or the fire of elemental animal passion, fire at white heat. In these experiments he sometimes arrives at states of the human mind as novel and seemingly impossible as liquefied air. Such a state of mind *may* exist, because the spiritual world, like the material, "is full," to use Leonardo da Vinci's words, "of countless possibilities, as yet unembodied." It has never been known, yet it is more than natural that *it should be;* to give the unembodied a body is a natural proceeding.

What is called Dostoievski's psychology is therefore a huge laboratory of the most delicate and exact apparatus and contrivances for measuring, testing, and weighing humanity. It is easy to imagine that to the uninitiated such a laboratory must seem something of a "devil's smithy."

Some of his scientific experiments are dangerous to the experimenter himself. We sometimes feel alarmed for him. His eyes are the first to see the unpermitted. He ventures into "depths" into which no one ventured before. Will he come back? Will he be able to manage the forces he has called up? In this daring of inquiry there is something especially modern and characteristic, it may be, of European science in general. It is also a Russian quality that we find in Tolstoi as well. With the same audacious curiosity Tolstoi scrutinizes the body and its past. The two writers supplement each other's work: "deep calleth unto deep."

In Dostoievski's novels there are peculiar passages as to which it is difficult to decide (compare some poems of Goethe's and drawings of Leonardo da Vinci's) whether they are Art or Science. At any rate they are not pure Art nor pure Science. Here accuracy of knowledge and the instinct of genius are mingled. It is a new "blend," of which the greatest artists and men of science had a pre-vision, and for which there is, as yet, no name.

And yet we have here "a cruel genius." This reproach, like some feeling of vague yet personal vexation, remains in the hearts of readers blessed with what is called "mental warmth," which we sometimes feel inclined to call "mental thaw." Why these sharp "shafts," these extremes, this "ice and fire"? Why not a little more good-heartedness, a little more warmth? Perhaps these readers are right; perhaps he really is "cruel," yet he is assuredly more merciful than they can conceive, for the object of his cruelty is knowledge. There are poisons which kill men, but have no effect on animals. Those to whom Dostoievski seems cruel will probably survive.

There remains the question, more worthy of our attention— the question of the cruelty of Dostoievski towards himself, his morbidity as an artist.

What a strange writer, in good sooth, with insatiable curiosity exploring only the maladies of the human soul, and for ever raving about plagues, as if he could not, or would not, speak of anything else! And what strange heroes these "lucky dogs," hysterical women, sensualists, deformed creatures possessed of the devil, idiots, lunatics! Perhaps it is not so much the painter as the healer of mental diseases we have here, and withal such a healer that to him we must say, "Physician, heal thyself." What have we that are whole to do with these, this plague-stricken collection of clinical cases?

But then we know tests of shameful disease have proved permanent sources of healing. Of a truth, it is only "by his sickness that we are healed." Ought not we, who have had such a warning from the history of the world, though we are only nominally Christians, to deal with less careless self-confidence, with more civilized caution, with all maladies?

For instance, we see too clearly the connexion between health and strength, an *abundance* of vitality on the one side and between disease and weakness and the *loss* of vitality on the other. Yet does there not exist a less obvious but not less real connexion between disease and strength, between what seems disease and real strength? If the seed does not sicken and die and decay, then it does not bear fruit. If the wingless insect in the chrysalis does not sicken, then it never gets wings. And "a woman when she is in travail suffereth pain because her hour is come." There is a sickness, not unto death, but unto life. Whole generations, civilizations, and nations are like to die for pain, but this too may be the birth-pang and the natural and wholesome sickness. In societies, true, it is immeasurably more difficult to distinguish apparent from real sickness, Decay from New Birth. Here we must feel our way. But there are dangerous diseases of society, which depend not on the want, but the excess of undeveloped life, of accumulated and unvented inward power, from the superabundance of health. Our national champions have sometimes felt "burdened with strength," as with a load, and seemed ailing because too strong.

The reverse is, of course, also true. Temporary excess of vitality and the sharpening of the natural capacities is the outcome of real sickness. The too strained cord sounds more loudly before it snaps.

Yes, the more deeply we ponder it the more difficult and enigmatical becomes the question of social maladies, and of the "sacred," or not sacred, malady of Dostoievski in particular. Yet it seems clear that whether he be great or little, at any rate he is unlike any of the family of world-famous writers. Does his strength come from his ailment, or his ailment from his strength? Is the real holiness—if not of the author himself (though those that were about him declare that there were times when he, too, seemed almost a saint) yet that of the *Idiot*—the result of apparent disease? Or does undoubted disease result from the doubtful sanctity?

" 'Go to the doctor,' Raskolnikov advises Svidrigailov, who has told him about his 'presentiments.'

" 'I know, without your telling me,' is the reply 'that I am out of health, though really I don't know in what way. *In my own way*, I feel sure, I am five times as well as you.'

"I asked, 'Do you believe in previsions—presentiments?'

" 'No; nothing will induce me to believe in them,' cried the other, with a touch of anger.

" 'Well now, what is the usual remark on the subject?' growled Svidrigailov, as if to himself, looking on one side and hanging his head down. 'They say, "You are ill: it is all your fancies—nothing but imagination, delirium." *But there's no strict logic in that.* I admit that previsions only appear to sick men, but then that only argues that previsions appear only to sick men, and not that they have no existence in themselves.'

" 'Certainly they have none,' persisted Raskolnikov irritably.

" 'No? You think so?' resumed the other, slowly gazing at him. 'Well, how if you settle it this way (there, help me): previsions are, so to say, fragments—pieces of other worlds, beginnings. The healthy man, of course, can't see them anyhow, because a healthy man is the most earthly man. He must, of course, live only the life of this world for completeness and order's sake. But no sooner does he fall ill, no sooner is the normal earthly order broken in his organism, than straightway the possibility of another world begins to dawn on him. The more ailing he is, the closer, I suggest, his contact with the other world.' "[1]

We can understand why Raskolnikov is irritated: although he himself has a dialectic on which he places his whole reliance, "sharpened like a razor," he feels that Svidrigailov, whom he despises as a moonstruck dreamer, has one still keener. Is Svidrigailov simply laughing at Raskolnikov? Is he merely teasing him with his previsions? Or is he exceedingly serious? Has he arrived at finally doubting even *unbelief?* He once admits that the idea of eternity sometimes seems to him discomforting: "a chamber something like a village bathhouse, long neglected, and with spiders' webs in all its corners."

It is curious that Dostoievski in his last diary, when expressing his stray thoughts about Christianity, repeats almost word for word the expression of Svidrigailov: "The firm belief of mankind in the contact with other worlds, obstinate and enduring, is also very significant." Not only so, these words of Svidrigailov's are also echoed by the "saintly" old Zosima in *The Brothers Karamazov:* "Grown creatures live and are kept alive only by the sense of contact with other and mysterious worlds."

In his thoughts about illness as the source of some higher life, or at least a state of insight not attainable in health, Svidrigailov and the Idiot agree with the "holy" Prince Myshkine.

"He thought, amongst other things, how, in his epileptic condition, there was one stage, just before the actual attack, when suddenly in the midst of sadness, mental darkness, and

[1] From *Crime and Punishment.*

oppression, his brain, as it were, flamed up, and with an unwonted outburst all his vital powers were vivified simultaneously. The sensation of living and of self-consciousness at such moments was almost decupled. They were moments like prolonged lightning. As he thought over this afterwards, when in a normal state, he often said to himself that all these flashes and beams of the highest self-realization and self-consciousness and doubtless 'highest existence' were nothing but a disease, the interruption of the normal state; *and if so, it was by no means the highest state, but on the contrary must be reckoned as the very lowest.* And yet he came at last to the exceedingly paradoxical conclusion, *'What matter if it is a morbid state?'* Finally he decided, *'What difference can it make that the tension is abnormal, if the result itself, if the moment of sensation, when remembered and examined in the healthy state, proves to be in the highest degree harmony and beauty; and gives an unheard of and undreamed of feeling of completion of balance, of satisfaction, and exultant prayerful fusion with the highest synthesis of life?'* If at that, the last instant of consciousness before the attack, he had happened to say to himself lucidly and deliberately 'Yes, for this moment one might give one's whole life,' then certainly that instant of itself would be worth a lifetime. However, he did not stand out for dialectics: obfuscation, mental darkness and idiocy stand before him as the obvious consequence of these loftiest moments."

It is a pity that Prince Myshkine did not stand out for the dialectical part of his deduction. For there is a vast importance attaching to the question, whether it is worth while to give for "a moment of the highest existence" the life, not merely of a man, but of all mankind? In other words, *"Is the goal of the world's evolution an endless continuation in time, in the succession of civilizations,* in the sequence of the generations, or some *final culmination* of all the destinies of history, all 'times and seasons,' *in a moment of 'the highest existence'; in what Christian mysticism calls 'the ending of the world'?"* This question seems mystical, abstract, aloof from actuality, but cannot fail, sooner or later, to have an effect on social life of the whole of mankind.

Before Christianity came mankind lived as the beasts live, without thought of death, with a sense of animal perdurability. The first, and so far the only religion which has felt the *im-*

perativeness of the thought of the end, of death—not only for man in particular, but also *for the whole of mankind*—has been Christianity. And perhaps it is just in this that lies the main distinction of the influence of Christianity (an influence that, even yet, is not complete) on the moral and political destinies of Europe.

And here the idea of the end of the world, the last consummation of all earthly destinies in a moment, when the angel of the Apocalypse "shall declare to all living that there shall be no more time," the moment of the highest harmony of "higher existence"—last pinnacle of all the civilization of the world—draws near to another idea. To the crowning idea of the religion of Christ the God-man draws near from another shore the religion, the solution of the man-God. Its preacher in Dostoievski's pages is the Nihilist Kirillov in the book called *The Possessed*—Kirillov whom all his life "God has tortured," who repeats even to the startling coincidence in the turns of expression the "extreme paradox" uttered on this point by Prince Myshkine.

"Have you moments of eternal harmony, my friend? There are seconds—five or six of them at most go by at a time—and you feel suddenly the presence of eternal harmony. It is not earthly, and I do not say that it is heavenly, but man in his earthly guise cannot bear them. *It is necessary to be transformed physically or to die.* This is a distinct feeling and one that cannot be disputed. It is as if you suddenly had the sense of all Nature and exclaimed 'Yes, it is true'; just as God, when He created the world, at the end of every day said, 'Behold, it is good.' It is not softening of heart, but just a kind of delight. You do not forgive anything, for there is nothing to forgive. Neither do you 'love,' for it is a feeling higher than love. The most terrible part is that it is so terribly distinct and joyful. For more than five seconds the mind cannot bear it, and must break down. In those five seconds I live a lifetime, *and for them I would give my lifetime.*

"In order to hold out ten seconds you must be transformed physically. I think men ought to cease to propagate. What is the use of children, or of progress, seeing the goal has been attained? In the New Testament it is written that in the resurrection they shall not have children, but be as the angels of God."

91

Here, in reality, Kirillov merely carries to its farthest consequences the dialectic of Prince Myshkine when he says "For that moment a man might give his whole life." Kirillov carries it on and concludes, *"For that moment you might give the life of all mankind."* However, Prince Myshkine too at times seems to approach this pinnacle. He dreads it, but it is nevertheless inevitable. "At that moment," he says to an intimate old friend, "there somehow became intelligible to me that hard saying, *'There shall be no more time.'* "

"Seriously, of course, he would not have maintained it," unexpectedly and timidly concludes Dostoievski. "In his appreciation of that minute doubtless there was an error." What error? "Obfuscation, mental darkness, and idiocy stood before him as the evident consequence of these loftiest minutes." But is not this obfuscation, this mental darkness, the prospect for every man living? Might not all mankind voluntarily give up its continued life for a brief epoch of intensest harmony with God? Would not that be a solution of both Pagan and Christian doctrine? This question is rooted in the very heart of Christian, nay, of *all* religion.

"Does this state often come to you?" asks Shatov of Kirillov, after his admission as to his moments of eternal harmony.

"Once in three days, or once in a week."

"Have you not got epilepsy?"

"No."

"Well, it means that you will have it. Take care, Kirillov; I have heard that is just the way epilepsy begins. An epileptic described to me in detail his sensations before an attack, exactly as you have: he mentioned the five seconds, and declared he could not stand more."

In Prince Myshkine[2] also the spiritual beauty of nature (undoubted in Dostoievski's eyes) results from these very flashes of "eternal harmony."

Kirillov anticipates a gradual but literal "physical transformation of man." We seem actually to hear echoes of apocalyptic prophecies: "Behold, I make all things new. There shall be a new heaven and a new earth." "In Christ Jesus—*a new*

---

[2] In *The Idiot.* "The theory put forward in *The Idiot* is, that a brain in which some of those springs which we consider essential are weakened may yet remain superior, both intellectually and morally, to others less affected."—WALISZEWSKI.

creature." The "physical transformation of man" is the new birth of the flesh—the real "resurrection of the body." "I tell you a mystery. We shall not all die, but we shall all be changed."

"Then there will be a new life on earth," says Kirillov. *"Then History will be seen divided into two vast epochs, the first from the gorilla to the annihilation of the conception of God, and, secondly, from the extinction of God to—"*

"To the gorilla?" suggested Stavrogine, with cold mockery.

"To the transformation of the earth and of man physically," resumed Kirillov calmly. "Man will be a god, and be physically transformed in his powers. The world will be changed, and all things will be changed, including thought and emotion."

The idea of the physical transformation of man gives Kirillov no rest, and haunts him like a fixed idea.

"I begin and end and open the door. And I save," he says to Peter Verkhovenski just before his suicide, in prophetic and pitiful enthusiasm. "Only this one thing can save all men, and in the next generation regenerate them physically; for in his present physical guise, as far as my conceptions take me, it is impossible for man to exist anyway without a previous God. I have sought for three years the attributes of my deity, and have found it: his attribute is self-will! That is the only way I can materially show my insubmission and my new and terrible liberty."

To Dostoievski Kirillov is a madman, "possessed, perhaps, of some spirit," one of those possessed that even Pushkin had foresight of:

> Endless, shapeless, soundless,
> In the moon's dim rays
> Demons circled, many
> As the leaves of November.

Not for nothing were these lines of Pushkin's taken by Dostoievski as a motto for his *Possessed.* He tried to discover in Kirillov to what monstrous extremes it is possible for the Russian nature to carry the logical dialectics of atheism.

But then, even Prince Myshkine is also a madman, possessed of devils, though only in the eyes of "this world," the wisdom of which is "foolishness with the Lord," and not in the eyes of his Creator. The "moments of highest harmony" which light up the figure of the Idiot with such a glow of unearthly beauty and sanctity are due also, according to his own admission, to the "sacred," or daemonic, sickness. The most profound and vital thoughts of Kirillov and Prince Myshkine both are in connexion with the prophecy "There shall be no more time," i.e. that the aim of universal, historical evolution is not an endless, earthly continuance, *but the ending of mankind.* Here Dostoievski hesitates. He will not fully utter his own thoughts; he draws back before some gulf, and closes his eyes: the thinker is lost in the artist. The Idiot and Kirillov are two sides of his own being, his two faces—one open, the other mysterious. Kirillov is the double of the Idiot.

"To recognize that there is no God, and at the same time not to recognize that you yourself have become a God, is folly; otherwise you would infallibly kill yourself." So says the daring Kirillov. "If there *is* a God, how can I bear the thought that *I* am not that God?" So says Friedrich Nietzsche. "There is no God. He is dead. And we have killed him. Ought we not to turn ourselves into deities? *Never was a deed done greater than this. He who shall be born after us by this alone will belong to a higher stage in history than any that has gone before.*" Who says this? Kirillov again? No, Friedrich Nietzsche. But Kirillov, as we have seen, says the same, with his two main epochs of history—including the extinction of the present conception of God. He too foretells the transformation of the earth and of the "physical nature of man," i.e. in other words, the appearance of the "Man-god," the "Uebermensch."

Although Nietszche called Dostoievski "his great master," we know that the principal ideas of Nietzsche were framed independently of the latter, under the influence of the Hellenic world, and mainly of ancient Tragedy, the philosophy of Kant and Schopenhauer on the one hand, and on the other the conclusions of modern experimental science, the ideas of Darwin, Spencer, and Haeckel on the biological transformation of species, the world's progress, natural metamorphosis, and Evolution, as it is called. Nietzsche merely carried on these scientific deductions and applied them to questions of sociology and universal history. *Man to him is not the end, the last link of the chain, but only one of the links of cosmic progress: just as man was the outcome of the transmutation of animal species, so a new creature will result from the transmutation of civilized human species.* This very being, the "new creature," is the "more than man," or, as with ingenious cynicism Dostoievski's Nihilist puts it, our world proceeds "from the gorilla to the man, and from man to the extinction of God," to the Man-god.

Here, of course, we have only the generally accessible, obvious, and outward aspect of Nietzsche—one which, in the long run, seemed to himself a coarse outer shell. He has also another more profound and hidden aspect. "As regards my complaint," he owns in one place, "I am undoubtedly more indebted to it than to health. I am indebted to it for *the highest kind of health,* the kind *in which a man is the stronger for whatever does not kill him.* I owe all my philosophy to it. Great pain alone is the final emancipator of the soul. Only great agony—that long-drawn, slow torture in which we seem to be burning over damp faggots, a pain which is in no hurry —only such lets us who are philosophers descend to our lowest depths and makes us rely on nothing of faith, good will, concealment, softness and directness, on which, perhaps, we previously based our humanity." This Nietzsche, like the Idiot and Kirillov, finds in the birth-pang, in his illness, "moments of eternal harmony," the source of "the highest state." *In the death of the human* he finds the first lightnings and glimpses of the "superhuman."

"Man is what must be overcome," says Zarathustra. Only by overcoming, by mortifying, both in his spirit and in his flesh, all that is "human, too human," only by casting off "the old man" with the animal serpent-like wisdom as an old dead slough, can man rise to incorruptibility, attain to the divine existence for which "there is a new heaven and a new earth."

Pushkin certainly—the most healthy and sane of our countrymen—had already pondered on this "physical transformation of man," physical and spiritual at once, this regeneration and turning of the "fleshly" flesh into spiritual flesh.

> And to my lips he stooped,
> Removed my sinful tongue:
> (Idle of speech and crafty)
> And placed with his blood-stained hand,
> Within my palsied lips,
> The serpent's sting of wisdom.
>
> Clove my breast with his glaive,
> My fluttering heart drew forth,

> And a burning fiery coal
> Forced into my bared breast.
> Like a corpse in the desert I lay—
> Then God's voice called to me:
> "Prophet, arise!"

But the Man lying in the desert will arise *no longer man* as we know him.

If the seed does not die, then it does not germinate. The constructive agony of birth is like the destructive agony of death.

"There come, as it were, unnecessary and gratuitous sufferings," says Tolstoi in *The Kingdom of God*, with regard to the inward state, "passing into a new form of life, untried as yet by man as he is to-day. Something happens akin to childbearing. All is ready for the new life, but this life still does not make its appearance. The situation seems one from which there is no issue." And a few lines later he speaks *of the flight, the wings, of the new man,* who "feels himself perfectly free, just as a bird would feel in a fenced-round close, *as soon as it chose to spread its wings.*"

Who knows? In others (not in himself) Tolstoi has sometimes found this illness of the present day—the pang of birth, the pain of the bursting of wings. Is he himself as free from such pain as he avers, as he would wish to be? Or is he only more skilful than others in hiding weakness by reproving the weakness of others?

"Every man of our day, if we penetrate the contrast of his judgment and his life, is in a desperate condition," he says, as usual speaking of others, of the people of "this world." But is there another "man of our day" whose reason and life are at greater variance than his own? In him the old struggle still continues in the subterranean quakings and echoes, like the dull roar of earthquake. In Tolstoi's *Resurrection* old Akim celebrates his "new birth" and the death of the "animal" in him—what he believes to be his final victory over the Beast. But if it be a victory, what a poor one! Does not Tolstoi realize in the penetralia of his artistic conscience that it is just here, at the decisive moment, that something has broken down and betrayed him? In this "regeneration," the mortification of the flesh has led to what it always leads to, the mortification of the spirit. Before our eyes is taking place the suicide of a man's genius.

Was this the "Resurrection" that we expected of him, that he expected of himself? It is not for nothing that he abjures those of his works which he owes to his "world-wide fame." *In him there was, or might have been, a prophet, though by no means such a one as he considered himself to be.* He must content himself with his fame as mere artist.

Tolstoi has human fame, but not God's fame, which is man's absence of fame, the persecution of prophets. His pride must be scourged by the servile praises of "innumerable pigmies." The spectacle recalls the torments of those wretches who, stripped naked, bound and smeared with honey, were exposed in the sun for insects to devour.

He is always silent. Silence is his last refuge. He will not admit his sufferings. But yet he knows that the hour is at hand when One, to whom nothing can be refused, will demand an account. We owe pity to this man of the day in his most desperate condition, the most lonely, deserted, and unregarded, in spite of all this fame. But sometimes one fancies that, being so great, he deserves no pity. In any case, only those who do not *love* him will believe in the health, the peace, and happiness, the "regeneration" of this man.

His illness is shown by a gradually increasing silence, callousness, decline, ossification, and petrification of the heart, once the warmest of human hearts.

It is because his ailment is inward, because he himself is scarcely conscious of it, that it is more grievous than the malady of Dostoievski or the madness of Nietzsche. Pushkin carried to the grave the secret of his great health; Dostoievski that of his great sickness. Nietzsche, the corpse of the "more-than-man," has gone from us, carrying the secret of his wisdom into the madhouse. And Tolstoi, too, has deserted us.

This generation is thrice-deserted, timid, ailing, ridiculous even in its own eyes. We have to solve a riddle which Gods and Titans could not solve—to draw the line which separates health in us from sickness, life from death, resurrection from decay. We can evade this riddle. Have we courage to solve it?

An almost unbearable burden of responsibility is thus laid on our generation. Perhaps the destinies of the world never hung so finely in the balance before, as if on the edge of a sword between two chasms. The spirit of man is faintly conscious that the beginning of the end is at hand.

Woe to them who awake too early, when all others are still asleep. But even if we wished we can no longer deceive ourselves and ignore the blinding light we behold.

Among the common people, far down out of hearing, there are those who are awaking as we.* Who will be the first to arise and say that he is awake? Who has overcome the fine delusion of our day, which confounds in each of us, in minds and life, the withering of the seed with its revival, the birthpang with the death-pang, the sickness of Regeneration with the sickness of Degeneration, the true "symbolism" with "decadence"? Action is first needed; and only when we have acted can we *speak*. Meanwhile here is an end of our open course, our words, our contemplation; and a beginning of our secrecy, our silence, and our action.

* Merezhkovsky is thinking of Maxim Gorky.—EDITOR'S NOTE.

VII

D. H. LAWRENCE

On Dostoievsky and Rozanov

We are told on the wrapper of this book that Prince Mirsky considered Rozanov "one of the greatest Russians of modern times. . . . Rozanov is the greatest revelation of the Russian mind yet to be shown to the West."

We become diffident, confronted with these superlatives. And when we have read E. Gollerbach's long "Critico-Biographical Study," forty-three pages, we are more suspicious still, in spite of the occasionally profound and striking quotations from *Solitaria* and from the same author's *Fallen Leaves*. But there we are; we've got another of these morbidly introspective Russians, morbidly wallowing in adoration of Jesus, then getting up and spitting in His beard, or in His back hair, at least; characters such as Dostoievsky has familiarized us with, and of whom we are tired. Of these self-divided, *gamin*-religious Russians who are so absorbedly concerned with their own dirty linen and their own piebald souls we have had a little more than enough. The contradictions in them are not so very mysterious, or edifying, after all. They have a spurting, *gamin* hatred of civilization, of Europe, of Christianity, of governments, and of everything else, in their moments of energy; and in their inevitable relapses into weakness, they make the inevitable recantation; they whine, they humiliate themselves, they seek unspeakable humiliation for themselves, and call it Christ-like, and then with the left hand commit some dirty little crime or meanness, and call it the mysterious complexity of the human soul. It's all masturbation, half-baked, and one gets tired of it. One gets tired of being told that Dostoievsky's *Legend of the Grand Inquisitor* "is the most

A review of V. V. Rozanov's *Solitaria*, by D. H. Lawrence, published in *Phoenix* (London: Heinemann; New York: Viking Press, 1936). Reprinted by permission of Laurence Pollinger, Ltd., and the Estate of the late Frieda Lawrence.

profound declaration which ever was made about man and life." As far as I'm concerned, in proportion as a man gets more profoundly and personally interested in himself, so does my interest in him wane. The more Dostoievsky gets worked up about the tragic nature of the human soul, the more I lose interest. I have read the *Grand Inquisitor* three times, and never can remember what it's really about. This I make as a confession, not as a vaunt. It always seems to me, as the Germans say, *mehr Schrei wie Wert*.

And in Rozanov one fears one has got a pup out of the Dostoievsky kennel. *Solitaria* is a sort of philosophical work, about a hundred pages, of a kind not uncommon in Russia, consisting in fragmentary jottings of thoughts which occurred to the author, mostly during the years 1910 and 1911, apparently, and scribbled down where they came, in a cab, in the train, in the w.c., on the sole of a bathing-slipper. But the thought that came in a cab might just as well have come in the w.c. or "examining my coins," so what's the odds? If Rozanov wanted to give the physical context to the thought, he'd have to create the scene. "In a cab," or "examining my coins" means nothing.

Then we get a whole lot of bits, some of them interesting, some not; many of them to be classified under the heading of: To Jesus or not to Jesus! if we may profanely parody Hamlet's To be or not to be. But it is the Russian's own parody. Then you get a lot of self-conscious personal bits: "The only *masculine* thing about you—is your trousers": which was said to Rozanov by a girl: though, as it isn't particularly true, there was no point in his repeating it. However, he has that "self-probing" nature we have become acquainted with. "Teaching is form, and I am formless. In teaching there must be order and a system, and I am systemless and even disorderly. There is duty—and to me any duty at the bottom of my heart always seemed comical, and on any duty, at the bottom of my heart, I always wanted to play a trick (except tragic duty). . . ."

Here we have the pup of the Dostoievsky kennel, a so-called nihilist: in reality, a Mary-Mary-quite-contrary. It is largely tiresome contrariness, even if it is spontaneous and not self-induced.

And, of course, in Mary-Mary-quite-contrary we have the ever-recurrent whimper: I want to be good! I *am* good: Oh,

I *am so* good, I'm better than anybody! I love Jesus and all the saints, and above all, the blessed Virgin! Oh, how I love purity!—and so forth. Then they give a loud *crepitus ventris* as a punctuation.

Dostoievsky has accustomed us to it, and we are hard-boiled. Poor Voltaire, if he recanted, he only recanted once, when his strength had left him, and he was neither here nor there. But these Russians are for ever on their death-beds, and neither here nor there.

Rozanov's talk about "lovely faces and dear souls" of children, and "for two years I have been 'in Easter,' in the pealing of bells," truly "arrayed in white raiment," just makes me feel more hard-boiled than ever. It's a cold egg.

Yet, in *Solitaria* there are occasional profound things. "I am not such a scoundrel yet as to think about morals"—"Try to crucify the Sun, and you will see which is God"—and many others. But to me, self-conscious personal revelations, touched with the gutter-snipe and the actor, are not very interesting. One has lived too long.

So that I come to the end of Gollerbach's "Critico-Biographical Study" sick of the self-fingering sort of sloppiness, and I have very much the same feeling at the end of *Solitaria*, though occasionally Rozanov hits the nail on the head and makes it jump.

Then come twenty pages extracted from Rozanov's *The Apocalypse of Our Times*, and at once the style changes, at once you have a real thing to deal with. *The Apocalypse* must be a far more important book than *Solitaria*, and we wish to heaven we had been given it instead. Now at last we see Rozanov as a real thinker, and "the greatest revelation of the Russian mind yet to be shown to the West."

Rozanov had a real man in him, and it is true, what he says of himself, that he did not feel in himself that touch of the criminal which Dostoievsky felt in *himself*. Rozanov was not a criminal. Somewhere, he was integral, and grave, and a seer, a true one, not a *gamin*. We see it all in his *Apocalypse*. He is not really a Dostoievskian. That's only his Russianitis.

The book is an attack on Christianity, and as far as we are given to see, there is no canting or recanting in it. It is passionate, and suddenly valid. It is not jibing or criticism or pulling to pieces. It is a real passion. Rozanov has more or less recovered the genuine pagan vision, the phallic vision, and with those eyes he looks, in amazement and consternation, on the mess of Christianity.

For the first time we get what we have got from no Russian, neither Tolstoi nor Dostoievsky nor any of them, a real, positive view on life. It is as if the pagan Russian had wakened up in Rozanov, a kind of Rip van Winkle, and was just staggering at what he saw. His background is the vast old pagan background, the phallic. And in front of this, the tortured complexity of Christian civilization—what else can we call it?—is a kind of phantasmagoria to him.

He is the first Russian, as far as I am concerned, who has ever said anything to me. And his vision is full of passion, vivid, valid. He is the first to see that immortality is in the vividness of life, not in the loss of life. The butterfly becomes a whole revelation to him: and to us.

When Rozanov is wholly awake, and a new man, a risen man, the living and resurrected pagan, then he is a great man and a great seer, and perhaps, as he says himself, the first Russian to emerge. Speaking of Tolstoi and Leontiev and Dostoievsky, Rozanov says: "I speak straight out what they dared not even suspect. I speak because after all I am more of a thinker than they. That is all." . . . "But the problem (in the case of Leontiev and Dostoievsky) is and was about anti-Christianity, about the victory over the very essence of Christianity, over that terrible avitalism. Whereas from him, from the phallus everything flows."

When Rozanov is in this mood, and in this vision, he is not dual, nor divided against himself. He is one complete thing. His vision and his passion are positive, non-tragical.

Then again he starts to Russianize, and he comes in two. When he becomes aware of himself, and personal, he is often ridiculous, sometimes pathetic, sometimes a bore, and almost always "dual." Oh, how they love to be dual, and divided against themselves, these Dostoievskian Russians! It is as good as a pose: always a Mary-Mary-quite-contrary business. "The great horror of the human soul consists in this, that while thinking of the Madonna it at the same time does not cease thinking of Sodom and of its sins; and the still greater horror is that even in the very midst of Sodom it does not forget the

Madonna, it yearns for Sodom and the Madonna, and this at one and the same time, without any discord."

The answer to that is, that Sodom and Madonna-ism are two halves of the same movement, the mere tick-tack of lust and asceticism, pietism and pornography. If you're not pious, you won't be pornographical, and *vice versa*. If there are no saints, there'll be no sinners. If there were no ascetics, there'd be no lewd people. If you divide the human psyche into two halves, one half will be white, the other black. It's the division itself which is pernicious. The swing to one extreme causes the swing to the other. The swing towards Immaculate Madonna-ism inevitably causes the swing back to the whore of prostitution, then back again to the Madonna, and so *ad infinitum*. But you can't blame the soul for this. All you have to blame is the craven, cretin human intelligence, which is always seeking to get away from its own centre.

But Rozanov, when he isn't Russianizing, is the first Russian really to see it, and to recover, if unstably, the old human wholeness.

So that this book is extremely interesting, and really important. We get impatient with the Russianizing. And yet, with Gollerbach's Introduction and the letters at the end, we do get to know all we want to know about Rozanov, personally. It is not of vast importance, what he was personally. If he behaved perversely, he was never, like Dostoievsky, inwardly perverse, and when he says he was not "born rightly," he is only yelping like a Dostoievsky pup.

It is the voice of the new man in him, not the Dostoievsky whelp, that means something. And it means a great deal. We shall wait for a full translation of *The Apocalypse of Our Times*, and of *Oriental Motifs*. Rozanov matters, for the future.

The Contrary Traffic

VIII

V. G. KOROLENKO

My First Encounter with Dickens

V. G. Korolenko (1853–1921) was as much Polish by blood as he was Russian. A native of Zhitomir, in a disputed border area between Russia and Poland, he was educated in Petersburg and Moscow. Arrested and deported to Siberia in 1879, Korolenko was not permitted to return to Russia until 1885, when he published *Makar's Dream*. From 1900 until his death he lived in Poltava, and in this period almost gave up storytelling, though in his last years he wrote an autobiography, *The History of My Contemporary*, of which the later parts were published posthumously. Russian critics frequently discover a Dickensian note in some of Korolenko's best stories.

The first book which I began to read of my own volition, and which I read through to the end with some fluency, was a novel by the Polish writer Korzhenewski—a talented production and written on a high enough literary level. No one after that guided my choice of reading, and at one time this took on a diverse, arbitrary, one might even say an adventurous, character.

In this I was following in the steps of my elder brother.

He was two and a half years older than I was. In childhood this difference in age is a notable one, but my brother was presumptuous on this account. Striving to distinguish himself in every way from "the kids," he took for himself various privileges. In the first place he took to a walking-stick, with which he strolled along the street, brandishing it in a distinctive manner. This was recognized as his privilege. The older people laughed, but the walking-sticks did not disappear. It

This essay was translated by Donald Davie. It is a kind of appendix to *The History of My Contemporary* and first appeared in *Nedelya Sovremmenovo Slova* (a weekly supplement to the newspaper *Sovremennoe Slovo*), January 30, 1912. It is included in Korolenko's *Collected Essays* (Vol. II), published by A. F. Marx, and also appears in Korolenko's *Collected Works*, edited by N. V. and G. V. Korolenko (Moscow: OGIZ, 1947).

was somewhat worse when he supplied himself likewise with tobacco, and began to train himself to smoke, keeping it secret from his parents, but practicing openly before us, his juniors. Nothing came of this: he was sick, and he only kept more tobacco out of pride. But when my father came in some way to learn of it, he was at first very annoyed, and later decided: "Let the child be better employed in reading a book." My brother received "2 zloty" (30 kopeks) and subscribed by the month to the library of Pan Butkevich, a tradesman in Kiev Street, who sold newspapers, pictures, notepaper, reading primers, exercise books, and who likewise issued, against cash, library books for reading. The books were not very numerous, and for the most part consisted of the stock in trade which commanded the most ready sale at that period: Dumas, Eugene Sue, Cooper, "mysteries" of various sorts and, it seems, the then already well-known *Rocambole*.*

To this new ruling my brother gave the appearance of a further privilege. When I tried sometimes to glance into a book left by him on the table, he would snatch it from my hand and tell me:

"Be off! It's too early yet for you to be reading novels."

After that it was only in secret, and in his absence, that I took a book, and, keeping thoroughly alert, devoured page after page.

This was a strangely varied, and a very highly-flavored sort of reading. Never was there question of reading uninterruptedly, becoming familiar with the plot and then following from that to the exposition. And now much of what I read then appears to me like a landscape below raining mists. As if I looked down a forest glade, brightly shining islets appear and fade . . . D'Artagnan, riding out of a small town on a ridiculous jade, the figures of his friends the musketeers, the assassination of Queen Margot, some villainies of the Jesuits, from Sue . . . All these pictures appear and fade, scared off by the steps of my brother, only to reappear thereafter in a different place already (in the subsequent volume), without any link in the action, without any definite characters. Duelists, assaults, ambuscades, lovers' intrigues, crimes and their inevita-

---

* *Rocambole* was the creation of Ponson du Terrail, who enjoyed a vogue as the pasteboard Dumas of the Second Empire.—EDITOR'S NOTE.

ble penalty. Now and then it befell me to take leave of the hero at the most critical moment, when they were running him through with a sword, and meantime the novel was still unfinished, and that meant that a place was left for the most excruciating conjectures. To my diffident questions—did the hero recover? and what became of his beloved while he was dragging out a miserable existence with a sword in his breast?—my brother replied with officious severity:

"Don't touch my books! It's too early yet for you to be reading novels."

And he would hide his books in another place.

After some little time, however, it inconvenienced him to run to the library, and he took advantage of one more of the privileges of his age: he began to send me to fetch the books for him.

I was very glad of this. The library was quite a long way from our home, and the book was thus at my disposal throughout this stretch. I began to read on the way.

This sort of procedure gave to the very process of reading a peculiar, and, as it were, a venturesome character. From the first I did not know how to look out for what was going forward in the traffic of the street, and I ran the risk of plunging under the hooves of the cabbies and carters, bumping against passers-by. I remember to this day the burly figure of a certain Pole, with gray cropped whiskers and a broad face, who, when I jostled him, took me by the collar and regarded me for some time with amused curiosity, letting me go then with some sententious maxim proper to the occasion. But with time I learned to be expert in maneuvering among perils, noting from afar, between the covers of my book, the legs that came to meet me. Slowly I went on, halting from time to time behind corners, greedily looking out for developments in the plot, and approaching the bookshop all the while. Arrived there, I hurriedly looked at the denouement and with a sigh went in to Butkevich. Of course, many lacunae remained. Knights, robbers, champions of innocence, beautiful ladies— all this, as in a sort of whirlwind, as if on the witches' sabbath, whirled through my head beneath the roar of the movement in the street, and was cut short disconnectedly, strangely and enigmatically, provoking and inflaming the imagination, but never satisfying it. Out of all the *Chevalier de Maison Rouge* I remembered only how he was disguised as a Jacobin, and paced out the flagstones in a hall of some sort, emerging in the end from beneath the scaffold, on which they had executed the most beautiful of queens, bringing with him a handkerchief steeped in her blood. What he was aiming at, and in what manner he had got himself beneath the scaffold, I did not know for a very long time.

I think that this reading did me much harm, stuffing my head with strange incongruous coils of intrigue, shadowy figures and personalities, inuring me to superficiality.

Once I brought my brother a book, sewn together apparently from a newspaper, in which, as I leafed it through on my way, I could discover with my accustomed eye no usual thread of events. The characterization was of some lofty individual, severe and unpleasant. A Merchant. He has a store in which "they were used to dealing in hides, but they never had any dealings with the female heart." Indeed! What have I to do with this uninteresting person! Then some Uncle Sol or other carries on strange conversations with his nephew in a workshop for marine equipment. Here, at last . . . the old man abducts a maiden, the merchant's daughter. But here too the whole matter boils itself down to a beggar-woman relieving her of her clothes and giving her rags in exchange. She comes home, they give her something warm to drink, and pack her off to bed. A woeful and uninteresting plot which I laid aside with great disdain: why, adventures such as that occurred in broad daylight. The book inspired me with a decided prejudice against it, and I did not take advantage of my opportunities when my brother put it by.

But lo and behold, I noticed at one time that my brother burst out laughing while reading, and then frequently flung himself back, laughing, upon the back of the rocking chair. When his companions came for him, I seized upon the book to find out what that was so funny could have happened to this merchant dealing in skins. For some time I wandered fumbling through the book, coming, just as in the street, upon whole throngs of people, upon their conversations, but still not grasping the important thing: the make-up of the Dickensian humor. Before me gleamed the small shape of little Paul, of his sister Florence, of Uncle Sol, of Captain Cuttle with his iron hook in place of a hand . . . No, still everything was of no interest . . . Toots with his passion for the waistcoat . . . The blockhead . . . Was it worthwhile writing about such a booby?

But look, skipping through Paul's death (in general I did not care for descriptions of death), I suddenly stopped in my headlong career down the page and froze, as if bewitched:

" 'Tomorrow morning, Miss Floy, papa will be going away.'

" 'You know, Susan, where he is going to?'—asked Florence, bending her eyes upon the ground."

The reader, of course, remembers the rest! Florence is mourning for the death of her brother. Mr. Dombey mourns for a son . . . A damp night. The soft rain mournfully beat upon the weeping panes. A baleful wind whined piercingly and groaned around the house, as if it too were agitated by the night's gloom. Florence sat alone in her mournful bed-chamber and was bathed in tears. From the clock-towers midnight struck.

I don't know how this happened, but with the mere first lines of this picture, the whole of it stood before me, as if in life, throwing a lurid light upon everything until then read through in fits and starts.

Suddenly I felt in life both the death of the unknown boy and that night, and that melancholy of loneliness and gloom, and the solitude in that place, blown through with the grief of death not far away . . . And the mournful fall of the dripping rain, and the groan, and the wailing of the wind, and the sickly shaking of the consumptive trees . . . And the poignant grief of the loneliness of the poor girl and the severe father. And her love for that dry, hard individual, and his fearsome indifference.

The door of the chamber stands open—not more than a hair's breadth, but all the same open—and always it was closed. The daughter with a faltering of the heart goes up to the chink. In the depth flickers a lamp, throwing an uncertain light upon the surrounding objects. The girl stands at the door. To go in or not to go in? Very softly she goes away. But the beam of light, falling in a narrow thread upon the marble floor, shines for her as a beam of celestial hope. She turned back, hardly knowing what she was doing, caught hold with her hands of the half-opened door and—went through.

My brother came back into the room for something or other, and I hardly managed to go out before he came. I stopped and waited. Is he taking the book? And I still do not know what happens further. What will this severe individual do with the poor girl, who comes to implore of him some drops of paternal love. Does he repulse her? No, it cannot be. My heart beat painfully and strongly. Yes, it cannot be. There are no such cruel people in the world. After all, surely this depends upon the author, and he will not bring himself to drive the poor girl once again back to the loneliness of that frightful and awful night . . . I felt a poignant concern that she should have met, at last, with love and tenderness. It would be so good . . . And if?

My brother ran out with his cap, and quickly his whole company went out through the court. They went off somewhere, surely for a long time. I rushed again into the room and seized upon the book.

"—Her father sat upon a chair in the depths of the study and turned over papers, one after another . . . The piercing wind wailed about the house . . . But Mr. Dombey heard nothing. He sat, absorbed in his thoughts, and those thoughts were heavier than the light step of the diffident girl. Yet his face met hers, a stern, clouded face, to which the flickering lamp communicated a somewhat wild appearance. His morose glance took on a corresponding expression.

" 'Papa! Papa! speak to me.'

"He started and sprang to the table.

" 'What do you want? Why have you come here?'

"Florence saw he knew why—and how did she know? His mind flamed in bitter letters upon his wild face . . . She took a fiery dart to her unwanted breast and a long heart-rending cry burst out of her fearful despair.

"Ah, this would be remembered by Mr. Dombey in the years to come. The cry of his daughter vanished and sank upon the air, but it does not vanish and sink away in the recesses of his soul. Yes, Mr. Dombey would remember this in the years to come!"

I stood with the book in my hands, stunned and shaken by the heart-rending cry of that girl, and by the spark of anger, and by the despair of the author himself . . . Now why, why did he write that? . . . So horrible and so cruel. Surely he might have written differently . . . Yet no. I felt then that he could not, that it was in fact thus, and he only saw this horror and was himself shaken, just as I was . . . And behold, to the heart-rending cry of the poor solitary girl was added the despair, pain, and rage of his own heart.

And I repeated for him, with hatred and a thirst for vengeance: Yes, yes, yes! He would remember, undoubtedly, undoubtedly he would remember this in years to come.

This picture straightway illumined for me, like a lightning-flash, all the fragments glimpsed so insensibly in the superficiality of reading. With grief I remembered what I had passed by so many times . . . Now I resolved to consume the remainder: I read greedily for two hours more, not tearing myself away right up to the arrival of my brother . . . I was introduced to dear Polly, the nurse, who consoled poor Florence, to the sick boy, inquiring on the shore, with the precocious wisdom of an ailing child, what the sea is talking about . . . And even the amorous Toots seemed to me now not so much of a booby. Feeling that my brother would soon return I nervously devoured page upon page, getting closer acquaintance with Florence's friends and enemies . . . And in the background all the time the figure of Mr. Dombey, already remarkable because doomed to a horrible punishment. Tomorrow on the road I should read how he, at last, "remembered in the years to come" . . . He would remember, but, of course, it would be late . . . Thus it had to be!

My brother read through the novel that night, and I heard once again how he now burst out laughing, and now in a gust of rage struck the table with his fist.

In the morning he told me:

"Now here, take it. And look at me: don't be long."

"Listen—" I brought myself to ask, "what were you laughing about yesterday?"

"You're silly as yet, and in any case, you wouldn't understand. You don't know what this humor—Anyhow, read just here—Mister Toots is having an explanation with Florence, and yet the whole business in hand never sees the light of day."

And again he took to laughing infectiously and loudly.

"Well, come here. I know: you read in the streets, and the Jews already call you 'meshiginer.' As regards that, it's still too early for you to be reading novels. But as for this one, if you understand it, you may. Only just the same, look here, don't be gone too long. You're to be back here in half an hour. Look, I'll take note of the time."

My brother was, for me, a great authority, but all the same I knew quite well that I should not return within half an hour nor yet within an hour. All I did not foresee was that for the first time in my life I was preparing something in the nature of a public scandal.

With my usual gait, but more slowly than usual, I maneuvered myself along the street, entirely absorbed in reading, but nonetheless adroitly tacking as usual among the passers-by. I stopped in corners, sat down on the benches, where they stood by the gates, came automatically to my senses and again moved on, poring over the book. It was already hard for me to attend, in the old way, only to the action along one line, not glancing aside and not stopping for the secondary characters. Everything became of unusual interest, every person lived his own life, every movement, as it were, every gesture, was engraved upon the memory. I laughed out in spite of myself when the sagacious Captain Bunsby, during the visit of the elegant Florence to his ship, inquires of Captain Cuttle: "Comrade, what would the lady have to drink?" Then I came across the explanation of the amorous Toots, discharging his salvo: "How do you do, Miss Dombey, how do you do? How are you, Miss Dombey? I am well, God be praised, Miss Dombey, and how are you?"

After this, in his famous manner, the young gentleman made a happy face, but, finding that there was nothing to be gay about, fetched a deep sigh, and judging that grief was no more to the purpose, again made a happy face and in the end, relapsed into the silence of the grave for the whole day.

Like my brother, I burst out laughing at poor Toots, drawing onto myself the attention of the passers-by. It seemed that my foresight, under the guidance of which I directed my heedless steps in sufficiently populous streets, took me almost to the end of my journey. In front was to be seen Kiev Street, where the library was. But I, in my enthusiasm for following through the separate stages, had still not reached by far those "years to come" when Mr. Dombey was to remember his sternness toward his daughter.

To this day, probably, not far from Kiev Street, in Zhitomir, stands the church of St. Pantaleimon (I think that was it). At that time, between some projecting wing of that church and the next house there was a recess, like a niche. Catching sight of this secluded nook, I went over there, leaned against the wall and . . . time flowed over my head . . . Now I noticed neither the roar of the streets nor the quiet flight of the minutes. As if spellbound I devoured scene upon scene, with no hope of reading right through to the end and yet without the power to break off. From the church rang out the vespers. The passers-by halted in passing and looked with astonishment at me in my retreat . . . Their figures, like vaguely irritating specks, were painted upon my field of vision, recalling me to the street. The young Jews—a lively, nimble, mocking tribe—threw ironical remarks and importunately inquired about something or other. Some went on, others remained . . . A crowd gathered.

Once I started up. It seemed to me that my brother approached with precipitate gait and swinging his walking-stick . . . "It cannot be," I consoled myself, but all the same I took to turning the pages more quickly . . . Mr. Dombey's second marriage . . . the proud Edith . . . She loves Florence and despises Mr. Dombey. Now, now, here it starts . . . "Then Mr. Dombey remembered . . ."

But here my enchantment was unexpectedly interrupted: my brother, having found time to go to the library, was returning thence in perplexity, not having found me, when he turned his attention upon the crowd of Jewish youths, clustered around my refuge. Ignorant as yet of the subject of their curiosity, he shouldered his way through them and . . . My brother was hot-tempered and took cognizance of any infringements of his privileged position. On this account he came swiftly into my refuge and snatched the book. Instinctively I began to hold on to it, not letting it out of my hands and not taking my eyes off it . . . The spectators exulted noisily, announcing the affair to the street with shouts and laughter.

"You dolt! Now they are closing the library—" cried my brother, and wrenching the book away, ran off down the street. In shame and confusion I followed after him, still altogether under the influence of my reading, escorted by the throng of Jewish boys. On the last pages, hurriedly turned over, had gleamed before me an idyllic picture: Florence married. She has a boy and a daughter, and . . . a certain gray old man walks with the children and looks upon his grandchild with fondness and sorrow.

"Surely—they made it up, didn't they?" I asked my brother, whom I met on the return journey from the library, satisfied because after all he had succeeded in taking a new novel and would not, in other words, be left without reading for the holiday. He had regained his composure and already only laughed at me.

"Now you are already a complete 'meshiginer' . . . You have acquired lasting fame . . . You ask: did Florence forgive? Yes, yes . . . She forgave. With Dickens the work always finishes in virtue and reconciliation."

Dickens . . . Childhood is ungrateful: I did not look at the names of the authors of books which afforded me pleasure, but this name, so silvery-sounding and pleasant, at once fixed itself upon my memory.

So there it is, how I first became acquainted—as you might say, in the street—with Dickens.

IX

A RUSSIAN CORRESPONDENT

Dickens in Russia, a Moral Educator

Nadeshda Krupskaya's unsuccessful attempt, as recorded in her book of reminiscences, to entertain Lenin during his last illness by reading him the *Christmas Carol*, the "bourgeois sentiment" of which revolted the Communist leader, is by no means a typical Russian reaction to Dickens. Lenin's purely ideological aversion contrasts strangely with the great gusto with which the wide Russian reading public used to swallow Dickens's long novels and the place which was assigned to the great English master in the established literary order.

To read the last volume of Fenimore Cooper or Mayne Reid meant for a boy in pre-war Russia more than the end of his happy prairie days and a sad farewell to the wigwams and gallant feathered chieftains. With the wild West, boyhood itself was left behind. The first novel of Dickens, who followed the two great masters of Red Indian lore in the time-honoured hierarchy of authors every self-respecting young man had to read, marked the beginning of youth and the initiation into a world of a more variegated scale of emotional values than good horsemanship and bravery. It was a red-letter day when the bespectacled, soft-spoken librarian, shyly asked to recommend a book, cast a gravely scrutinizing look at the youthful reader and then, still slightly hesitating, picked a copy of *Dombey and Son* from the crowded shelves and put the volume in a glossy uniform binding on the counter. For such an act was tantamount to a solemn recognition of one's mature age and good literary education, and consecrated as definitely as the puberty rites of the primitive tribes the achievement of a higher social standing.

To enter the quaintly crowded Dickensian world through the wealthy but not very cosy drawing-room of stiff Mr.

Reprinted, by permission, from the *Times Literary Supplement*, September 7, 1940.

Dombey was for some obscure reason regarded by Russian teachers and librarians as a minor but nevertheless binding detail of the ritual. It was considered the sign of a somewhat disrespectful mind, of dangerous anarchistic leanings, ill-breeding and bad taste to relish the eccentricities of the Pickwick Club before having paid homage to the more serious aspects of Dickens's genius by studying rather than reading the life of the prosperous city merchant.

But once this preliminary stage of the formalities was over, one was at liberty to follow the heart's desire and to roam freely through the highways and by-ways of Dickens's odd universe. Odd, indeed, to the mind of a Russian boy of fifteen appeared this remote English world with its unfamiliar institutions so surprisingly different from his own surroundings, far more puzzling than the life of the Red Indians, its strangeness enhanced by the queer names of the heroes—to which the Russian transliteration added a grotesque twist through the necessity of transcribing the letter *h*, which is lacking in the Russian alphabet, by a *g*, so that Humphrey, e.g., became Gumphrey.

Clerks and solicitors were not a common type in a commercially and industrially under-developed Russia, and the abundance of such characters, the exact vocation of which it was nearly impossible to imagine, cast a spell of mystery over these two professions, which seemed to be powerful casts or orders engaged in hatching out sinister plots against orphans and schoolboys. Clubs were entirely unknown in Russia and so were taverns of the Victorian type. Lacking the adequate Russian terms, the English names had to be preserved in the translation, their exotic sound stimulating the fancy of the youthful reader, and, not unlike the curious breed of clerks and solicitors, clubs and taverns were difficult to hold apart, their sense oscillating between mad-houses for the mildly insane and dens of iniquity.

The soft Russian tongue with its rich choice of endearing words, its wide gamut of emotional expressions and its passionate tinge enhances the sentimental aspect of Dickens's art. The translator's poetic licence in rendering the title of *Little Dorrit* by *Kroshka Dorrit*, which really means "Tiny Dorrit," is revealing in that respect. Transplanted into the new linguistic medium permeated with the breath of wide, melancholy steppes, the whimsical human fauna and flora of Dickens's fancy seemed to grow more lusciously, the local colour of the alien tongue rather adding to than detracting from the bizarre and picturesque shapes of the original. Against the backgrounds of a profoundly different reality Mr. Pickwick's antics and Mr. Micawber's exploits appeared nearly superhuman in their ridiculous or heroic forms.

Looking back, from a distance of twenty years, at those hours of the long Russian winter afternoons spent over the bulky volumes of *David Copperfield, Nicholas Nickleby, Martin Chuzzlewit* and *Master Humphrey's Clock*, and musing to-day over the first impressions gathered from the novels and the lasting benefit derived from the intense spell of Dickens's art, it becomes increasingly clear that the dramatic element in his work leaves deeper traces in the mind than the purely farcical side. The sufferings of little Nell and little Dorrit, the adversities experienced by David Copperfield and Mr. Micawber's daring ventures have a stronger and more fertile hold on the imagination than Mr. Pickwick's eccentricities. The intense melodramatic form and the lachrymose effects, albeit inferior from the purely artistic point of view, vigorously stimulate the growth of moral consciousness in the young mind. Good and evil are so clearly contrasted that there can be no doubt about the right choice and the duty to which one is by honour bound. Dickens's melodrama of human entanglements in the social sphere set the stage, as it were, for the tragedy of man divided against himself. It was not before the tragic mask of Dostoevsky appeared that the glittering world of Dickens seemed to fade, though these were the shadows of a temporary eclipse and not of oblivion.

Tolstoy

X

D. S. MEREZHKOVSKY

Tolstoy as Artist

The Princess Volkonski, wife of Prince Andrei, as we learn from the first pages of Tolstoi's great novel *Peace and War*, was rather pretty, with a slight dark down on her upper lip, which was short to the teeth, but opened all the more sweetly, and still more sweetly lengthened at times and met the lower lip. For twenty chapters this lip keeps reappearing. Some months have passed since the opening of the story: "The little princess, who was *enceinte*, had meanwhile grown stout, but her eyes and the short downy lip and its smile, were curled up just as gaily and sweetly." And two pages later, "The princess talked incessantly: her short upper lip with its down constantly descended for a moment, touched at the right point the red lower one, and then again parted in a dazzling smile of eyes and teeth." The princess tells her sister-in-law, Prince Andrei's sister, Princess Maria, of the departure of her husband for the war. Princess Maria turns to her, with caressing eyes on her person; "Really?" The princess's face changed, and she sighed. "Yes, really!" she replied, "Ah, it is all very terrible!" and the lip of the little princess descended. In the course of one hundred and fifty pages we have already four times seen that upper lip with its distinguishing qualifications. Two hundred pages later we have again, "There was a general and brisk conversation, thanks to the voice and the smiling downy lip that rose above the white teeth of the little princess." In the second part of the novel she dies in a confinement. Prince Andrei entered his wife's room: she lay dead in the very attitude in which he had seen her five minutes before, and the same expression, in spite of the still eyes and the paleness of the cheeks, was on this charming child-like face with the lips covered with dark down.

From *Tolstoi as Man and Artist*, by D. S. Merezhkovsky, Chapter IX (London: Constable, 1902). Reprinted by permission of the publisher.

"I love you all, have harmed nobody. What have you done with me?" This takes place in the year 1805.

The war had broken out, and the scene of it was drawing near the Russian frontiers. In the midst of its dangers the author does not forget to tell us that over the grave of the little princess there had been placed a marble monument: an angel that had a slightly raised *upper lip*, and the expression which Prince Andrei had read on the face of his dead wife, "Why have you done this to me?"

Years pass. Napoleon has completed his conquests in Europe. He is already crossing the frontier of Russia. In the retirement of the Bare Hills, the son of the dead princess "grew up, changed, grew rosy, grew a crop of curly dark hair, and without knowing, smiling and gay, raised the *upper lip* of his well-shaped mouth just like the little dead princess." Thanks to these underlinings of one physical feature first in the living, then in the dead, and then again on the face of her statue and in her son the upper lip of the little princess is engraved on our memory with ineffaceable distinctness. We cannot remember her without also recalling that feature.

Princess Maria Volkonski, Prince Andrei's sister, has a heavy footstep which can be heard from afar. "They were the heavy steps of the Princess Maria." She came into the room "with her heavy walk, going on her heels." Her face "grows red in patches." During a delicate conversation with her brother about his wife, she "turned red in patches." When they are preparing to dress her up upon the occasion of the coming betrothed, she feels herself insulted: "she flashed out, and her face became flushed in patches."

In the following volume, in a talk with Pierre about his old men and beggars, about his "bedesmen," she becomes confused and "grew red in patches." Between these two last reminders of the patches of the princess is the description of the battle of Austerlitz, the victory of Napoleon, the gigantic struggle of nations, events that decided the destiny of the world, yet the artist does not forget, and will not to the end, the physical trait he finds so interesting. We are forced to remember the glaring eyes, heavy footsteps, and red patches of the Princess Maria. True, these traits, unimportant as they may seem, are really bound up with deep-seated spiritual characteristics of the *dramatis personae*. The upper lip, now gaily tilted, now piteously dropped, expresses the childlike carelessness and help-lessness of the little princess. The clumsy gait of the Princess Maria expresses an absence of external feminine charm; both the glaring eyes and the fact that she blushes in patches are connected with her inward womanly charm and spiritual modesty. Sometimes these stray characteristics light up a vast and complex picture, and give it startling clearness and relief.

At the time of the popular rising in deserted Moscow, before Napoleon's entry, when Count Rostopchin, wishing to allay the bestial fury of the crowd, points to the political criminal Verestchagin (who happened to be at hand and was totally innocent) as a spy, and the scoundrel who had ruined Moscow, the thin long neck and the general thinness, weakness and fragility of his frame of course express the defencelessness of the victim in face of the coarse mass of the crowd.

"Where is he?" said the Count, and instantly saw round the corner of a house a young man with a long thin neck coming out between two dragoons. He had "dirty, down at heel, thin boots. On his lean, weak legs the fetters clanked heavily. 'Bring him here,' said Rostopchin, pointing to the lower step of the *perron*. The young man, walking heavily to the step indicated, sighed with a humble gesture, crossed his thin hands, unused to work, before his body. 'Children,' said Rostopchin, in a metallic ringing voice, 'this man is Verestchagin, the very scoundrel that ruined Moscow.' Verestchagin raised his face and endeavoured to meet the Count's eyes, but he was not looking at him. On *the long thin neck* of the young man a vein behind the ear stood out like a blue cord. The people were silent, only pressed more closely together. 'Kill him! Let the traitor perish, and save from slur the Russian name,' cried Rostopchin. 'Count!' was heard saying amid the renewed stillness the timid yet theatrical voice of Verestchagin, 'Count, one God is above us.' And again the large vein in his *thin neck* was swollen with blood. One of the soldiers struck him with the flat of the sword on the head. Verestchagin, with a cry of terror, with outstretched hands plunged forward towards the people. A tall youth against whom he struck clung with his hands to his *thin neck* and with a wild cry, fell with him under the feet of the onrushing roaring populace." After the crime, the very people who committed it with hang-dog and piteous looks gazed on the dead body with the purple bloodstained and dusty face and the mangled *long thin neck*. Scarce a word of the inward state of the victim, but in five pages the word *thin* eight times repeated in various connexions—and this outward sign fully depicts the inward condition of Verestchagin in relation to the crowd. Such is the ordinary artistic resource of Tolstoi, from the seen to the unseen, from the external to the internal, from the bodily to the spiritual, or at any rate to the emotional.

Sometimes in these recurrent traits are implicated deeper fundamental ideas, main motives of the book. For instance, the weight of the corpulent general Kutuzov, his leisurely old man's slowness and want of mobility, express the apathetic, meditative stolidity of his mind, his Christian or more truly Buddhistic renunciation of his own will, the submission to the will of Fate or the God of this primitive hero; in the eyes of Tolstoi, a hero pre-eminently Russian and national, the hero of inaction or inertia. He is in contrast with the fruitlessly energetic, light, active, and self-confident hero of Western culture, Napoleon.

Prince Andrei watches the commander in chief at the time of the review of the troops at Tsarevoe Jaimishche: "Since Andrei had last seen him Kutuzov had grown still stouter and unwieldy with fat." An air of weariness was on his face and in his figure. "*Snorting and tossing heavily* he sat his charger." When after finishing the inspection he entered the court, on his face sat "the joy of a man set free, purposing to take his ease after acting a part. He drew his left leg out of the stirrup, rolling his whole body and, frowning from the effort, with difficulty raised it over the horse's back. Then he gasped and sank into the arms of supporting Cossacks and aides-de-camp; stepped out with a plunging gait and heavily ascended the staircase creaking under his weight." When he learns from Prince Andrei of the death of his father, he sighs "profoundly, heaving his whole chest, and is silent for a time." Then he "embraced Prince Andrei, pressed him to his stout chest, and for long would not let him go. When he did so, the prince saw that the swollen lips of Kutuzov quivered, and tears were in his eyes." He sighs, and grasping the bench with both hands to rise, rises heavily and *the folds of his swollen neck disappear*.

Even more profound is the significance of *rotundity* in the frame of another Russian hero, Platon Karataev. This rotundity typifies the eternal completeness of all that is simple, natural and artificial, a self-sufficingness, which seems to the artist the primary element of the Russian national genius. "Platon Karataev always remained in Pierre's mind as the strongest and dearest memory and personification of all that is Russian, good, and *rounded off.*" When next day, at dawn, Pierre saw his neighbour, the first impression of something round was fully confirmed; the whole figure of Platon in his French cloak, with a cord girdle, a forage-cap and bast shoes, was *round,* the head was completely *round,* the back, the chest, the shoulders, even the arms, which he carried as if he was always going to lift something, all were *round:* the pleasant smile and the great brown tender eyes were *round.* Pierre felt something "*round, if one might strain language, in the whole savour of the man.*" Here, by one physical trait, carried to the last degree of geometrical simplicity and obviousness, is expressed a huge abstract generalization. Tolstoi's religion and metaphysics enter into the delineation by this single trait.

Similar deep expressiveness is given by him to the hands of Napoleon and Speranski, the hands of men that wield power. At the time of the meeting of the Emperors in face of the assembled armies, the former gives a Russian soldier the Legion of Honour, he "draws off the glove from his *white small hand,* and tearing it, throws it away." A few lines later, "Napoleon reaches back *his small plump hand.*" Nicolai Rostov remembers "that self-satisfied Bonaparte with *his little white hand.*" And in the next volume, when talking with the Russian diplomat Balashiev, Napoleon makes "an energetic gesture of inquiry with *his little white, plump hand.*"

He sketches, too, the whole body of the Emperor, stripping the studious demi-god, till he stands, like other men, food for cannon.

In the morning, just before the battle of Borodino, the Emperor, in his tent, is finishing his toilette. "Snorting and panting, he turned, now his plump back, now his overgrown fatty chest to the brush with which the valet was rubbing him down. Another valet, holding the mouth of the bottle with his finger, was sprinkling the pampered little body with eau-de-cologne, with an air that said he alone could know how much and where to sprinkle. Napoleon's short hair was damp and hanging over his forehead. But his face, though bloated and yellow, expressed physical well-being. 'More now, harder now!' he cried, stretching and puffing, to the valet who was rubbing him, then bending and presenting his fat shoulders."

This white hand denotes the upstart hero who exploits the masses.

Speranski too, has white fat hands, in the description of which Tolstoi plainly somewhat abuses his favourite device of repetition and emphasis. 'Prince Andrei watched all Speranski's movements; but lately he was an insignificant seminarist, and now in his hands, those white plump hands, he held the fate of Russia, as Volkonski reflected." "In no one had the Prince seen such delicate whiteness of the face, and still more the hands, which were rather large, but unusually plump, delicate and white. Such whiteness and delicacy of complexion he had only seen in soldiers who had been long in hospital." A little later he again "looks involuntarily at the white delicate hands of Speranski, as men look generally at the hands of people in power. The mirror-like glance and the delicate hand somehow irritated Prince Andrei."

The detail is repeated with unwearying insistence till in the long run this white hand begins to haunt one like a spectral being.

In comparing himself with Pushkin as an artist, Tolstoi said to Bers that the difference between them, amongst other things, was this, that Pushkin in depicting a characteristic detail does it lightly, not troubling whether it will be noticed or understood by the reader, while he himself, as it were, stood over the reader with this artistic detail, until he had set it forth distinctly. The comparison is acute. He *does* "stand over the reader," not afraid of sickening him, and flogs in the trait, repeats, lays on colours, layer after layer, thickening them more and more, where Pushkin, barely touching, slides his brush over in light and careless, but invariably sure and faithful strokes. It seems as if Pushkin, especially in prose harsh, and even niggardly, gave little, that we might want the more. But Tolstoi gives so much that there is nothing more for us to want; we are sated, if not glutted.

The descriptions of Pushkin remind one of the light watery tempera of the old Florentine masters of Pompeian frescoes, dim, airily translucent colours, like the veil of morning mist. Tolstoi paints in the more powerful oil colours of the great

Northern Masters. And side by side with the dense black and living shadows we have sudden rays of the blinding all-penetrating light, drawing out of the dark some distinct feature, the nakedness of the body, a fold of drapery, a keen, quick movement, part of a face stamped with passion or suffering. We get a startling, almost repulsive and alarming vividness. The artist seeks through the natural, strongly emphasized, the supernatural; through the physical exaggerated, the hyperphysical.

In all literature there is no writer equal to Tolstoi in depicting the human body. Though he misuses repetitions, he usually attains what he needs by them, and he never suffers from the *longueurs* so common to other vigorous masters. He is accurate, simple, and as short as possible, selecting only the few, small, unnoticed facial or personal features and producing them, not all at once, but gradually and one by one, distributing them over the whole course of the story, weaving them into the living web of the action. Thus at the first appearance of old Prince Volkonski we get only a fleeting sketch, in four or five lines, "the short figure of the old man with the powdered wig, small *dry hands* and grey, overhanging brows that sometimes, when he was roused, dimmed the flash of the clever youthful eyes." When he sits down to the lathe "by the movement of his small foot, the firm pressure of his thin veined hand" (we already know his hands are dry, but Tolstoi loves to go back to the hands of his heroes), "you could still see in the Prince the obstinate and long-enduring force of hale old age." When he talks to his daughter, Princess Maria, "he shows in a cold smile, his strong but yellowish teeth." When he sits at the table and bends over her, beginning the usual lesson in geometry, she "feels herself surrounded with the snuffy, old-age, acrid savour of her father," which had long been a sign to her. There he is all before us as if alive, height, build, hands, feet, eyes, gestures, brows, even the peculiar savour belonging to each man.

Or take the effect on Vronski when he first sees Anna Karénina. You could see at a glance she belonged to the well-born; that she was very beautiful, that she had red lips, flashing grey eyes, which looked dark from the thickness of the lashes, and that "an excess of life had so filled her being that in spite of herself it showed, now in the flash of her eyes, now in her smile." And again as the story progresses, gradually, impreceptibly, trait is added to trait, feature to feature: when she gives her hand to Vronski he is delighted "as by something exceptional with the vigorous clasp with which she boldly shook his own." When she is talking to her sister-in-law Dolly, Anna takes her hand in "her own vigorous little one." The wrist of this hand is "thin and tiny," we see the "slender tapering fingers," off which the rings slip easily.

In the hands of Karénina, as in those of other characters (it may be because the hands are the only part of the human body always bare and near elemental nature, and unconscious as the animal), there is yet greater expressiveness than in the face. In the hands of Anna lies the whole charm of her person, the union of strength and delicacy. We learn when she is standing in the crowd at the ball "that she always held herself exceptionally erect"; when she leaves the railway carriage or walks through the room she has "a quick, decisive gait, carrying with strange ease her full and perfectly proportioned body." When she dances she has "a distinguishing grace, sureness and lightness of movement"; when, having gone on a visit to Dolly, she takes off her hat, her black hair, that catches in everything, "ripples into waves all over," and on another occasion "the unruly short waves of her curly hair keep fluttering at the nape and on the temples."

In these unruly curls, so easily becoming unkempt, there is the same tension, "the excess of something" ever ready for passion, as in the too bright flash of the eyes, or the smile, breaking out involuntarily and "fluctuating between the eyes and the lips." And lastly, when she goes to the ball, we see her skin: "The black, low-cut velvet bodice showed her full shoulders and breast polished like old ivory, and *rounded* arms." This polishedness, firmness, and *roundness* of the body, as with Platon Karataev, is to Tolstoi very important and subtle, a mysterious trait. All these scattered, single features complete and tally with one another, as in beautiful statues the shape of one limb always corresponds to the shape of another. The traits are so harmonized that they naturally and involuntarily unite, in the fancy of the reader, into one living, personal whole: so that when we finish the book we cannot but recognize Anna Karénina.

This gift of *insight into the body* at times, though seldom, leads Tolstoi into excess. It is easy and pleasant to him to describe living bodies and their movements. He depicts exactly how a horse begins to start when touched by the spur: "Jarkov touched his horse with the spurs and it thrice in irritation shifted its legs, not knowing with which to begin, reared and leaped." In the first lines of *Anna Karénina* Tolstoi is in a hurry to tell us how Stepan Arcadievich Oblonski, of whom we as yet know nothing, "draws plenty of air into his broad pectoral structure," and how he walks with "his usual brisk step, turning out the feet which so lightly carry his full frame." This last feature is significant, because it records the family likeness of the brother Stepan with his sister Anna. Even if all this seems extravagant, yet extravagance in art is not excess, it is even in many cases the most needful of all things. But here is a character of third-rate importance, one of those which vanish almost as soon as they appear, some paltry regimental commander in *Peace and War*, who has no sooner flitted before us than we have already seen that he "is broader from the chest to the back than from one shoulder to the other," and he stalks before the front "with a gait that shakes at every step and his back slightly bent." This shaky walk is repeated four times in five pages. Perhaps the observation is both true and picturesque, but it is here an inappropriate touch and in excess. Anna Karénina's fingers, which "taper at the ends," are important; but we should not have lost much if he had not told us that the Tartar footmen who hand dinner to Levine and Oblonski were broad-hipped. Sometimes the distinguishing quality of an artist is shown, not so much by what he has in due proportion as by the gift which he has to excess.

The language of gesture, if less varied than words, is more direct, expressive and suggestive. It is easier to lie in words than by gesture or facial expression. One glance, one wrinkle, one quiver of a muscle in the face, may express the unutterable. Succeeding series of these unconscious, involuntary movements, impressing and stratifying themselves on the face and physique, form the expression of the face and the countenance of the body. Certain feelings impel us to corresponding movements, and, on the other hand, certain habitual movements impel to the corresponding *internal* states. The man who prays, folds his hands and bends his knees, and the man too who folds his hands and bends his knees is near to the praying frame of mind. Thus there exists an uninterrupted current, not only from the internal to the external, but from the external to the internal.

Tolstoi, with inimitable art, uses this convertible connexion between the external and the internal. By the same law of mechanical sympathy which makes a stationary tense chord vibrate in answer to a neighbouring chord, the sight of another crying or laughing awakes in us the desire to cry or laugh; we experience when we read similar descriptions in the nerves and muscles. And so by the motions of muscles or nerves we enter shortly and directly into the internal world of his characters, begin to live with them, and in them.

When we learn that Ivan Ilyich cried out three days for pain "Ugh, U-ugh, Ugh!" because when he began to cry "I don't want to!" he prolonged the sound "o-o-o," it is easy for us, not only to picture to ourselves, but ourselves physically experience this terrible transition from human speech to a senseless animal howl. And what an endlessly complex, variegated sense at times a single movement, a single attitude of human limbs receives at his hands!

After the battle of Borodino, in the marquee for the wounded, the doctor, in his bloodstained apron with hands covered with blood "holds in one of them a cigar between the middle and fore-finger, so as not to mess it." This position of the fingers implies both the uninterruptedness of his terrible employment, and the absence of repugnance for it; indifference to wounds and blood, owing to long habit, weariness, and desire to forget. The complexity of these internal states is concentrated in one little physical detail, in the position of the two fingers, the description of which fills half a line.

When Prince Andrei, learning that Kutuzov is sending Bagration's force to certain death, feels a doubt whether the commander-in-chief has the right to sacrifice, in this self-confident way, the lives of thousands of men, he "looks at Kutuzov, and what involuntarily strikes his eye at a yard's distance is the clean-washed sutures of the scar on Kutuzov's temple, where the bullet at Ismail penetrated his head, and his lost eye." "Yes, he has the right," thinks Volkonski.

More than anything which science tells Ivan Ilyich about his illness by the mouth of the doctors, more than all his own wonted conventional ideas about death, does a chance look reveal the actual horror of his state. "Ivan Ilyich began to brush his hair and looked in the mirror: he was horrified by the way that his hair clung closely to his long forehead." No words would suffice to express animal fear of death, as this state of the hair noticed in the mirror. The indifference of the healthy to the sick, or the living to the dying, is realized by Ivan Ilyich, not from the words people use, but only by "the brawny, full-veined neck, closely girt by its white collar, and the powerful limbs habited in tight black breeches, of Fedor Petrovich" (his daughter's betrothed).

Between Pierre and Prince Vasili the relations are very strained and delicate. Prince Vasili wishes to give Pierre his daughter Ellen and is waiting impatiently for Pierre to make her an offer. The latter cannot make up his mind. One day, finding himself alone with the father and daughter, he rises and is for going away, saying it is late. "Prince Vasili looked at him with stern inquiry, as if the remark was so strange that it was impossible to believe his ears. But presently the look of sternness changed. He took Pierre by the arm, put him in a chair and smiled caressingly, 'Well, what of Lelia?' he said, turning at once to his daughter and then again to Pierre, reminding him, not at all to the point, of a stupid anecdote of a certain Sergyè Kuzmich. Pierre smiled, *but it was plain from his smile* that he knew that it was not the story of Sergyè Kuzmich that interested Prince Vasili at the moment: and Prince Vasili was aware that Pierre saw this. The former suddenly muttered something and left the room. It seemed to Pierre that Prince Vasili, too, felt confused. He looked at Ellen, and she too seemed embarrassed, and her eye said, 'Well you yourself are to blame.'" What complex and many-sided significance evoked by a single smile! It is repeated and mirrored in the minds of those around, in a series of scarcely perceptible half-conscious thoughts and feelings, like a ray or a sound.

Pierre sees Natasha after a long separation, and the death of her first betrothed, Prince Andrei. She is so changed that he does not recognize her. " 'But no, it cannot be,' he thinks. 'This stern, thin, pale, aged face? It cannot be she. It is only the memory of a face.' " But at that moment Princess Maria says, 'Natasha.' "And the face with the observant eyes, with difficulty, with an effort, as a stuck door is opened, smiled at him and from this opened door suddenly, startlingly, came the breath, floating round Pierre, of that long forgotten happiness.

It came and took hold of and swallowed him whole. When she smiled, there could no longer be a doubt; it was Natasha, and he loved her." During this scene, one of the most important and decisive in the action of this novel, only *five* words are pronounced by Princess Maria, "Then don't you recognize her?" But the silent smile of Natasha is stronger than words; it decides the fate of Pierre.

Tolstoi depicts by gesture such intangible peculiarity of sensation as a bar of music, or of a song. "The drummer and choir leader looked sternly over the soldiers of his band and frowned. Then having convinced himself that all eyes were fixed on him, he appeared carefully to raise in both hands some unseen precious object above their heads, held it there some seconds and suddenly threw it away desperately. 'Ah! alackaday, my tent, my tent! my new tent!' took up twenty men's voices."

He has equally at command the primal elemental masses and the lightest molecules scattered, like dust, over our inward atmosphere, the very atoms of feeling. The same hand which moves mountains guides these atoms as well. And perhaps the second operation is more wonderful than the first. Putting aside all that is general, literary, conventional, and artificial, Tolstoi explores in sensation what is most private, personal, and particular; takes subtle shafts of feeling, and whets and sharpens these shafts to an almost excessive sharpness, so that they penetrate and pierce like ineradicable needles; the peculiarity of his sensation will become for ever our own peculiarity. We feel Tolstoi afterwards, when we return to real life. We may say that the nervous susceptibility of people who have read the books of Tolstoi becomes different from what it was before reading them.

The secret of his effects consists, amongst other things, in his noticing what others do not, as too commonplace, and which, when illumined by consciousness, precisely in consequence of this commonplace character, seems unusual. Thus he first made the discovery, apparently so simple and easy, but which for thousands of years had evaded all observers, that the smile is reflected, not only on the face, but in the sound of the voice, that the voice as well as the face can be smiling. Platon Karataev at night, when Pierre cannot see his face, says something to him, "in a voice changed by a smile." The living web of art consists in such small but striking observations and discoveries.

He was the first to notice that the sound of horse-hoofs is, as it were, a "transparent sound."

His language, usually simple and measured, does not suffer from an excess of epithet. When the sensation to be described is so subtle and new that by no combination of words can it possibly be expressed, he uses concatenations of onomatopoeic sounds, which serve children and primitive people in the construction of language.

In his delirium, Prince Andrei heard a low, whispering voice, ceaselessly affirming in time "I piti piti piti," and then "i ti ti," and again "i piti piti piti," and once more "i ti ti." At the same time at the sound of his whispered music Prince Andrei felt that over his face, over the very middle of it, moved some strange airy edifice of fine needles or chips. He felt, although it was hard for him, that he must assiduously maintain his equilibrium in order that this delicate fabric might not fall down. But still it did fall down, and slowly rose again to the sounds of the rhythmically whispering music. "It rises, it rises! It falls to pieces and yet spreads," said he to himself. "I piti piti piti, i ti ti, a piti piti—bang, a fly has knocked against it."

Ivan Ilyich, remembering before his death the stewed plums "which they advise me to eat now," remembered also the "dry, crinkled French prunes when I was a child." It would seem the detail was sufficiently definite. But the artist enforces it still more. Ivan remembered the peculiar taste of plums and "the abundance of saliva when you got to the stones." With this sensation of saliva from plum stones is connected in his mind a whole series of memories, of his nurse, his brother, his toys, of his whole childhood, and these memories in their turn evoke in him a comparison of the then happiness of his life with his present despair and dread of death. "No need for that, too painful," he says to himself. Such are the generalizations to which, in us all, trifling details lead.

Sonia, when in love with Nicolai Rostov, kisses him. Pushkin would have stopped at recording the kiss. But Tolstoi, not content, looks for more exactness. The thing took place at Christmas, Sonia was disguised as a hussar, and moustaches had been marked on her lips with burnt cork. And so Nicolai remembers "the smell of cork, mixed with the feel of the kiss."

The most intangible gradations and peculiarities of sensation are distinguished by him to correspond with the character, sex, age, bringing up, and status of the person experiencing them. It seems that in this region there are no hidden ways for him. His sensual experience is inexhaustible, as if he had lived hundreds of lives in various shapes of men and animals. He fathoms the unusual sensation of her bared body to a young girl, before going to her first ball. So, too, the feelings of a woman growing old and worn out with child bearing, who "shudders as she remembers the pain of her quivering breasts, experienced with almost every child." Also of a nursing mother, who has not yet severed the mysterious connexion of her body with that of her child, and who "knows for a certainty, by the excess of milk in her, that the child is insufficiently fed." Lastly, the sensations and thoughts of animals, for instance the sporting dog of Levine, to whom the face of her master seems "familiar," but his eyes "always strange."

Not only the old Greeks and Romans, but in all probability the people of the eighteenth century, would not have understood the meaning of the "transparent" sound of horsehoofs, or how there can be "a savour of burnt cork mixed with the feel of a kiss," or how dishes "reflect" an expression of the human countenance, a pleasant smile, or how there can be "a roundness" in the savour of a man. If our critics, the Draconian judges of the new so-called "decadence" of Art, were consistent throughout, should they not accuse even Tolstoi of "morbid obliquity"? But the truth is that to determine the fixed units of the healthy and the morbid in Art is much more difficult than it seems to the guardians of the Classical canons. Is not the "obliquity" they presuppose only an *intensifying*, the natural and inevitable development, refinement, and deepening of healthy sensuality? Perhaps our children, with their unimpaired susceptibility, will understand what is unintelligible to our critics and will justify Tolstoi. Children are well aware of what some fathers have forgotten, viz.: that the different branches of what are called "the five senses" are by no means so sharply divided from one another, but blend, interweave, cover and supplement one another, so that sounds may seem bright and coloured ("the bright voice of the nightingale," Pushkin has it) and concatenations of movements, colours, or even scents may have the effect of music (what is called "eurhythmia,") the harmony of movement, as of colours in painting. It is usually thought that the physical sensations, as opposed to mental, are a constant quantity throughout time in the historical development of mankind. In reality, the care of physical sensation changes with the development of intellect. We see and hear what our ancestors did not see or hear. However much the admirers of classical antiquity may complain of the physical degeneracy of the men of to-day, it is scarcely possible to doubt that we are creatures more keen-sighted, keen of hearing and physically acute, than the heroes of the *Iliad* and the *Odyssey*. Does not science, too, conjecture that certain sensations, for instance, the last colours of the spectrum, have become the general achievement of men, only at a comparatively recent and historical stage of their existence, and that perhaps even Homer confused green with dark blue in one epithet, for the hue of seawater? Does there not still go on a similar natural growth and *intensification* in other branches of human sentience? Will not our children's children see and hear what we as yet do not see and hear? Will not the unseen be seen to them, though undreamed of by our fathers, our critics, men of worn-out sensitiveness to impression, nay, even the boldest and most advanced of ourselves? Will not our present "decadent" over-refinement, which so alarms the old believers of the day on Art, then seem in its turn obvious, primitive, Homeric healthiness and coarseness? In this unchecked development, movement and flow, where is the fixed standard for dividing the lawful from the unlawful, wholesome from morbid, natural from corrupt? Yesterday's exception becomes to-day's rule. And who shall dare to say to the living body, the living spirit, "Here shall you stop, no further may you go"? Why particularly here? Why not farther on?

However this may be, the special glory of Tolstoi lies exactly in the fact that he was the first to express (and with what fearless sincerity!), new branches, unexhausted and inexhaustible,—of over-stabilizing physical and mental consciousness. We may say that he gave us new bodily sensations, new vessels for new wine.

The Apostle Paul divides human existence into three branches, borrowing the division from the philosophers of the Alexandrian School, the physical man, the spiritual and the natural. The last is the connecting link between the first two, something intermediate, double, transitional, like twilight; neither Flesh nor Spirit, that in which the Flesh is completed and the Spirit begins, in the language of psycho-physiology the physico-spiritual phenomenon.

Tolstoi is the greatest depictor of this physico-spiritual region in the natural man; that side of the flesh which approaches the spirit, and that side of the spirit which approaches the flesh, the mysterious border-region where the struggle between the animal and the God in man takes place. Therein lies the struggle and the tragedy of his own life. He is a "man of the senses," half-heathen, half-Christian; neither to the full.

In proportion as he recedes from this neutral ground in either direction, it matters not whether towards the region of the cold "pre-animal" Nature, that region which *seems* inorganic, insentient, inanimate, "material" (the terrible and beatific calm of which Turgeniev and Pushkin have told so well); or as he essays the opposite region, human spirituality, almost set free from the body, released from animal nature, the region of pure thought (the passionate workings of which are so well embodied by Dostoievski and Tiutchev), the power of artistic delineation in Tolstoi decreases, and in the end collapses, so that there are limits which are for him wholly unattainable. But within the limits of the purely natural man he is the supreme artist of the world.

In other provinces of Art, for instance the painting of the Italian Renaissance and the sculpture of the ancient Greeks, there have been artists who with greater completeness than Tolstoi depicted the bodily man. The music of the present day, and in part the literature, penetrate us more deeply. But nowhere, and at no time, has the "natural man" appeared with such startling truth and nakedness as he appears in the creations of Tolstoi.

XI

D. H. LAWRENCE

Thomas Hardy, Verga, and Tolstoy

From "Study of Thomas Hardy," Chapter III.

This is a constant revelation in Hardy's novels: that there exists a great background, vital and vivid, which matters more than the people who move upon it. Against the background of dark, passionate Egdon, of the leafy, sappy passion and sentiment of the woodlands, of the unfathomed stars, is drawn the lesser scheme of lives: *The Return of the Native, The Woodlanders,* or *Two on a Tower.* Upon the vast, incomprehensible pattern of some primal morality greater than ever the human mind can grasp, is drawn the little, pathetic pattern of man's moral life and struggle, pathetic, almost ridiculous. The little fold of law and order, the little walled city within which man has to defend himself from the waste enormity of nature, becomes always too small, and the pioneers venturing out with the code of the walled city upon them, die in the bonds of that code, free and yet unfree, preaching the walled city and looking to the waste.

This is the wonder of Hardy's novels, and gives them their beauty. The vast unexplored morality of life itself, what we call the immorality of nature, surrounds us in its eternal incomprehensibility, and in its midst goes on the little human morality play, with its queer frame of morality and its mechanized movement; seriously, portentously, till some one of the protagonists chances to look out of the charmed circle, weary of the stage, to look into the wilderness raging round. Then he is lost, his little drama falls to pieces, or becomes mere repetition, but the stupendous theatre outside goes on enacting its own incomprehensible drama, untouched. There is this quality in almost all Hardy's work, and this is the magnificent irony it

From *Phoenix*, by D. H. Lawrence (London: Heinemann; New York: Viking Press, 1936). Reprinted by permission of Laurence Pollinger, Ltd., and the Estate of the late Mrs. Frieda Lawrence.

all contains, the challenge, the contempt. Not the deliberate ironies, little tales of widows or widowers, contain the irony of human life as we live it in our self-aggrandized gravity, but the big novels, *The Return of the Native*, and the others.

And this is the quality Hardy shares with the great writers, Shakespeare or Sophocles or Tolstoi, this setting behind the small action of his protagonists the terrific action of unfathomed nature; setting a smaller system of morality, the one grasped and formulated by the human consciousness, within the vast, uncomprehended and incomprehensible morality of nature or of life itself, surpassing human consciousness. The difference is, that whereas in Shakespeare or Sophocles the greater, uncomprehended morality, or fate, is actively transgressed and gives active punishment, in Hardy and Tolstoi the lesser, human morality, the mechanical system, is transgressed, and holds, and punishes the protagonist, whilst the greater morality is only passively, negatively transgressed, it is represented merely as being present in background, in scenery, not taking any active part, having no direct connexion with the protagonist. Oedipus, Hamlet, Macbeth set themselves up against, or find themselves set up against, the unfathomed moral forces of nature, and out of this unfathomed force comes their death. Whereas Anna Karenina, Eustacia, Tess, Sue, and Jude find themselves up against the established system of human government and morality, they cannot detach themselves, and are brought down. Their real tragedy is that they are unfaithful to the greater unwritten morality, which would have bidden Anna Karenina be patient and wait until she, by virtue of greater right, could take what she needed from society; would have bidden Vronsky detach himself from the system, become an individual, creating a new colony of morality with Anna; would have bidden Eustacia fight Clym for his own soul, and Tess take and claim her Angel, since she had the greater light; would have bidden Jude and Sue endure for very honour's sake, since one must bide by the best that one has known, and not succumb to the lesser good.

Had Oedipus, Hamlet, Macbeth been weaker, less full of real, potent life, they would have made no tragedy; they would have comprehended and contrived some arrangement of their affairs, sheltering in the human morality from the great stress and attack of the unknown morality. But being, as they are, men to the fullest capacity, when they find themselves, daggers drawn, with the very forces of life itself, they can only fight till they themselves are killed, since the morality of life, the greater morality, is eternally unalterable and invincible. It can be dodged for some time, but not opposed. On the other hand, Anna, Eustacia, Tess or Sue—what was there in their position that was necessarily tragic? Necessarily painful it was, but they were not at war with God, only with Society. Yet they were all cowed by the mere judgment of man upon them, and all the while by their own souls they were right. And the judgment of men killed them, not the judgment of their own souls or the judgment of Eternal God.

Which is the weakness of modern tragedy, where transgression against the social code is made to bring destruction, as though the social code worked our irreparable fate. Like Clym, the map appears to us more real than the land. Shortsighted almost to blindness, we pore over the chart, map out journeys, and confirm them: and we cannot see life itself giving us the lie the whole time.

From "Study of Thomas Hardy," Chapter IX.

Most fascinating in all artists is this antinomy between Law and Love, between the Flesh and the Spirit, between the Father and the Son.

For the moralist it is easy. He can insist on that aspect of the Law or Love which is in the immediate line of development for his age, and he can sternly and severely exclude or suppress all the rest.

So that all morality is of temporary value, useful to its times. But Art must give a deeper satisfaction. It must give fair play all round.

Yet every work of art adheres to some system of morality. But if it be really a work of art, it must contain the essential criticism on the morality to which it adheres. And hence the antinomy, hence the conflict necessary to every tragic conception.

The degree to which the system of morality, or the metaphysic, of any work of art is submitted to criticism within the work of art makes the lasting value and satisfaction of that work. Aeschylus, having caught the oriental idea of Love, correcting the tremendous Greek conception of the Law with this new idea, produces the intoxicating satisfaction of the Orestean trilogy. The Law, and Love, they are here the Two-in-One in all their magnificence. But Euripides, with his aspiration towards Love, Love the supreme, and his almost hatred of the Law, Law the Triumphant but Base Closer of Doom, is less satisfactory, because of the very fact that he holds Love always Supreme, and yet must endure the chagrin of seeing Love perpetually transgressed and overthrown. So he makes his tragedy: the higher thing eternally pulled down by the lower. And this unfairness in the use of terms, higher and lower, but above all, the unfairness of showing Love always violated and suffering, never supreme and triumphant, makes us disbelieve Euripides in the end. For we have to bring in pity, we must admit that Love is at a fundamental disadvantage before the Law, and cannot therefore hold its own. Which is weak philosophy.

If Aeschylus has a metaphysic to his art, this metaphysic is that Love and Law are Two, eternally in conflict, and eternally being reconciled. This is the tragic significance of Aeschylus.

But the metaphysic of Euripides is that the Law and Love are two eternally in conflict, and unequally matched, so that Love must always be borne down. In Love a man shall only suffer. There is also a Reconciliation, otherwise Euripides were not so great. But there is always the unfair matching, this disposition insisted on, which at last leaves one cold and unbelieving.

The moments of pure satisfaction come in the choruses, in the pure lyrics, when Love is put into true relations with the Law, apart from knowledge, transcending the metaphysic, where the aspiration to Love meets the acknowledgment of the Law in a consummate marriage, for the moment.

Where Euripides adheres to his metaphysic, he is unsatisfactory. Where he transcends his metaphysic, he gives that supreme equilibrium wherein we know satisfaction.

The adherence to a metaphysic does not necessarily give artistic form. Indeed the over-strong adherence to a metaphysic usually destroys any possibility of artistic form. Artistic form is a revelation of the two principles of Love and the Law in a state of conflict and yet reconciled: pure motion struggling against and yet reconciled with the Spirit: active force meeting and overcoming and yet not overcoming inertia. It is the conjunction of the two which makes form. And since the two must always meet under fresh conditions, form must always be different. Each work of art has its own form, which has no relation to any other form. When a young painter studies an old master, he studies, not the form, that is an abstraction which does not exist: he studies maybe the method of the old great artist: but he studies chiefly to understand how the old great artist suffered in himself the conflict of Love and Law, and brought them to a reconciliation. Apart from artistic method, it is not Art that the young man is studying, but the State of Soul of the great old artist, so that he, the young artist, may understand his own soul and gain a reconciliation between the aspiration and the resistant.

It is most wonderful in poetry, this sense of conflict contained within a reconciliation:

> Hail to thee, blithe Spirit!
>   Bird thou never wert,
> That from Heaven, or near it,
>   Pourest thy full heart
> In profuse strains of unpremeditated art.

Shelley wishes to say, the skylark is a pure, untrammelled spirit, a pure motion. But the very "Bird thou never wert" admits that the skylark *is* in very fact a bird, a concrete, momentary thing. If the line ran, "Bird thou never art," that would spoil it all. Shelley wishes to say, the song is poured out of heaven: but "or near it," he admits. There is the perfect relation between heaven and earth. And the last line is the tumbling sound of a lark's singing, the real Two-in-One.

The very adherence to rhyme and regular rhythm is a concession to the Law, a concession to the body, to the being and requirements of the body. They are an admission of the living, positive inertia which is the other half of life, other than the pure will to motion. In this consummation, they are the resistance and response of the Bride in the arms of the Bridegroom. And according as the Bride and Bridegroom come closer together, so is the response and resistance more fine, indistinguishable, so much the more, in this act of consummation, is the movement that of Two-in-One, indistinguishable each from the other, and not the movement of two brought together clumsily.

So that in Swinburne, where almost all is concession to the

body, so that the poetry becomes almost a sensation and not an experience or a consummation, justifying Spinoza's "Amor est titillatio, concomitante idea causae externae," we find continual adherence to the body, to the Rose, to the Flesh, the physical in everything, in the sea, in the marshes; there is an overbalance in the favour of Supreme Law; Love is not Love, but passion, part of the Law; there is no Love, there is only Supreme Law. And the poet sings the Supreme Law to gain rebalance in himself, for he hovers always on the edge of death, of Not-Being, he is always out of reach of the Law, bodiless, in the faintness of Love that has triumphed and denied the Law, in the dread of an over-developed, over-sensitive soul which exists always on the point of dissolution from the body.

But he is not divided against himself. It is the novelists and dramatists who have the hardest task in reconciling their metaphysic, their theory of being and knowing, with their living sense of being. Because a novel is a microcosm, and because man in viewing the universe must view it in the light of a theory, therefore every novel must have the background or the structural skeleton of some theory of being, some metaphysic. But the metaphysic must always subserve the artistic purpose beyond the artist's conscious aim. Otherwise the novel becomes a treatise.

And the danger is, that a man shall make himself a metaphysic to excuse or cover his own faults or failure. Indeed, a sense of fault or failure is the usual cause of a man's making himself a metaphysic, to justify himself.

Then, having made himself a metaphysic of self-justification, or a metaphysic of self-denial, the novelist proceeds to apply the world to this, instead of applying this to the world.

Tolstoi is a flagrant example of this. Probably because of profligacy in his youth, because he had disgusted himself in his own flesh, by excess or by prostitution, therefore Tolstoi, in his metaphysic, renounced the flesh altogether, later on, when he had tried and had failed to achieve complete marriage in the flesh. But above all things, Tolstoi was a child of the Law, he belonged to the Father. He had a marvellous sensuous understanding, and very little clarity of mind.

So that, in his metaphysic, he had to deny himself, his own being, in order to escape his own disgust of what he had done to himself, and to escape admission of his own failure.

Which made all the later part of his life a crying falsity and shame. Reading the reminiscences of Tolstoi, one can only feel shame at the way Tolstoi denied all that was great in him, with vehement cowardice. He degraded himself infinitely, he perjured himself far more than did Peter when he denied Christ. Peter repented. But Tolstoi denied the Father, and propagated a great system of his recusancy, elaborating his own weakness, blaspheming his own strength. "What difficulty is there in writing about how an officer fell in love with a married woman?" he used to say of his *Anna Karenina;* "there's no difficulty in it, and, above all, no good in it."

Because he was mouthpiece to the Father in uttering the law of passion, he said there was no difficulty in it, because it came naturally to him. Christ might just as easily have said, there was no difficulty in the Parable of the Sower, and no good in it, either, because it flowed out of him without effort.

And Thomas Hardy's metaphysic is something like Tolstoi's. "There is no reconciliation between Love and the Law," says Hardy. "The spirit of Love must always succumb before the blind, stupid, but overwhelming power of the Law."

Already as early as *The Return of the Native* he has come to this theory, in order to explain his own sense of failure. But before that time, from the very start, he has had an overweening theoretic antagonism to the Law. "That which is physical, of the body, is weak, despicable, bad," he said at the very start. He represented his fleshy heroes as villains, but very weak and maundering villains. At its worst, the Law is a weak, craven sensuality: at its best, it is a passive inertia. It is the gap in the armour, it is the hole in the foundation.

Such a metaphysic is almost silly. If it were not that man is much stronger in feeling than in thought, the Wessex novels would be sheer rubbish, as they are already in parts. *The Well-Beloved* is sheer rubbish, fatuity, as is a good deal of *The Dynasts* conception.

But it is not as a metaphysician that one must consider Hardy. He makes a poor show there. For nothing in his work is so pitiable as his clumsy efforts to push events into line with his theory of being, and to make calamity fall on those who represent the principle of Love. He does it exceedingly badly, and owing to this effort his form is execrable in the extreme.

His feeling, his instinct, his sensuous understanding is, however, apart from his metaphysic, very great and deep, deeper than that, perhaps, of any other English novelist. Putting aside his metaphysic, which must always obtrude when he thinks of people, and turning to the earth, to landscape, then he is true to himself.

Always he must start from the earth, from the great source of the Law, and his people move in his landscape almost insignificantly, somewhat like tame animals wandering in the wild. The earth is the manifestation of the Father, of the Creator, Who made us in the Law. God still speaks aloud in His Works, as to Job, so to Hardy, surpassing human conception and the human law. "Dost thou know the balancings of the clouds, the wondrous works of him which is perfect in knowledge? How thy garments are warm, when he quieteth the earth by the south wind? Hast thou with him spread out the sky, which is strong?"

This is the true attitude of Hardy—"With God is terrible majesty." The theory of knowledge, the metaphysic of the man, is much smaller than the man himself. So with Tolstoi.

From Introduction to *Cavalleria Rusticana*, by Giovanni Verga.

It may be urged that Verga commits the Tolstoian fallacy, of repudiating the educated world and exalting the peasant. But this is not the case. Verga is very much the gentleman, exclusively so, to the end of his days. He did not dream of putting on a peasant's smock, or following the plough. What Tolstoi somewhat perversely worshipped in the peasants was poverty itself, and humility, and what Tolstoi perversely hated was instinctive pride or spontaneous passion. Tolstoi has a perverse pleasure in making the later Vronsky abject and pitiable: because Tolstoi so meanly envied the healthy passionate male in the young Vronsky. Tolstoi cut off his own nose to spite his face. He envied the reckless passionate male with a carking envy, because he must have felt himself in some way wanting in comparison. So he exalts the peasant: not because the peasant may be a more natural and spontaneous creature than the city man or the guardsman, but just because the peasant is poverty-stricken and humble. This is malice, the envy of weakness and deformity.

We know now that the peasant is no better than anybody else; no better than a prince or a selfish young army officer or a governor or a merchant. In fact, in the mass, the peasant is worse than any of these. The peasant mass is the ugliest of all human masses, most greedily selfish and brutal of all. Which Tolstoi, leaning down from the gold bar of heaven, will have had opportunity to observe. If we have to trust to a *mass*, then better trust the upper or middle-class mass, all masses being odious.

But Verga by no means exalts the peasants as a class: nor does he believe in their poverty and humility. Verga's peasants are certainly not Christ-like, whatever else they are. They are most normally ugly and low, the bulk of them. And individuals are sensitive and simple.

Verga turns to the peasants only to seek for a certain something which, as a healthy artist, he worshipped. Even Tolstoi, as a healthy artist, worshipped it the same. It was only as a moralist and a personal being that Tolstoi was perverse. As a true artist, he worshipped, as Verga did, every manifestation of pure, spontaneous, passionate life, life kindled to vividness. As a perverse moralist with a sense of some subtle deficiency in himself, Tolstoi tries to insult and to damp out the vividness of life. Imagine any great artist making the vulgar social condemnation of Anna and Vronsky figure as divine punishment! Where now is the society that turned its back on Vronsky and Anna? Where is it? And what is its condemnation worth, to-day?

XII

D. H. Lawrence and "Anna Karenina"

Anna, Lawrence and 'The Law'

BY HENRY GIFFORD

Lawrence came to self-realisation, I think, in some part through wrestling with Tolstoy, whose 'marvellous sensuous under-standing' he rated highly, but whose 'metaphysic' he thought ignoble. The struggle centres on *Anna Karenina*, a book that had engrossed him in student days, and that later bore closely upon his own situation when he married Frieda. Tolstoy be-trayed Anna, in Lawrence's view. He denied thereby his 'in-stinct for life' which should transcend any mere 'theory of right and wrong.' The doctrine of *Anna Karenina* Lawrence held to be blasphemous: and perhaps his final effort at rectifi-cation was made in *Lady Chatterley's Lover*.

What is meant by the 'instinct of life,' and how does it show in the novel? One episode defines it excellently: Anna has returned to St. Petersburg and is appalled at the sight of her husband:

'Oh heavens, why has he such ears?' she thought, looking at his cold and imposing figure, and particularly with amazement at the fleshy parts of his ears, as they propped up the rim of his round hat. On seeing her he came forward to meet her, forming his lips into his habitual mocking smile and gazing straight at her with his large weary eyes. A certain unpleasant feeling caught at her heart, when she encountered his fixed and weary gaze, as though she had ex-pected to find him different. What struck her particularly was the feeling of dissatisfaction with herself which she experienced on meet-ing him. The feeling was an old and familiar one akin to a sense of hypocrisy, which she experienced in her relations with her husband; but before she had not noticed this feeling, now she clearly and painfully recognized it.

Similar to her feeling is that of her newly declared lover Vronsky, who looks on Karenin as a dog, sheep or pig fouling

From the *Critical Quarterly*, Vol. I, No. 3.

the spring where he longs to slake his own thirst. Their reaction belongs to 'the body's life'—the body that 'feels real hunger, real thirst, real joy in the sun or the snow, real pleasure in the smell of roses or the look of a lilac bush,' and real emotions. Karenin's aspect—the fleshy ears, the tired eyes and bantering voice—are signs of his damnation. He is a 'social being' —one who fails to possess himself, but who, after forgiving Anna and Vronsky, is soon parted from his fine intentions by the 'brute force' of social opinion. Anna confesses to her brother 'I can't live with him. Understand, the sight of him affects me physically. . . .' This response is the truer, Lawrence would claim, for being involuntary, like the response of Miss Louisa to the withered clergyman in his own story *Daughters of the Vicar*. Such instinctive judgments, as Leavis observes, 'express a moral sense that speaks out of the fulness of life.'

We can distinguish between the 'goodness' of Stiva (which enrages Dolly in the opening scene) and the 'virtue' of Karenin. Stiva, for all his moral insouciance, has no truck with falsehood; Karenin, the self-consciously upright man, lives with it comfortably enough. Anna is like her brother in radiating this quality of 'goodness.' She has the same effortless charm, and she appeals by her candour. 'Apart from intelligence, grace, beauty,' Levin reflected on first meeting her, 'she had truthfulness.' Under necessity, of course, she may abuse this instinct for truth, living with Karenin while she is expecting Vronsky's child; but ultimately she cannot disguise from herself the truth. As Lawrence said in the *Fantasia*, 'let it be a great passion and death, rather than a false or faked purpose.'

It is possible to see Anna's conduct as a challenge to a false and faking society (which she braves at the theatre in Moscow), or as an affront to the family and traditional pieties. Tolstoy does indeed show up the triviality and insincerity of the 'great world' by Anna's example of passionate and serious loving. As Berdyaev says, we are given 'the truth and rightness of the love between Anna Karenina and Vronsky as against the falsehood of Karenin's legalism and pharisaism.' 'By their own souls,' Lawrence insisted, 'they were right.' Yet Tolstoy could not admit that 'truth and rightness' belong to this love. Anna—a consideration that hardly occurs to Lawrence—had broken her home, and worse, abandoned the child of her marriage to Karenin. Tolstoy judges her in the cherished name of the family, the idea which possessed him at the time of writing this novel. The supreme test is Dolly's visit to Anna in her second home—a visit that contrasts tellingly with Anna's mission to her in the opening scenes of unhappiness. Dolly is prepared to forgive, even to side, with Anna. But she at once divines that the whole establishment is false, to the extent of Anna's not knowing how many teeth the baby has. Dolly returns from illusory happiness of the lovers, to the solid content of her own home. She has been weary on her drive to Anna; but this is wholly unlike the weariness of Anna's own last drive to destruction. Her soul is tired rather than sick; and she owes salvation to the family. She has that inward 'peace of mind' so deeply desired by many characters in the book.

The ideal of the family is honoured by the Shcherbatskys and by Levin whose old home represents for him 'a whole world'—the world that had been the life and death of his parents. It is the world of Moscow tradition, rather than of Petersburg novelty, and these two cities are here, as elsewhere in Russian literature, used to symbolise the conflict between old pieties and modern pressures. Tolstoy shocked Turgenev by the tenacity of his prejudice. *Anna Karenina* no less than *War and Peace*, combines a wonderful candour with a highly tendentious design. 'When the novelist puts his thumb in the scale,' warned Lawrence, 'to pull down the balance to his own predilections, that is immorality.' About Tolstoy's predilections there can be no doubt. The strategy of the novel is directed against Anna. Has Tolstoy tampered then with his natural feelings?

'Vengeance is mine,' runs the epigraph, 'and I will repay.' The text can be taken variously. It shames the judgment of man (the judgment of the theatre audience who feel insulted by Anna's sitting among them). It may hint at the mercy of God. Yet as the story develops, this promise of vengeance rings ever more terribly in the reader's ears. Anna is doomed to the train wheels, which, as we are reminded by too many hints, have been waiting for her from the start of her infidelity —even since that first shriek of the engine whistle in the blizzard when Vronsky declared his love for her. This is the logic of guilty passion, which breeds in turn frenzy, bitterness, shame and mutual hatred; finally a cynical despair, the moral nihilism of the rake Yashvin, whose words seem so true to Anna.

Levin's wife Kitty is allowed to describe her as 'a vile woman'—and the judgment goes uncontradicted. A few hours before, Levin had been completely won over to Anna, by the spell of 'her beauty and intelligence, her culture, and with these her straightforwardness and sincerity.' Anna was indeed aiming to captivate him; yet the reader, despite Tolstoy's implication that something is subtly wrong, responds to her in the same way as Levin does. Therefore Kitty's outburst—the resentment of a pregnant wife who fears that her husband is being deluded—comes as a shock to us. Lawrence complained (in his essay on *Cavalleria Rusticana*) that Tolstoy deliberately seeks to humiliate Vronsky, that he 'has a perverse pleasure in making the later Vronsky abject and pitiable.' The same might be said of his attitude towards Anna, at this point.

Lawrence's own case makes him a far from unimpeachable witness. Still, a close reading of the book raises certain doubts in our minds: we ask the question that Tolstoy himself asked about one of Maupassant's heroines: 'Why was this beautiful being destroyed? Must it really be so?' Anna, the delinquent, yet captures our allegiance. 'It is the triumph of Anna's charm that remains paramount,' wrote Arnold, '. . . the impression of her large, fresh, rich, generous, delightful nature never leaves us . . . keeps our sympathy, keeps even, I had almost said, our respect.' To have done this, she must have appealed more strongly to her creator than the moralist in him would allow. When he set in motion that iron wheel of retribution, the 'something enormous and inexorable' that crushed Anna, he shrank from her total destruction. As Arnold noted, 'the graceful head is untouched.'

Tolstoy seems to have isolated in Anna, and to some extent in her brother, the pride of the individual life, the 'quickness' that Lawrence so deeply cared for. Dolly, and Kitty too, are good women, mainstays of the family, but they lack the compelling charm of Anna. Indeed, Dolly is ground down by family cares, so that nothing of the bride remains in her, she becomes wholly the anxious mother. And Tolstoy pits her, shabby and timorous, against the invincible beauty of Anna. He does not shrink from presenting the contrast in its most truthful terms. That is to be expected from Tolstoy's honesty.

But in a deeper sense he is not honest; or rather he cannot face the issue, which will not work out for him in accordance with his moral beliefs. Anna must be destroyed. She has been forced into a hideous marriage with Karenin, and there is no way out except through her own destruction. Lawrence was perfectly right in sensing that Tolstoy is already waging war on the flesh. After all, Anna's final reflections on sexual love, disordered though her mind is shown to be, quite simply anticipate Tolstoy's own later views. There is something like a self-mutilation in his punishment of Anna. Lawrence says that he 'denied the Father, and propagated a great system of his recusancy, elaborating his own weakness, blaspheming his strength.' Certainly the Tolstoy of subsequent years—the old man, for instance, whom Gorky knew at Yalta—was often perverse, seldom found peace in himself, clung obstinately to his system, 'a man for whom all questions were settled.'

'The real tragedy of Anna, and of certain characters in Hardy's novels who perished like her,' said Lawrence, 'is that they are unfaithful to the greater unwritten morality,' which he also called 'the Law.' 'All the while,' he contends, 'by their own souls they were right.' Two views of life were at issue in Tolstoy's mind, one of them later to be expressed by Lawrence ('Any creature that attains to its own fulness of being, its own *living* self, becomes unique, a non-pareil') and the other by Eliot ('Those who glitter in the glory of the humming bird, meaning Death'). He affirms them both; and his torment as to which he should follow constitutes perhaps 'the real tragedy' of *Anna Karenina.*

Lawrence and Tolstoy

BY RAYMOND WILLIAMS

Certainly Tolstoy's influence on Lawrence is important. Once we are given the beginning of the thread, we are surprised how far it leads us: especially from *Anna Karenina* to *The Rainbow, St. Mawr* and *Lady Chatterley's Lover.* Lawrence's attack on Tolstoy's working-out of *Anna Karenina* is only one clear and conscious incident in a long, complicated and partly

A reply to Henry Gifford, "Anna, Lawrence and 'The Law,'" *Critical Quarterly,* Vol. I, No. 3.

unconscious process, but it is useful to isolate it, for the time being, because of its exceptional interest. Yet let us leave out the possibility that in attacking *Anna Karenina* Lawrence was defending his own life with Frieda, and the similar interpretation of Tolstoy's own attack on *King Lear*. The novel and the criticism are general facts, and everything that needs to be said can be said in their terms.

We have to consider first a formulation by Lawrence that has become very popular: 'when the novelist puts his thumb in the scale to pull down the balance to his own predilections that is immorality.' The metaphor is vivid, and we all like repeating it, but the issue it raises is very difficult. It seems to be often assumed that the scale in question is some general model, which if we like we can call reality, and hence that we can all take readings on it and watch when the thumb is applied. Obviously we have to work on some such general sense of reality, and some consequent criterion of probability. But if we take the question of *Anna Karenina* as it has been usually posed—the morality of a woman leaving an unsympathetic husband for a man who really awakens her love—we must surely see that there is no simple general-purpose scale. We know from evidence, in actual cases, that this can lead to a creative relationship, or to new forms of frustration and inadequacy, or to disaster. If somebody got out the statistics, we should still have no useful scale for any particular reading. Since we know that in any actual case the outcome will depend on the qualities of the people concerned, and on their actual circumstances, the most we can ask, in literature, is that the event corresponds to the given balance: that the internal logic of the voluntarily created situation should be obeyed. There are cases, undoubtedly, in which we can see this logic being broken, for external reasons such as compatibility to a public or a formula: think, in particular, of the routine 'happy ending,' though the routine 'unhappy ending' and the routine ending of isolation and indecision are also relevant. But this is something different from the author's 'own predilections,' where we are saying either that the author is too weak or stupid to revise his general views in the light of the particular experience he is exploring, or (more insidiously) that we find his general views unacceptable. In the case of Tolstoy, we are surely bound to say that the charge of distorting *Anna Karenina* can only be sustained if we find evidence, from the constituent characters and circumstances of the book, that either for external reasons, or through weakness or stupidity, the given logic of the situation was falsified. But this is very different from any such metaphor as 'the scale.'

Two facts about the general reading of *Anna Karenina* are very noticeable. First, there is the common isolation of characters from their context, as if the tragedy of Anna could be considered apart from the actual relationships with Karenin and Vronsky, and without reference to the society in which these are lived out. The tone of many critics in their comments on Anna, is suspiciously rhapsodical: for to see the novel as a mere framework for the story of a beautiful woman sacrificed to convention is as narrow and sentimental as a similar reading of the *Antigone*. Secondly, there is the extraordinary isolation of the Anna-Vronsky-Karenin story from the novel as a whole, in which it occupies rather less than half the actual narrative. The exclusion of Levin, and of the Levin-Kitty and Stiva-Dolly marriages, is tacit but inadmissible. It is sometimes rationalised by the argument that Anna-Vronsky is the real story, and that the story of Levin (though of course occupying a great deal of space) is simply the result of Tolstoy's incurable autobiographical itch: he had to record his discursive observations on work and faith even though the real story was about the lovers. Actually, this tells us more about the sensibility from which Tolstoy has been read—a sensibility which sustains most modern English fiction and criticism—than it helps in any way with the actual novel. Even in its less obvious form—the tacit exclusion of the Levin story, and of its relevance to the story of Anna and Vronsky—the narrowness is still evident. This is, really, the fashionable 'personal relationships' dogma, in which certain kinds of relationship are abstracted from their context of society, work and belief, in obedience to strong and obscure pressures from our own kind of society. It is worth repeating a fact fairly obvious in reading the novel: that it is a whole structure in which all the elements are closely related and that the complexity of this structure is Tolstoy's actual scale—his basic reading of experience at this time. Readers and critics who isolate the Anna-Vronsky story should consider as just one example of this structure, the sequence of chapters in Part Five, where the marriage of Levin and Kitty is followed by the Italian 'honeymoon' of Anna and Vronsky and then by Levin and Kitty setting up house and living through the first difficulties of their marriage, to the crucial death of Nikolay and the discovery that Kitty is with child. This is not the interweaving of plot and sub-plot, or of two separate stories, but the enactment of a single design.

The strength of Lawrence's case is his recognition of the quickening of life in Anna, after her meeting with Vronsky, but from this point on the actual elements of the novel are distorted, not by Tolstoy, but by his critic. The rejection of Karenin is certainly part of Anna's new 'instinct for life,' but it is much too crudely realised if Karenin is seen as simply damned (the crudeness of the physical disablement of Sir Clifford Chatterley is relevant here). Tolstoy created in Karenin, a memorable figure of the avoidance of love, but he was concerned to analyse rather than simply to damn. All his adult life, Karenin has been afraid of open emotion, of any kind, because of a characteristic fear that in exposing himself he will be hurt. This fear is once, and once only, overcome, in the great stress of the expectation of Anna's death after bearing Vronsky's child, and her powerful appeal to Karenin, accompanied by a temporary rejection of Vronsky:

> There is another woman in me, I'm afraid of her: she loved that man, and I tried to hate you, and could not forget about her that used to be. I'm not that woman. Now I'm my real self, all myself.

To this declaration, Karenin responds, for once breaking his habit and his fear, only to be told by Anna, after her recovery, that she has gone back to her previous position. Thus the pattern of Karenin's whole character has been confirmed: he has 'given way' to emotion, and he has been deeply hurt. His subsequent deterioration is then hardly surprising. The point here is, not that Anna's 'instinct for life' is disproved, but that Tolstoy, quite evidently, is not dealing with cardboard figures of the 'quick' and the 'dead,' but with actual processes of relationship in which love and hate are confirmed or denied. By letting us see this situation from each point of view in turn, rather than predicating the 'quick' and the 'dead'—the 'quick' to be forgiven their weaknesses, the 'dead' to be ritually damned—Tolstoy shows an absence of 'predilections' that is characteristic of his extraordinary maturity as an artist.

The next crucial element is the character of Vronsky. It is true to say that he awakens Anna, but it is one thing to wake somebody, another to live through the day. Lawrence tells us that Tolstoy has a 'perverse pleasure' in humiliating Vronsky, but the question that has to be asked is whether the Vronsky created by Tolstoy (and no other is admissible) is in fact capable of meeting the demands of the love which he has started in Anna. It is worth remembering that our introduction to Vronsky is, in the abortive relationship with Kitty, an introduction if not to a trifler at least to a man unprepared for a relationship of any permanence. Anna's own comment, just before her death, seems in retrospect an accurate account of a relationship with such a man:

We walked to meet each other up to the time of our love, and since then we have been irresistibly drifting in different directions. And there's no altering that. He tells me I'm insanely jealous, but it's not true. I'm not jealous, but I'm unsatisfied.

Vronsky's qualities are obvious, but it becomes clear, as the relationship with Anna develops, that he lives in a single and limited dimension, in which there is no real place for enduring passion. We can be misled, as Lawrence was often misled, by too simple an idea of 'masculinity.' Tolstoy raises the point in the novel, in Vronsky's reflections on the character of the foreign prince (is being a man something more than being a piece of healthy beef?) More fully, it is raised throughout the novel, by the comparison between Vronsky and Levin, which is surely one of Tolstoy's major themes, and from which Levin emerges as undoubtedly the stronger man. It is quite easy, in a highly civilised society, to be carried away by phrases like 'animal vigour,' but this, as Lawrence sometimes told it, is frankly a cock-and-bull story. A man's strength has to include the tenderness of protection and the warmth of continuing care which are biologically necessary in the human condition. Without these, vigour can be merely destructive, as Tolstoy shows on a small scale in the killing of the mare, and on a larger scale in Vronsky's contribution to the destruction of Anna. When she is isolated, in the country and in Moscow, he repeatedly leaves her alone, to play at politics or to watch Yashvin's gambling. The cold regularity of his reply to her desperate appeals, on the day of her death, is just another 'moment of carelessness,' but it is characteristic of his limited and powerful determination (which, ironically, had first enabled him to break through to Anna). It is significant that Lawrence, reworking this situation in *Lady Chatterley's Lover*, created in Mellors not a Vronsky, but a Levin. Mellors is strong and live, but he is also capable of deep tenderness, and interestingly, has that quality which Tolstoy saw as the means of health in Levin—an intimate and deeply respecting contact with the world of natural growth. Lawrence the critic was, after all, put right by Lawrence the artist, and we can leave it at that.

And yet, in spite of everything, did Tolstoy kill Anna, as a kind of renunciation of love? It is certainly true that Tolstoy insisted, much more than Lawrence, on the social consequences of primary relationships, but then, unlike Lawrence, he set all his fiction in real societies, and could hardly avoid what they were showing him: a network of actual and continuing relationships which could not be simply dismissed as puritanism and the grey North. The convention invoked against Anna is indeed shallow and hypocritical, but take a society in which there is no difficulty of divorce, in which an Anna would not be pointed at and avoided, and the human difficulty in substance remains. The child is there, in any society. Frustration and hatred are there, under any laws, if the real relationships are wrong. The tragedy of Anna is affected by her society, but the roots of the tragedy lie much deeper, in a specific relationship (just as, in modern societies in which the old sexual laws and conventions have been practically abandoned, men and women still kill themselves in despair of love). The action of Anna's tragedy is that she leaves one inadequate man for another; but the inadequacy of Karenin lay with an unawakened woman, the inadequacy of Vronsky with a woman grown to passion and demanding it as the continuing centre of her life. The characteristic of Anna, at the highest point of her growth, is that she must live her feelings right through. Living on a limited commitment had been possible once, but it was from this that she broke out. Of course, not as a mature woman: the maturity seemed to be there, when she lived by her limited commitment to Karenin, but it is not there once her full energy is released. One of the few things we do not know enough about in the novel is her original attitude to the marriage to Karenin (this is usually left out of romantic and anti-romantic stories alike). But it is at least clear that she has become a wife and mother without ever having been a girl in love, but now in a situation where much more is needed. The rush of feeling is awakened by and attached to Vronsky, but this is not the whole story; there is also evidence, in her attitude to Vronsky, of the familiar adolescent condition in which overwhelming feeling as it were collides with an object rather than grows towards it. This can be disastrous, even for a girl, if the object is inadequate or irrelevant to the real force of the feeling. But Anna is not a girl; she is still in part the guilty wife and mother, and the combination is terrifying. The ordinary married woman's affair, as with her friends in Petersburg, is a characteristically limited commitment. We see this again in her brother Stiva, in many ways so like her, but unhurt because always essentially uncommitted. Anna shames the half-life of this society, but half-life is often a protection for the weak and the immature. Stiva slips away from diffi- culty, from any real demand on himself, with his 'almond-oil smile.' Anna, in her delayed rush of feeling, must give herself wholly, without regard for safety, and whether she then sur- vives depends on the quality of the man she is giving herself to. Nothing less is thinkable; the demand is quite absolute. Even her death is a revengeful move to make Vronsky love her more, and this tragic error (common enough in certain kinds of suicide) combines the wholeness and the immaturity which, falling on weak hands, unite to destroy her.

Tolstoy's logic, given the elements he has created, is sound. But of course Lawrence is right to imply that in choosing these elements Tolstoy was revealing himself. Yet it is no simple question of 'being' and 'social being.' Tolstoy was torn by very deep tensions, not only because he was a particular kind of man, but because he went on living in his own society, with its own deep tensions, and in touch with his own errors, which he did not simply move on from. Aksinia, the serf-girl he had loved, scrubbed floors in his wife's house, and his son by her lived nearby. It is not, as it is sometimes put, a case of a young rake turned old Puritan. It is a man watching his own life, in terms of a society which divided people and exacerbated their necessary difficulties. I agree with Edmund Wilson that there were elements in this complex that he failed to recognize completely, and that there is a consequent dark area in his work, both in its shaping and in its omissions. But we must notice that in *Anna Karenina*, in relation to the tragedy of Anna, there is in the story of Levin an account of the fulfilment of a man who gives himself and commits himself completely. Significantly, this is a slow growth, learned as much from the death of his brother as from the love of Kitty, learned also in work and in the effort towards right working relations with other men. The density of this life of Levin's makes an obvious contrast with the single dimension in which, in their different ways, Vronsky and Karenin and Stiva live (in each of these men the attitude to work, and thence to other men, is seen as related to the differing yet inadequate attitudes to love). Levin translating a hundred-rouble note, lightly spent in Moscow, into the work of men in the fields, is involved with values in a sense equally opposed to the conventions of fashionable society and the mere flouting of them. In learning a reverence towards all that lives, Levin is learning something deeper than either respectability or personal honour. His ability to love Kitty as a wife, and then to love their child, grows from this whole attachment, which is more mature than anything Anna is allowed to live. Vronsky, in the end, wants marriage and a stake in the country, but in these terms the offer is both too much and too little for Anna: she does not want marriage and Vronsky's children, but she needs passion, which on Vronsky's side has gone. A meaningful society, and therefore a meaningful place in it, is for different reasons, beyond both of them. Here is the moving field of all Tolstoy's greatest writing, and there are few writers who can live with him in it. The irony is that Lawrence addressed himself to just these problems, though with less strength and in any case with less time (he died in the year of life in which *Anna Karenina* was begun). It is vitally important that we do not scale Tolstoy down to the limited sensibility (the separation of work from life, and of personal meanings from social meanings) which has recently governed our own culture. We can see the sense of Lawrence's protest, though he had to rework the book to sustain it (first in a critical error, second in a creative transformation). But while Lawrence's strength is of

Tolstoy's kind, his weakness is that of our own majority culture, and must be analysed rather than merely repeated. (How dare Mr. Gifford, for example, write such a stale salon sentence as 'Dolly, and Kitty too, are good women, mainstays of the family, but they lack the compelling charm of Anna'? Consider that contrast between 'mainstay' and 'charm.' Does Mr. Gifford really live in that world, or if he does, does he want to?) 'Fulness of being' is when we live as ourselves with others and in our world, and no writer more than Tolstoy, no book more than *Anna Karenina*, illuminates its substance, its consequences, and its demands. As in all tragedy, it is not the fate of characters we rest on, but the living patterns of experience that can help us to live.

Further Notes on "*Anna Karenina*"

by HENRY GIFFORD

There is a sense of outrage in Mr. Williams' reply to my article, *Anna, Lawrence and 'The Law*,' with which one must sympathise. Lawrence's views are too often repeated by admirers who never stop to inspect them; great and complicated novels like *Anna Karenina* do not get the responsible reading, the full view, they deserve; personal relationships too often, in our culture, try to escape from the necessities of communal living. We must agree with Mr. Williams that the Levin side of Tolstoy's novel bears directly upon the predicament of Anna: home, the family, rural ways, the realities of work stand over against the insecure relationships of the St. Petersburg salon, the world of railway trains and 'escape from it all' to Italy. He is right too in stressing Anna's immaturity, and the fulfilment in Levin's experience, which is denied to her. A just reading of the book will recognize all these values. Why, then, invoke Lawrence and his accusations of blasphemy?

In the twentieth volume of the Russian 'Jubilee' edition of Tolstoy, one may study the suppressed earlier drafts from which, after five years of intermittent toil, *Anna Karenina* as we know it emerged. A novel should be judged by its final form; but Lawrence's sense of a certain unresolved conflict in the work (shared surely by many readers) finds a good deal of support in the evidence of these earlier drafts. Fortunately there is to hand an extremely careful study by Vladimir A. Zhdanov, published in Moscow three years ago, the title of which may be translated as *The Making of Anna Karenina*. From its analyses one may see, perhaps, what is meant by the novelist putting his thumb in the scale. Tolstoy, as George Steiner reminds us in his recent book, nearly always wrote with a 'palpable design.' He distrusted art, and could never fend off the didactic impulse for long. *Anna Karenina* bears the ravages of that ceaseless civil war in its author, though, as Steiner points out, the double plot structure allows Tolstoy to release most of his didactic energies in the Levin story, and to treat Anna more freely and generously than he had intended.

Anna was always, of course, at the book's centre. (Note that even when, subsequently, Levin's story was added, Tolstoy chose to name the book still after her, and contrast this with the thematic titles of his other great works: *War and Peace, The Power of Darkness, Resurrection.*) Her story was to be that of an adulteress, who, is first seen in a drawing-room behaving not only indiscreetly but shamelessly with her lover. The husband decides that she is possessed by the devil. And this notion appears in more than one of the earlier attempts. An unrepentant Anna (then called Tatyana) returns to her husband after the race-meeting 'with a diabolical glitter in her eyes.' And the husband, in another variant which still keeps the diabolical motive, tells her: 'Our life has been united, and united not by men but by God. . . . In our opinion there is a mystery, and you and I, we feel it. . . . I shall do nothing, I cannot and indeed I do not wish to punish. Vengeance is God's.' There can be little doubt that it was Tolstoy, the rigid moralist who planned this story. It might have issued as a crude tract against adultery. The annals of adultery are almost without exception squalid; but there is always 'the possible other case.' Tolstoy by prejudging the matter had suppressed that possibility; and this is what I call putting a thumb in the balance.

But the balance rose against his thumb, all the same. Gradually Karenin (who wasn't so called at first) underwent a change. At the beginning he was a gentle, easily put out, weak and almost unworldly figure, with a kind smile and kind blue eyes. Slowly he turned into the official; the 'goodness' was taken away from him; his eyes and his bearing became *cold;*

he is Karenin, after, it seems, the Greek word *karenon*, the head. And so we get the evasive but imposing figure who meets Anna at the station. Karenin lives like Casaubon in a paper world, and I would suggest that the author has far less sympathy for him than George Eliot shows for Casaubon. He is ranged with Levin's half-brother, who also prepares cut-and-dried formulations to meet the unexpected in life. True, there is once for Karenin 'the awful daring of a moment's surrender,' when he forgives Anna on her supposed death-bed, and Vronsky too. But very soon after he recognises in the Princess Betsy's tone and smile that force of social opinion to which he has always bowed. Karenin *is* a 'social being': he cares more for appearances than the truth. In that scene to which Mr. Williams has alluded, when Anna speaks of that other woman who has possessed her, and Karenin melts in forgiveness, I believe the didactic impulse has taken control. It seems to me a contrived moment (like the manifestation of Platon Karataev in *War and Peace*) but Tolstoy was too honest not to go back on it. Basically I am sure he was hostile to Karenin, who lives by the head, and is an emanation of Petersburg.

The counterbalance to Petersburg is Levin's world, Muscovite and rural. Mr. Williams has every reason for saying that here Tolstoy gets down to his real values: marriage, the family, the daily order of work in the fields. Anna, as we know, is condemned to live in a false society; and it is doubly tragic for her that the lover whom she chooses, in her denial of that society, should himself be infected deeply with its prejudices: he shows indeed what George Eliot called 'spots of commonness.' Anna, in fact, cannot enter the responsible world of Levin: we know—and Dolly's visit reveals this—how glossily unreal is the establishment that she and Vronsky set up in the country, when Vronsky needs occupation. Nobody can dispute the logic of Anna's case: she is necessarily excluded from some of the richest experiences in human life. When, therefore, critics like Arnold speak of her 'charm that remains paramount,' are they forgetting the full context? Perhaps—and yet surely it is not romantic to insist that Anna (even though she has deserted her child, and virtually destroyed both husband and lover) somehow evades human judgment? 'Vengeance is mine, saith the Lord.' Anna has done wrong; nonetheless she stands for qualities of truthfulness and generous feeling, even of dedication, that are found nowhere else in her milieu. Anna's protest against the Karenin set, its limited risks and saving hypocrisies, surely wins assent from the reader. But I believe in a more profound sense Tolstoy felt an involvement with Anna. We may recall that Levin originally fell in love with the Shcherbatsky family as a whole, and it is scarcely an exaggeration to say that he married Kitty on grounds of principle: he thought first of children and the married state, then of the woman who could provide these. Now Anna has an endowment of life—call it, as I perhaps unwisely did, a 'compelling charm'—a spontaneity, which obviously attracted Tolstoy. Anna and Levin are the two most complete beings in the novel, and whereas Levin sometimes wearies the reader with his irritable probings after certainty, Anna disarms our prejudice against her: Tolstoy gave her, in spite of himself, an undeniable presence—she is no common creature. Tolstoy, as Pasternak has said in the *Essay in Autobiography*, though 'a moralist, a leveller, a preacher of a system of justice applicable to every human being without exception, and in equal measure,' yet was in himself startlingly original. An egalitarian, yes, but he always saw himself as *primus inter impares*. We know of the crisis that followed *Anna Karenina:* the long years ensuing which were marked by what Lawrence has termed 'recusancy.' Tolstoy never achieved the balance of Shakespeare after *King Lear*. We must not allow our knowledge of his later extremes to read overmuch into Anna Karenina. Was he lacerating himself when he drove Anna to her destruction? It is difficult to prove. Certainly he has pursued relentlessly the logic of her situation: one might contend (especially in the light of his earlier drafts) that he argues the case against Anna. His logical victory is complete; but why did he need to embark on such an argument? What led him to conceive Anna, to endow her so lavishly, and then to force her into an ugly marriage and a career of shame ending in a bloody death? There is an agony of spirit here which is never quite subdued by all the affirmations of virtue and responsibility in Levin's world.

XIII

DONALD DAVIE

Tolstoy, Lermontov, and Others

"THE KREUTZER SONATA"

In general, we regard *The Kreutzer Sonata* as a didactic tract disguised as a novel. Such tracts in disguise can be works of literary and artistic value. Perhaps they are necessarily of the second rank as works of art. But at least the novel of ideas is a thoroughly respectable literary kind, having methods and conventions proper to it. One may cite, in our day, the novels of Mr. Arthur Koestler. But is *The Kreutzer Sonata* a novel of ideas, of this sort? I think that it is not. It is a novel and a tract at once, or it essays to be both at once. It is both and neither. And the conventions which govern it are confused, so that the reader does not know "which way to take it." Nor, so far as we can see, was this ambiguity intended by the author. It is therefore a grossly imperfect work.

The scene in the railway-carriage is set, in the first two chapters, with pleasing skill. Thereafter, until chapter xxi, the initial convention is not altogether sustained; the reader begins to wonder why the scene should have been set at all. These chapters constitute the first part of Pozdnishchev's confessional monologue, and the sentences interjected from time to time, reminding the reader of the setting, seem only perfunctory. Still, this part is read, with no discomfort, as within the convention of the novel of ideas; and the reader hopes that the significance of the setting will emerge later. We infer, meanwhile, that the sentiments expressed by Pozdnishchev are not to be taken as being "in character," that the sentiments expressed are the sentiments of Tolstoy himself. In chapter xxi Pozdnishchev tells how he introduced into his home the man who was to cause him to murder his wife:

"I disliked him exceedingly from the first moment I looked upon him. But some strange fatal force moved me not only to refrain from repelling him, but to draw him nearer to me. What could be simpler than to exchange a few words with him, to bid him good-bye chillingly, and not to introduce him to my wife? But no; I must talk about his playing, and tell him that I had heard he had given up music. He said it was not so; that he had never practised more assiduously all his life than at that moment; and passing from himself to me, reminded me that I too had played in times gone by. To this I replied that I did not play now, but that my wife was a good musician. It is very curious! From the very first day, from the very first hour I saw him, my relations towards him were such as they could only have been subsequently to everything that occurred later on. There was something very strained in my intercourse with him; I took note of every word, every expression uttered by him or by myself, and invested them with a significance justified by nothing that I then knew."

It is very curious indeed. It is very curious that Pozdnishchev who in previous chapters has been so empirically reasonable, impatient of idealism and illusion, should here show himself as believing, not only in precise foreboding, but also in "some strange fatal force." He believes in these, moreover, against the run of the empirical evidence. There was apparent, as he says, nothing to prevent him from keeping his rival away. Yet in the earlier chapters the appeal was always to the empirical evidence, to milliners' shop-windows and the social usages of the Russian gentry, against any preconceived notions. If we are to believe, despite all appearance to the contrary, in "some strange fatal force," why must we not believe, despite appearances to the contrary, in the quite general existence of ennobling and permanent love between the sexes?

Three pages later, the "strange fatal force" reappears as "an invisible power":

"I could not help noticing all this, and I suffered horribly in consequence. And yet, in spite of this, or rather, perhaps, by reason of it, an invisible power compelled me against my will to be not only extremely courteous, but affectionate towards him. I am unable to specify the motive which prompted me to act thus; whether it was to prove to my wife and to him that I was not actuated by fear, or to deceive myself, I cannot say; I only know that from the very first my relations with him were not natural and unaffected."

The "power," it is plain, the "fatal force," is inward. And it is "strange" and "mysterious" only because it cannot be rationalized, brought into consciousness. But the contradiction remains. Whence this inability to specify the motive? The sudden humility is suspicious after the downrightness with which Pozdnishchev specified the motive in the earlier passages of courtship and honeymoon and parenthood. For the remainder of the novel, however, this humility is maintained. In the wonderful passages which describe the murder itself, we gape at the fluctuating and mysterious complexity in the mind of the murderer:

"I knew very well what I was doing, and did not for a single second cease to be conscious of it. The more I fanned the flame of my fury, the brighter burned within me the light of consciousness, lighting up every nook and corner of my soul, so that I could not help seeing everything I was doing. I cannot affirm that I knew in advance what I was going to do, but the very moment I was doing anything, and I fancy some seconds beforehand, I was conscious of what I was doing, in order, as it were, that I might repent of it in time, that I might afterwards have it to say that I could have stayed my hand. Thus, I was aware that I was striking her below the ribs, and that the blade would penetrate. The moment I was doing this, I knew that I was doing something terrible, a thing that I had never done before, an action that would be fraught with frightful consequences."

And again:

"I recollect the indescribable horror of this state of mind, and I infer from it, and in fact I may add that I have a dim remembrance, that having plunged the dagger into her body, I instantaneously drew it out again, anxious thereby to remedy what I had done, to stay my hand. I then stood motionless for an instant, waiting to see what would happen, and whether it was possible to undo it."

I suppose it is this in Tolstoy which we especially admire; on the one hand, the effortless accuracy about the processes of thought (as here first the recollection, then the inference from the recollection, last the corroboration from dim remembrance); on the other, the shocking honesty about the endless irrationality of motive—"I instantaneously drew it out again, anxious thereby to remedy what I had done. . . . I then stood motionless for an instant, waiting to see what would happen. . . ." And indeed it is fine—we are persuaded once again about the complexity of the mental life, and about the irrationality of motive.

All the more, then, are we indignant, on turning back to the earlier chapters, to find motive over an enormous field of human experience reduced bluntly to one simple proposition:

"Last spring a number of peasants were working in our neighbourhood on a railway embankment. The usual food of a strong peasant when engaged in light field labour consists of bread, kvass, onions, and this keeps him alive, active, and healthy. When he enters into the service of a railway company his food is porridge, and a pound of meat daily. This meat he gives out again in the form of sixteen hours' labour, driving a wheelbarrow of thirty poods, which is just as much as he is able to perform. We, on the other hand, eat game, meat, and fish, besides sundry other kinds of heat-giving food and drink. Now where, may I ask, does all this go? To produce excesses, abnormal excitement, which, passing through the prism of our artificial life, assumes the form of falling in love."

What we have learned from Tolstoy he appears never to have learned himself. Only in Tolstoy himself, he would have us think, are the processes of thought and the faculties of knowledge not muddled but naïve and clear. Only in himself, he implies, are the springs of action always reasonable.

But this is a monster. One really cannot believe that the man who knew so profoundly the minds of his fellows knew his own mind so little. There must be another reason why Tolstoy cheated the most valuable trait in himself, his plastic apprehension of irrationality and complexity. I think there is. For Tolstoy all thought was vicious, whether artistic or philosophical, so long as it did not lead to action:

"Music instantaneously throws me into the state of feeling in which the composer of it found himself when he wrote it. My soul blends with his, and together with him I am transported from one frame of mind to another. But why I am so ravished out of myself I know not. He who composed the piece—Beethoven, for instance, in the case of the Kreutzer Sonata—knew perfectly well why he was in that mood; it was that mood that determined him to do certain things, and therefore for him that state of mind has a meaning; for me it has absolutely none. This is why it is that music only causes irritation, never ends anything. It is a different thing if a military march is played, then the soldiers move forward, keeping time to the music, and the end is attained; if dance music is played people dance to it, and the object is also accomplished; if a Mass is sung I receive

Holy Communion, and here, too, the music is not in vain; but in other cases there is nothing but irritation, and no light how to act during this irritation."[1]

There is no disputing the puerility of this. The argument rests upon hypotheses about the mind of Beethoven in the act of composing, assumptions which are not, in the nature of the case, susceptible of proof. Nor can it be argued, I fear, that Tolstoy is aware of the puerility, that it is not his but his puppet's, Pozdnishchev's. This is a passage in which the plastic imagination breaks down, as in the earlier chapters, before the half-baked rationalist. What emerges, however, as the overriding preoccupation here, is the desire for art to prove its utility by leading to action. And since the passage was apparently crucial for Tolstoy in that it provides the title to the book, we are justified in supposing that what he says here of music he would have applied, with more or less qualification, to the other arts—to his own, for instance, the art of the novelist. There is corroboration of this in other pamphlets.

Now it is plain that passages of the kind we have admired from *The Kreutzer Sonata* do not lead to action. There is no need to argue a case that great art produces a stasis or an equilibrium, not a drive to the act. We need only say that we shall presumably be wary of intervening in any situation if that situation is presented as of great psychological complexity, and that we shall not be so wary if the issues are simplified for us. At bottom, the reason for inconsistency of method in Tolstoy is as simple as this. On the other hand, Tolstoy is not alone in supposing that, for the sophisticated individual of the nineteenth century, it was impossible to meet fully the claims of the will, demanding expression in action, and also the claims of the intelligence, demanding freedom and scope to analyze, weigh pros and cons, and scrutinize motive. On the contrary, this was a preoccupation common to most of the European Romantics. It was Shakespeare's Hamlet who talked of being "sicklied o'er with the pale cast of thought"; but it was Coleridge, the Romantic critic, who saw in this the problem debated in every line of the play. Tolstoy, again, was not alone in deciding that the rights of the will overrode the rights of the

[1] The style of the translator, who is anonymous in this first translation of *The Kreutzer Sonata*, is here extremely slipshod.

intelligence.[2] Most of the Romantics had agreed, and it is this which lends color to the contention that Romanticism was antirationalist, that it worked by impulse and intuition, not by intelligence. There is no question, therefore, of looking for a "source" for Tolstoy's attitude. The spirit of his age led him inevitably to think in these terms, to see the claims of the analyzing intelligence in conflict with the claims of the will to act.

In terms of this conflict Tolstoy saw life; and in terms of this conflict he lived his life. The conflict in the living spills over into *The Kreutzer Sonata* and breaks that book into two. From other books, earlier than *The Kreutzer Sonata*, and later, the conflict was excluded. Or rather, the conflict is present, as the theme which is debated, as the terms of the vision which is presented; but it is not present as the agony which was lived. In *The Cossacks*, in *War and Peace*, in *Hadji Murad*, the conflict which Tolstoy lived is kept separate from the conflict which was seen. In *The Kreutzer Sonata*, the conflict of the life distorts the conflict of the vision. When we discuss Tolstoy's narrative method and his style, we try to find out how the conflict of the life was kept out of the vision. In these, the great books, the conflict is seen as the conflict inside men, not in the first place as the conflict inside Tolstoy. We are concerned with Tolstoy the artist, not with Tolstoy the agonized titan. It has been said that this is impossible, and in general it is true. It is better to say, therefore, that we are concerned with Tolstoy's vision, not with Tolstoy's life, and with the means by which the vision was made independent of the life. The vision is not independent in *The Kreutzer Sonata*, and the novel suffers accordingly.

STENDHAL

There is no question of looking for a source for this attitude in Tolstoy, that is, his predisposition for seeing life as a conflict between the will and the intelligence. But, given the attitude, Tolstoy had to find a literary method most suitable for dealing

[2] *The Private Diary of Leo Tolstoy, 1853–1857*, ed. Aylmer Maude (London: Heinemann, 1927), p. 43: "To take the decisions of one's will as rules for oneself about everything is an excess, but in some cases such decisions are necessary." The cult of *l'absurde*, as practiced by Camus in our own day, is surely the same answer to the same problem.

with it. And in this limited sense a source can be found, in Stendhal. It was from Stendhal, says Prince Mirsky, that Tolstoy first learned how to cast into artistic form that analysis of motive and fluctuating feeling for which he had an equal or a greater flair. But there is another side to Stendhal. Romain Rolland, for example, finds in some of Tolstoy's early work "a quality of disorder, and at times a certain dryness of abstract analysis, which is increased by divisions and sub-divisions after the manner of Stendhal."[3] And he quotes in illustration two passages:

There are three kinds of love: 1, aesthetic love; 2, devoted love; 3, active love. . . . [Tolstoy's *Youth*.]

And again:

There are three kinds of soldiers: 1, the docile and subordinate; 2, the authoritative; 3, the boasters—who themselves are subdivided into: (a) the docile who are cold and lethargic; (b) those who are earnestly docile; (c) docile soldiers who drink. . . .

Now surely what disconcerts us in these passages is not the "dryness" (though that is an aspect, too, of inhumanity), but the arrogance. We just do not believe that Russian soldiers can be classified so simply, and we are cross with the writer who maintains the contrary, because he seems to betray the endless fecundity and diversity of life. In fact, these passages displease in just the same way as that passage from *The Kreutzer Sonata*, in which the difference between the sexual lives of the Russian gentry and the Russian peasant is accounted for in terms of the diet of each class. The author is too certain of himself. The problem cannot be so simple. And we dislike him as a doctrinaire.

It would not be altogether fair to blame Stendhal for this fault in Tolstoy. Quite apart from the fact that Tolstoy was innately disposed to this point of view, Stendhal only supplying the literary model appropriate to it, Stendhal, as it seems to me, was frequently tactful enough to keep "classification" out of his novels. It went into his treatise *De l'Amour* and out of *La Chartreuse de Parme*. On the other hand, this element

[3] Romain Rolland, *Tolstoy*, trans. B. Miall (London: T. Fisher Unwin, 1911), p. 50.

is certainly present in Stendhal, and it is accepted that Stendhal powerfully influenced the young Tolstoy; so that it is not a mistake to recall his name.[4]

Of course, the case in which Tolstoy's fidelity to fecundity and variety in life is most grossly at variance with his habit of doctrinaire generalization *about life* is *War and Peace*. Of *War and Peace* Tolstoy remarks that Stendhal had taught him all he knew about war. It is not true. Proudhon, for instance, had taught Tolstoy a great deal.[5] But it is certainly true, in one sense, that all the theories of history put forward in *War and Peace* no less than the battle-pieces themselves, are so many amplifications of what is implied by Stendhal when Fabrice del Dongo wanders bewildered about the field of Waterloo. All of the theorizing chapters, where Tolstoy is contending that the historian must not dogmatize, are themselves dogmatizing of the most shameless kind, affirming the most arrogant of generalizations about the whole of human history. When these chapters began to appear in the later volumes of *War and Peace*, Russian readers were dismayed, Flaubert and others were bitterly disappointed. Tolstoy himself later admitted the justness of these criticisms. This discrepancy in *War and Peace*, and the discomfort we feel in reading, are the same discrepancy and the same discomfort we found in reading *The Kreutzer Sonata*.

[4] Perhaps a propensity to arrogant generalization is inherent in the French genius. Those Frenchmen who have written on the Russian novel (Dupuy, De Vogüé, Gide) sometimes seem to admit as much. It is worth noting that Kafka disliked in Balzac something close to that with which we find fault in Tolstoy:

"There is no more pregnant contrast to Kafka than Balzac's sham preciseness, Balzac's superlatives and generalisations (something after this style: 'She walked along with that light tread with which every Paris woman walks between ten and ten-fifteen in the morning.')"

(Quoted by Max Brod, *Franz Kafka: A Biography*, trans. H. Roberts [London: Secker and Warburg, 1947], p. 44.) Brod comments:

"It is superfluous to point out . . . that Kafka found much to admire in Balzac. For he never lost the grand line in the mass of details, nor the sweep of a way of life. Kafka once said: Balzac carried a stick with the motto 'I break every obstacle'—my motto would rather be, 'every obstacle breaks me.'"

[5] See Boris Eichenbaum, "*War and Peace*: A New Theory," *Criterion*, October 1931, pp. 50–57.

DONALD DAVIE

GOGOL AND DICKENS

Tolstoy once made a list of the books which had influenced him in his early years.[6] This list is of great importance, for just as the influence of Stendhal can be traced to a point as late in Tolstoy's career as *The Kreutzer Sonata*, so can many other items of his youthful reading.

On the second page of *The Kreutzer Sonata* Pozdnishchev is described for the first time:

It was characteristic of this person that he uttered from time to time peculiar sounds resembling short coughs or laughter just begun and suddenly broken off.

Eleven pages later we are reminded of Pozdnishchev's presence when "a noise was heard as of suppressed laughter or a smothered sob." Seven pages later he is "making that strange noise to which he was addicted." And three pages later again he "uttered that peculiar sound which he apparently always made whenever a new thought occurred to him." The peculiar sound, between a cough and a laugh, is uttered thereafter every few pages. Pozdnishchev's "peculiar sound" is the ghost of the Princess Volkonski's short upper lip, which is always a little moist, and of Karenin's cracking finger-joints. It belongs with those details of physical appearance, apparently superfluous, which grow, by repetition, to become an emblem of the inward personality. The Princess's lip and Karenin's finger-joints have been noticed appreciatively by many critics, and it is true that they represent a device, a sort of metaphor, peculiar to Tolstoy, of which he made triumphantly successful use.

Yet the Russians recognize this device of "superfluous detail" as characteristic of the whole tradition of the Russian novel and as deriving from Gogol. And this is true. For instance, on the first page of *Dead Souls*, Chichikov, the hero,

[6] The list is as follows (from G. R. Noyes's *Tolstoy* [London: John Murray, 1919], pp. 16–17): Of "immense influence": Sermon on the Mount in Matthew's Gospel; Rousseau, *Confessions* and *Émile*; Dickens, *David Copperfield*; of "very great" influence: Sterne, *Sentimental Journey*; Rousseau, *Nouvelle Héloïse*; Pushkin, *Eugene Onegin*; Schiller, *The Robbers*; Gogol, *Dead Souls*; Turgenev, *A Sportsman's Sketches*; Grigorovich, *Anton Goremyka*; Lermontov, *A Hero of Our Time*; of "great" influence: Gogol, short stories; Prescott, *Conquest of Mexico*.

arrives at the provincial town where he is to start his adventures:

His arrival produced no commotion whatever in the town, and was not signalized by anything in particular; though two moujiks who were standing at the door of a pot-house opposite the inn, made some remarks, which had, however, more reference to the equipage than to the person seated in it. "Just look," said one of them to the other, "What a wheel that is! What do you think? Will that wheel last as far as Moscow or not?"—"Oh! it will hold out," replied the other. "But it won't hold out as far as Kazan, I fancy?"—"It will not," returned the other. And here the conversation ended. However, as the britchka drove into the inn yard, it was met by a young man in white duck trousers very narrow and very short, and a swallow-tailed coat with claims to fashion, beneath which was visible a shirt-front fastened with a Tula pin, in the shape of a bronze pistol. The young man turned round, surveyed the equipage, caught hold of his cap, which the wind was on the point of blowing off, and then went his way.[7]

That is all. The two moujiks and the dashing young man never reappear in the story; nor does the plot turn upon the breaking of a carriage-wheel or the necessity of traveling to Moscow or Kazan. The whole passage, detailed as it is ("a Tula pin, in the shape of a bronze pistol"), points nowhere. It is entirely "superfluous." But of course it is not really superfluous. In Gogol passages of this sort are made to serve purposes which arise from the very center of his genius. In the first place, the sheer wealth of invention, sustained without effort, takes away the breath. These passages are astonishing in themselves; and, occurring as here, on the first page, win over the reader before he can take his bearings. The hectic and tumultuous movement of Gogol's prose combines with this wealth of inventive detail to take the matter out of the reader's hands. From this point of view the passage just quoted may be compared with the first pages of *Martin Chuzzlewit*, where, as Taine noticed, Dickens' tour-de-force of inventive fantasy, woven about the dead leaves, has the same effect. Second, the passage is undeniably funny. That "however," in the middle of the passage, arousing hopes of logical relevance, which are immediately dashed, awakes in

[7] *Tchitchikoff's Journey*, or *Dead Souls*, trans. Isabel F. Hapgood (London, 1887).

the reader a rueful and reluctant smile which it is always Gogol's achievement to command. In the third place, all the images which Gogol evokes are mean, "diminishing images," as the Elizabethans called them, consistently destructive of stature and dignity. Hence arises the horrific-comic in Gogol's world. And it was this consistently "diminishing" effect of Gogol's writing which enabled the Russian critics of his age to present him as a critic of Russian society. Fourth, as a special mode of "diminishing" the human, Gogol treats of persons and of things as enjoying equal status. The Tula pin has as much attention, has as much of life, as the young man who wears it. Gogol's method drains his human figures of life and imbues his inanimate objects with a specious animation. He makes objects of human beings. Even the names of his characters suggest animated objects—Bashmatkin, from "bashmak," a slipper. Fifth (and this is of vast importance for all Russian fiction). Gogol constructs a lawless world. It is not bounded; it obeys no rules. At any moment an irrelevance may occur. It is open to the void, from which may come at any moment a meaningless intruder. It is a free world, so free that one is made to regret that freedom. In this it is at the opposite pole from the world of Balzac. And this is the aspect of Gogol which attracted Dostoievsky. Finally, there is in Gogol, though rarely, that use of the superfluous detail which was appropriated by Tolstoy. Chichikov's complicated writing-case, which has detailed treatment in the middle of the book, is a superfluous detail in itself and an accretion of superfluous details. In its vulgar and worn elegance it is in some sort, as Andrei Bely and Vladimir Nabokov have pointed out, a metaphor of Chichikov's soul, which is, precisely, vulgar and glossy, endlessly mean. And this function of the superfluous detail corresponds to the Princess's short upper lip and Karenin's cracking of the finger-joints. But these are only the most obvious examples of what Tolstoy could do with this device. He could make it betray a wholly new situation, a complicated change in human relationships, as when Anna Karenina, returning from Moscow where she has met Vronsky, notices for the first time the size of her husband's ears. One could find many more, and subtler, instances.

In this respect, however, it is likely that the influence of

Dickens was at least as great as that of Gogol. Tolstoy himself records the influence of *David Copperfield* as "immense," that of *Dead Souls* only as "very great." And he affirmed that the genius of Dickens was similar to that of Gogol, but greater because more humane. Certainly Dickens animates the inanimate as Gogol does, but he does not steal the animation from his human figures. They too are extravagantly animated, in scale. Dickens' world is not dehumanized. And again, nowhere but in Dickens do we find this tag of peculiar detail recurring continually to distinguish one character from another, as we have seen it in the cases of Pozdnishchev, the Princess Volkonski, and Karenin. In Dickens the superfluous detail by which the reader identifies a character is usually a conversational phrase—"waiting for something to turn up," "Barkis is willing," "I will not desert Mr. Micawber." In Tolstoy the tag is a physical characteristic. But the principle is the same.

Nevertheless, and while it is true that Tolstoy's world is not mean and vulgar with the deliberate vulgarity of Gogol's, there survived from Gogol the practice of "diminishing images," of making the superfluous detail mean. Karenin's ears, Pozdnishchev's cough, even the Princess's wet lip, are deliberately debasing details. This "meanness" in the Russian novelists can be called a vice of the age, which is to say, of the audience. For in an age which is skeptical and pessimistic about the ideal, the writer, if he wants to inculcate belief in some ideal, must first satisfy his readers that he is as mean and skeptical as they are. The reader will believe in the ideal presented only if it rises out of a skepticism as real as his own, which qualifies it. And Tolstoy, who always wanted to exert this sort of influence (*War and Peace*, said Leontiev, is not historical but political—the motive behind it is not, in the first place, attainment of accuracy, but exertion of influence), had therefore to present, as it were, his credentials as a skeptic. In 1896, Leontiev made the point thus:

For the Russian reader of our day (especially from the middle rank of society) there is little of that realism which says: this one is weak, but this one crafty; one is cruel, another is comical, tactless, pitiful, and so on. This, we agree, would be a realism sober and truthful; we are all helpless and sinful; but of this, I say, we have little. . . . For us it is essential that someone should snort through his nose and so on. It is no use saying that the reader himself must often already in the course of life have remarked that people snore, and splutter with rage and the rest. But his guides and mentors have already taught him so thoroughly that he should give greater credence to honour if it is painted warts and all, that he will feel greater love if the beloved snores, and so on, and by the same token, if someone "with a nervous movement pours out a glass of water for himself," and then does not smile but "smirks," then his belief will be the firmer! . . .

In my view,—I am ready to confess—all this is grossly unnecessary, and common, in more or less degree, to all the Russian story-tellers and novelists, starting with *Dead Souls* (here it is even in place) and continuing almost up to the "What men live by" of Count Tolstoy (and here, thank God, it does not appear at all.)[8]

After all, Leontiev is right. There is a dishonesty here, both in readers and in authors. Why should we believe in the spirituality of Alyosha Karamazov because, leaving Father Zossima's cell in a quiet and tender mood, he does not behave quietly and tenderly, but appears "with a wry smile, walking away with rapid steps"? Why should we believe in Pozdnishchev's seriousness because he speaks "smiling awkwardly, and displaying great timidity"? Why should we believe in the piety of Mr. Graham Greene's Mexican priest because his teeth are decaying and he swallows a mouthful of bile? It is all meanness, which we admire, calling it "concrete, immediate, specific."[9] But it is really a piece of legerdemain, and only an inelegant convention shared by reader and writer. Tolstoy is less to blame than others in this respect, but it does represent a serious blemish upon his work. And once again the vice is only the reverse side of one of his most splendid virtues as a novelist.

PUSHKIN AND STERNE

The Kreutzer Sonata starts well, *in medias res:*

It was early spring. We had passed two weary days and a night in the train. Passengers riding for short distances were continually

8 Konstantin Leontiev, *O Romanakh Grafa Tolstogo* (Moscow, 1896), pp. 21–22.

9 "Specific" is a very dangerous word. I cannot, for instance, share Merezhkovsky's admiration for Tolstoy's description of hoof-beats as "a

coming in and getting out, but there were three others besides myself who had come the whole way from the terminus at which the train had started: a lady, no longer young or attractive, addicted to smoking, attired in a man's greatcoat, and wearing a little soft hat on her head, and whose face spoke of long and profound suffering; an acquaintance of hers, a talkative gentleman of forty, faultlessly attired in brand new clothes; and another gentleman, short of stature, and of fitful, nervous movements, not yet old, although his curly hair was prematurely grey.

It seems artless. But this successful naïveté, the directness in attack, was not an endowment of Tolstoy from birth. He worked out the method with some difficulty. And he found his models among the names in his youthful reading list. In this case, the important names are those of Pushkin and of Sterne.[10]

It may seem to be a small enough matter. The start *in medias res* is, after all, only a trick of the trade. And it is not always a virtue. One can think of cases in which such an opening would be positively inappropriate. But to assess its importance for Tolstoy, we have to remember what Tolstoy was attempting in his major novels. He was concerned with painting the portrait of a whole society. In a sense, this is the object of all novelists. But in Tolstoy's case the portrait was to be attempted quite explicitly, in the most obvious way. Tolstoy attempted to portray society in explicit detail, like Balzac, not by implication from a study of relationships in a tiny group, like, for instance, Turgenev, in *A Nest of Gentlefolk*. As Balzac represented one way of going to work, Pushkin and Sterne represented another.

It is Balzac's method to set the stage, in space and in time, before ever his figures begin to move. In some of Balzac's novels, the setting of the stage occupies as much as a third of the book. Tolstoy never takes as long as that, but he certainly experimented with the method of Balzac in some of his works, for instance in the story "Two Hussars":

---

transparent sound." This conveys no clear impression, and I think it a very impure use of language. Still, Tolstoy seldom offends in this way.

[10] I mean here the Sterne of *Tristram Shandy*. Tolstoy's earliest literary undertaking was a translation, for his own use, of the *Sentimental Journey*, and references to this book are frequent in the earlier diaries. The influence of *A Sentimental Journey* upon *Childhood and Youth* is patent.

Early in the nineteenth century, when there were as yet no railways or macadamized roads, no gaslight, no stearine candles, no low couches with sprung cushions, no unvarnished furniture, no disillusioned youths with eye-glasses, no liberalizing women philosophers, nor any charming dames aux camelias of whom there are so many in our times, in those naive days, when leaving Moscow for Petersburg in a coach or carriage provided with a kitchen-full of homemade provisions one travelled for eight days along a soft, dusty or muddy road and believed in chopped cutlets, sledge-bells, and plain rolls; when in the long autumn evenings the tallow candles, around which family groups of twenty or thirty people gathered, had to be snuffed; when ball-rooms were illuminated by candelabra with wax or spermaceti candles, when furniture was arranged symmetrically, when our fathers were still young and proved it not only by the absence of wrinkles and grey hair but by fighting duels for the sake of a woman and rushing from the opposite corner of a room to pick up a bit of a handkerchief purposely or accidentally dropped; when our mothers wore short-waisted dresses and enormous sleeves and decided family affairs by drawing lots, when the charming dames aux camelias hid from the light of day—in those naive days of Masonic lodges, Martinists, and Tugendbunds, the days of Miloradoviches and Davydovs and Pushkins—a meeting was held in the Government town of K——, and the nobility elections were being concluded.

And at this point, not before, the story starts. The same method appears at the beginning of *The Decembrists:*

This happened not long ago, in the reign of Alexander II, in our days of civilization, progress, questions, regeneration of Russia, and so forth, and so forth; at a time when the victorious Russian army was returning from Sevastopol, surrendered to the enemy; when all of Russia celebrated the annihilation of the Black Sea fleet, and white-stoned Moscow received and congratulated on this happy event the remainders of the crews of that fleet, offering them a good Russian cup of vodka, and bread and salt, according to the good Russian custom, and bowing down to their feet. It was that time. . . .[11]

And so on, for the first three pages.

Now the disadvantages of this method are obvious. The sententious tone and sluggish movement, the ponderous hu-

---

11 For the comparison of these two passages, and for the extract which follows, from "A Ball at the Narishkins," I am indebted to Boris Eichenbaum, *Leo Tolstoi, Second Volume, The Sixties* (Leningrad, 1928).

mor ("purposely or accidentally dropped"), the constant risk of patronizing—all these are painfully apparent. And the irony is blunt and uncertain. Tolstoy finally worked his way out of this method in the course of his work on *War and Peace*. Among the sketches for *War and Peace*, posthumously published, appears a fragment entitled "A Ball at the Narishkins." It seems fairly plain that this was to be the first chapter. And it begins in the way with which we are now familiar:

> The events which we are about to describe took place in the period between the Peace of Tilsit and the great fire of Moscow, a time when the whole of Europe thought and talked of nothing but Napoleon, when it was considered smart in Russian Society to have a French tutor, when the St Petersburg ladies fought for precedence at the receptions of the Secretaries of the French Embassy, when every Russian spoke French better than the French themselves, and all squabbles and petty jealousies revolved around the French in general and Napoleon in particular.
> Those were days when. . . .[12]

And so on. If this is compared with the final version of chapter i of *War and Peace*, it becomes clear how thoroughly and deliberately Tolstoy weaned himself from this deep-rooted habit:

> "Well, Prince, so Genoa and Lucca are now just family estates of the Buonapartes. But I warn you, if you don't tell me that this means war, if you still try to defend the infamies and horrors perpetrated by that Antichrist—I really believe he is Antichrist—I will have nothing more to do with you and you are no longer my friend, no longer my faithful slave, as you call yourself! But how do you do? I see, I have frightened you—sit down and tell me all the news."
> It was in July 1805, and the speaker was the well-known Anna Pavlovna Scherer, maid of honour and favourite of the Empress Marya Fedorovna. With these words she greeted Prince Vasili, a man of high rank and importance, who was the first to arrive at her reception. Anna Pavlovna had had a cough for some days. She was,

---

[12] "A Ball at the Narishkins," an unpublished chapter of *War and Peace*, from *New Light on Tolstoy, literary fragments, letters and reminiscences not previously published. Issued under the authority of the Tolstoy family, edited by René Fülop-Miller, translated by Paul England.* (London: Harrap, 1931), p. 28.

It is interesting to note how Dickens infuses trenchancy and point into this convention, drawing it tautly together by paradox. Cf. *A Tale of Two Cities,* p. 1.

as she said, suffering from la grippe; "grippe" being then a new word in St Petersburg, used only by the elite.[13]

All the details of setting have now taken flesh. They breathe and move. The novel starts from the first line, in action. And the scene is set insidiously, *en passant*.[14] The speaking of French becomes vivid in "la grippe"; "the whole of Europe" becomes St. Petersburg, Genoa, and Lucca. And all the uncertainties of tone have vanished.

Tolstoy learned this improved method from Pushkin, or else from Sterne, or else from the one through the other. In Tolstoy's list of influences, Pushkin appears only as the author of *Eugene Onegin*, his "novel in verse." As a matter of fact we know that other works by Pushkin influenced Tolstoy. Some of his prose, for example, served as model for *Anna Karenina*. And of course Tolstoy's *Prisoner of the Caucasus* is a working-over of one of Pushkin's poems. In the present case, however, it is certainly *Eugene Onegin* which is in question. For, as Viktor Shklovsky has pointed out,[15] it is in *Eugene Onegin*, and only there, that the influence of Sterne can be detected in Pushkin. Sterne is a living influence in Russian fiction almost to the present day. He has exerted much greater influence in Russia than in England, and to trace all the ramifications of this influence would be an enormous task. The present case, however, presents no such difficulties. Pushkin's prose represents an astonishing effort toward an extreme of narrative bareness. The "thing," the described object, is pushed out of the picture almost completely. Instead the prose is concerned with the act, with the event, with occurrences.[16] It was this which influenced Mérimée. But

[13] *War and Peace*, trans. Aylmer Maude (London: H. Milford, 1933).

[14] Some similar revision occurred in relation to *The Cossacks*. Cf. the early version of that novel (in René Fülop-Miller, *New Light on Tolstoy*) with the final version. Here, however, the weaving together of narrative and setting is left in its early stages; in fact, Tolstoy was never satisfied with this novel and published it with reluctance.

[15] V. Shklovsky, *Zametki o proze Pushkina* (Moscow, 1937).

[16] See Tolstoy's diary, *op. cit.*, p. 34: "Read 'The Captain's Daughter' and, alas, I have to admit that Pushkin's prose is already old-fashioned, not in its language but in the manner of its exposition. It is true that the new tendency is for interest in details of feeling to predominate over interest in the events themselves. Pushkin's stories seem rather bare."

Pushkin's Russian is more austerely dynamic even than Mérimée's French. In all of this Sterne's example could play no part. But in *Eugene Onegin* Pushkin had to concern himself with objects. He set himself, as Tolstoy did, to portray a whole age and a whole society. He was thus confronted, as Tolstoy was, by the necessity of combining a great amount of descriptive material with the desire for the dynamic, the need to set in motion and to keep in motion a train of events. The demands of the verb had to be reconciled with the demands of the noun. The impedimenta must not impede; the upholstery must not cushion the impact or make for a sedentary prose. The style of Sterne, with its acrobatic digressions, extended allusions, and periphrases, supplied Pushkin with a means of reconciliation. By Balzac's method,[17] a bloc of descriptive setting precedes a bloc of narrative; the two sections are separate and distinct. By Sterne's method, the exposition of setting and the narrative of action are developed side by side; events are set in motion from the first line, and the description is dealt with in small units inserted into the narrative as digressions or asides. The first three stanzas of *Eugene Onegin* answer clearly to this analysis of the Sternean procedure and correspond almost exactly, as regards the disposition of material, with the first two paragraphs of *War and Peace:*

> "My uncle's shown his good intentions
> By falling desperately ill;
> His worth is proved; of all inventions
> Where will you find one better still?
> He's an example, I'm averring;
> But, God, what boredom—there, unstirring,
> By day, by night, thus to be bid
> To sit beside an invalid!
> Low cunning must assist devotion
> To one who is but half-alive:

[17] In associating this method in Tolstoy with the name of Balzac, I may be unfair. Certainly I would not suggest that it was from Balzac that Tolstoy adopted it. He set his face against the method of Balzac, the "veliki nabludatel," the "great observer," dealing with "things." If one is to find a model for this imperfect method, from among the names of the reading-list, a case could be made for Grigorovich. Leontiev quotes the first page of "Anton Goremyka," which betrays rather the same laborious discomfort as the passage quoted from "Two Hussars."

You puff his pillow and contrive
Amusement while you mix his potion;
You sigh, and think with furrowed brow—
'Why can't the devil take you now?' "

'Tis thus the gay dog's thoughts are freighted,
As through the dust his horses fare,
Who by the high gods' will is fated
To be his relative's sole heir.
You knew Ruslan and fair Ludmila;
For this new hero prithee feel a
Like fellowship, as I regale
You, readers, with another tale:
Onegin, meet him, born and nourished
Where old Neva's grey waters flow,
Where you were born, or, as a beau,
It may be, in your glory flourished.
I moved there also for a while,
But find the North is not my style.

A man of rank, his worthy father
Would always give three balls a year;
He lived in debt, and did not bother
To keep his hopeless ledgers clear.
Fate guarded Eugene, our young waster;
While in due time Monsieur replaced her,
At first Madame controlled the child;
The charming lad was rather wild.
Monsieur l'abbé, a Frenchman, seedy,
Thought sermons fashioned to annoy;
He spared the rod to spoil the boy,
And in a voice polite but reedy
Would chide him, would forgive him soon,
And walk him in the afternoon.[18]

The translation is far from happy. It serves our purpose, however, to note that the first stanza of Pushkin, like the first
paragraph in Tolstoy, does not set the scene but is concerned
with reported speech (whether inward or actual speech is no
matter). The speech sets the narrative in motion and arouses
in the reader a wish to know the context. This wish is satisfied in a digression which sets the scene. The action begins
before the stage is set and the two are then developed side

[18] *Eugene Onegin,* trans. Babette Deutsch (New York: Modern Library, 1936).

by side.[19] This means of course that the development will be slow, but at least it does not break the novel (or the poem) into two dissimilar parts. This complicated maneuver, in Tolstoy's more ambitious novels, is analogous to the start, *in medias res*, of *The Kreutzer Sonata*.

Pushkin and Lermontov

There is one respect, however, in which Tolstoy's method is widely different from that of Pushkin (in *Eugene Onegin*) and from that of Sterne. Pushkin does not hesitate to stand about inside his own poem referring to one of his past successes (*Ruslan and Ludmila*) and talking about the project he has in hand. So Byron appears, wagging a roguish finger, in *Don Juan*. So Sterne tugs at his reader's sleeve. And so does Gogol. This is made possible and successful by the deliberate idiosyncrasies of style, by breathless rhyming in Pushkin and in Byron, by the fantastic acrobatics of rhetoric and movement, in Sterne and in Gogol. But Pushkin's method in his prose had been the antithesis of Gogol's. As might be expected from what we have remarked of "bareness" in Pushkin's prose, the author is rigidly excluded from the book. The whole object is the attainment of the impersonal; there are to be no personal idiosyncrasies at all. Pushkin, in fact, aimed to create a model prose for Russian, as he had earlier created a model verse. It was to be classical, in the sense that it should be absolutely central to the nature of the language, colored by no personal leanings toward this or that theme, this or that mood. In fact, Pushkin did not altogether succeed. Many Russians feel that, if one may be paradoxical, the rigid exclusion of idiosyncrasy, carried to an extreme, became an idiosyncrasy in its own right. In other words, one becomes conscious in the reading of Pushkin's prose of all that he has contrived to exclude. It is, therefore, slightly self-conscious; and, to that extent, not so much pure Russian as purist Russian. Nevertheless, Pushkin's prose represents a vast labor of purification, and he is rightly regarded as the creator of

[19] Tolstoy seems to have seen this problem as early as 1853. In his diary for October 23, 1853, while writing *Boyhood*, he complains of that work: "The action is long-drawn, and too sequent in point of time and not sequent enough in thought. For instance, the method of describing past actions in the course of a narrative for the sake of clearness and relief, is quite sacrificed owing to my division of the chapters" (*op. cit.*, p. 28).

classical Russian, both in verse and in prose. Without the preliminary labors of Pushkin the prose of Lermontov could never have appeared. And Lermontov's is held to be the model style, absolutely impersonal. What it means for a prose style to be an impersonal model is something not often recognized; it may appear in due course.

Now, Tolstoy aimed at this impersonality, at a prose which should be "transparent" and which should never advertise itself. His language was never to be self-conscious in the least degree. He committed himself, as it were, to writing *War and Peace* using the narrative method of Sterne and the narrative prose of Lermontov. But this is an impossibility. It is impossible to write like Sterne except by writing like Sterne. One cannot write like Lermontov except by writing in Lermontov's way. In other words, the way a writer disposes his material (as, description here, narrative here) is inseparable from the way he disposes his sentences. Form and style are one and the same. Tolstoy then, did not achieve a pure Russian style in *War and Peace*, even if he modeled his prose upon *A Hero of Our Time*.[20] The Russian is good but it is "off center." And it rests with the reader to dismiss the peculiarities either as downright blemishes, or as idiosyncrasies, justified, as the different oddities of Gogol are justified, by what Tolstoy attempted to do. Tolstoy will not be "elegant," even where elegance is called for. Turgenev declared in 1862, "The fear of phrases has driven Tolstoy into the most desperate phrases."[21] And this is true. Merezhovsky gives two examples from *War and Peace*. Bezukhov speaks the first:

"What crime can there be in my having wished—to do good? Even though I did it badly, or only feebly, yet I did something for that end, and you will not only not persuade me of this, that that which I did was not good, but not even that you did not think so."[22]

[20] Prince Mirsky suggests that Lermontov was the model, but Tolstoy appears to compare himself more frequently with Pushkin. The argument holds in either case. If Tolstoy modeled his style on Pushkin's, then he was trying to construct his novel like *Eugene Onegin* (Pushkin's verse) and to write it like Pushkin's prose. On the other hand, *A Hero of Our Time* appears in the reading list. I refer to this later.

[21] Quoted in Noyes, *op. cit.*, p. 346.

[22] Quoted in D. S. Merezhkovsky, *Tolstoi as Man and Artist* (London: Constable, 1902), pp. 201–2.

And the second is concerned with Natasha's illness, and with the attitude toward it of her father and her cousin:

How would the Count have borne the illness of his beloved daughter if he had not known that if she did get better he would not grudge thousands more to take her abroad? What would Sonia have done if she had not had the pleasant consciousness of this that she had not undressed for three nights in order to be ready precisely to carry out all the directions of the doctor, and that she now did not get a night's sleep, in order not to let the time pass at which the pills ought to be given. And she was also pleased at this, that she, by neglecting to carry out the instructions, could show that she did not believe in doctors.

There is certainly clumsiness here. (It is not due to the translator, since Merezhkovsky noticed it.) And Turgenev's explanation of the clumsiness convinces. We may contrast the first sentence of *Anna Karenina:* "All happy families are more or less like one another; every unhappy family is unhappy in its own particular way." This, by comparison, is phrasemaking. But the phrase is a fine one and worth the making.[23] In general, the Russian of *Anna Karenina* is Tolstoy's style at its purest; and this purity is not to be understood apart from the arduous labor which we know to have gone into its making, nor from its formal unity, as compared with *War and Peace,* nor from its use of a conventional frame. The ghostly peasant tapping the wheels of the locomotive, who appears as an ill-omen near the beginning and again at the end of the book, is in the convention of supernatural agency, as used, for instance, by Pushkin in *The Captain's Daughter.* The use of this conventional and supernatural frame not only creates the sense of doom which draws the story together; it also forces the author to stand at some distance from his own creation so that he need not feel self-conscious when he allows his style to be neat, elegant, and even epigrammatic. In no work up to *Anna Karenina* had Tolstoy used a conventional frame, and in no

[23] Tolstoy recorded that, after wrestling unsuccessfully with the start of *Anna Karenina,* a chance reading of Pushkin's *Tales of Belkin* showed him "the way to start a story," whereafter all went well. But the epigram about happy and unhappy families was prefixed at a later stage. What really came from Pushkin was the second sentence, and those which follow, which are a fine example of how to start *in medias res.* Cf. Pushkin, "The Coffin-Maker" (*Tales of Belkin*).

work does he write so purely. This may not be his best novel, but it is his most nearly perfect work, the most classical.

We may agree with Turgenev that "the fear of phrases" produced "the most desperate phrases," or with Merezhkovsky, that "an excessive aiming at simplicity" produced "simplesse, and artificiality," but this is not the whole of the matter. For we cannot but notice that these failures in the prose occur always in relation with the same turn of the theme. They do *not* occur where Merezhkovsky says they do:

> But directly he enters on abstract psychology, not of the "natural" but the "spiritual" man—"philosophisings" in Flaubert's phrase, "lucubrations," to use his own words—as soon as we get to the moral transformations of Bezukhov, Nekhliudov, Pozdnychev, or Levine, something strange happens, *il dégringole affreusement*, he goes off terribly: his language seems to dry up, wither, and become helpless, to cling convulsively to the object depicted, and yet to let it escape, like a man half paralyzed.[24]

This is simply not true. Merezhkovsky's examples refute him.[25] It is not in abstract psychology or in moral transformations that Tolstoy's prose fails him. It fails him when he is analyzing a person's mood or action and finding hypocrisy beneath it. It is when this is called for, in concrete analysis, not in abstract psychology, and in unmasking of hypocrisies, not in moral transformations, that Tolstoy's false naïveté appears. And to understand why this should be so, we have to turn to another name from Tolstoy's reading list.

ROUSSEAU AND TURGENEV

To some extent, the influence of Rousseau on Tolstoy has been acknowledged for a long time. It is generally admitted that except for Tolstoy's early reading of Rousseau and Tolstoy's sustained admiration for Rousseau, not only would he not have created Uncle Yeroshka in *The Cossacks*, the compelling representative of carnal innocence and good in the

---

[24] Merezhkovsky, *op. cit.*, p. 201.

[25] Besides those we have copied from *War and Peace*, Merezhkovsky quotes from *The Death of Ivan Ilyich* (trans. Aylmer Maude): "Everything she did for him was entirely for her own sake, and she told him she was doing for herself what she actually was doing for herself, as if that was so incredible that he must understand the opposite."

"natural" man, but he would not have created Platon Karataev in *War and Peace*, nor would he have been so ready, in
The Kreutzer Sonata, to see the sex life of the peasant laborer
as more successful than the sex life of the gentleman, and as
morally superior. It is agreed that Tolstoy's notion of "the
natural man" is derived from Rousseau. But one considerable
artist does not infect another with characteristic ideas and attitudes except through transmitting, also, formal devices in disposition of material. In other words, if Tolstoy took over
Rousseau's "ideas," he also, it is probable, took over the very
construction and measure of Rousseau's sentence. This is not
generally admitted, but it is a conclusion forced upon any
critic who believes that in literature the form and the content
are ultimately inseparable.

To determine, in this way, Rousseau's influence upon Tolstoy would be a considerable undertaking. It is notable, for instance, that in his reading list Tolstoy distinguishes between
the *Confessions, La Nouvelle Héloise,* and *Émile;* and no doubt
a close examination could distinguish between the influences of
each of these books upon Tolstoy's method. For our more
modest purposes it will be sufficient to return to *The Kreutzer
Sonata,* with Rousseau in mind.

In a passage quoted already from *The Kreutzer Sonata,*
Pozdnishchev discussed his excessive friendliness toward a
man whom he disliked, who was destined to be the seducer of
his wife:

"I am unable to specify the motive which prompted me to act
thus; whether it was to prove to my wife and to him that I was not
actuated by fear, or to deceive myself, I cannot say; I only know that
from the very first my relations with him were not natural and
unaffected."

Earlier this passage was noticed on account of its modesty—"I
am unable to specify. . . ." Here we must notice, rather, that an
attitude of courtesy and friendship which others might have
counted unto themselves for virtue, as civility or even as courage, is by Pozdnishchev accounted for as unconscious hypocrisy. He is unable to specify the motive, but he is sure that the
motive was base. In the same way, when he is describing the
act of murder, Pozdnishchev rejects what would be, for most
men, an excuse or at least an extenuation, the commonly

accepted notion that in such a situation the man is no longer in control of himself, that his mind goes blank, that he does not know what he is doing:

"Whenever people assert that in a paroxysm of madness they do not remember what they are doing, they are either talking nonsense —or lying. I knew very well what I was doing, and did not for a single second cease to be conscious of it. The more I fanned the flame of my fury, the brighter burned within me the light of consciousness, lighting up every nook and corner of my soul, so that I could not help seeing everything I was doing. I cannot affirm that I knew in advance what I was going to do, but the very moment I was doing anything, and I fancy some seconds beforehand, I was conscious of what I was doing, in order, as it were, that I might repent of it in time, that I might afterwards have it to say that I could have stayed my hand."

Here too we notice the modesty, even the tentativeness—"I cannot affirm" . . . "I fancy" . . . "as it were."

Tolstoy was not always so tentative in uncovering the base motives below an apparently creditable act or intention. Thus, in *Youth*, describing Irteniev after confession:

"I felt that I was taking delight in the sensation of emotion; and, fearing that I might banish it in some way, I took leave of the priest in haste, and without glancing aside, in order not to distract my attention, quitted the enclosure, and seated myself again in the motley [*sic*] and jolting drozhky. But the jolts of the equipage, the variety of objects which flashed before my eyes, speedily dissipated that sensation, and I already began to think that the priest was probably thinking by this time that such a fine soul of a young man as I he had never met, and never would meet in all his life, and that there were no others like me. I was convinced of that, and this conviction called forth in me a feeling of cheerfulness of such a nature that it demanded communication to some one."[26]

There are no hesitations, no qualifying phrases here. And their absence makes a great difference. For why, if Irteniev felt complacent when he confessed his sins to the priest, should be not feel complacent at thus confessing to the reader his complacency? The coils of hypocrisy and self-deceit are endless. In pretending to be worse than he is, a man may be as much of a hypocrite as when he pretends to be better than he is.

[26] *Youth*, in *Childhood and Youth*, trans. Malwida von Meysenbug (London, 1862), p. 231.

This is precisely what we feel very often about Rousseau. Is he not smirking with complacency because he has confessed to his reader all his baseness?

Ces réflexions tristes, mais attendrissantes, me faisaient replier sur moi-même avec un regret qui n'était pas sans douceur. Il me semblait que la destinée me devait quelque chose qu'elle ne m'avait pas donné. À quoi bon m'avoir fait naître avec des facultés exquises, pour les laisser jusqu'à la fin sans emploi? Le sentiment de mon prix interne, en me donnant celui de cette injustice, m'en dédommageait en quelque sorte, et me faisait verser des larmes que j'aimais à laisser couler.[27]

The easy slip and cadence of Rousseau's sentence, its very accomplishment, prompts the suspicion that the author is preening himself upon his own honesty. And the passage from Tolstoy's *Childhood* is easy in the same way. When we contrast these passages with some from *The Kreutzer Sonata* we realize that the new modesty is not a matter of a few qualifying phrases, but rather, as we noted at the start, of a soul-felt accuracy about the processes of thought—first, the recollection ("I recollect the indescribable horror of this state of mind"); then, the inference from the recollection ("and I infer from it"); then, a check in mid-career by corroboration from memory ("and in fact I may add that I have a dim remembrance"); until finally the act and the state of mind, thus painfully reconstructed, are defined. It is not fanciful, perhaps, to compare this with Proust's examination of the processes of memory, thus, painfully, to reconstruct a train of past events.

This, then, is the way in which Tolstoy used the example of Rousseau and then worked his way out of writing in Rousseau's manner. But this way is only valid for writing in the first person. For if the author is telling the reader about the unconscious hypocrisies in a third person, he runs the risk of seeming to preen himself upon his omniscience, just as, when he is telling the reader of hypocrisies in himself, he runs the risk of

[27] *Les Confessions de J.-J. Rousseau*, Vol. II, Book IX (Paris: Garnier Frères, 1926), pp. 272–73.

Cf. Lermontov, *A Hero of Our Time*, trans. Martin Parker (Moscow, 1947), p. 82. Foreword to Part II: "The story of a human soul, even the pettiest of human souls, is no less interesting and instructive than the story of a nation, especially if it is the result of the observation of a mature mind and written without the vain desire to evoke compassion or wonder. One of the defects of Rousseau's Confessions is that he read it to his friends."

seeming to parade his honesty. The French novelists habitually take this risk. Stendhal tells his reader that at a certain point the mutual passion of Julien Sorel and his mistress changed its character; he tells him this, he does not present it as happening. Benjamin Constant tells his reader that Adolphe wanted to be in love; he tells him this, he does not leave it to be inferred from an accumulation of details, which at first seem superfluous but which later take on meaning.[28] In his early works in the third person, in the "Sevastopol" sketches, for example, Tolstoy takes this risk in the French manner. He is the omniscient author. The "Sevastopol" sketches, however, are not a novel but a sequence of imaginative reportage. And Tolstoy was not content for long to be omniscient, or to take the risk of seeming so.[29] From Pushkin or from Turgenev he had adopted the ideal of the transparent style which creates the illusion that the author does not intervene at all between the occurrence and the reader. As we have seen, the method of superfluous detail solved many of his problems. We are not told that Anna Karenina's attitude to her husband changed. We are told that for the first time she noticed the size of her husband's ears. This does just as well, and without our being conscious that the author has intervened, as it were, between us and the page. But "superfluous detail" could not enable Tolstoy to unveil those twists and turns of unconscious hypocrisy with which he was particularly concerned. In *The Cossacks* he found a way to do so, by making Olyenin write a long introspective letter. That is, he inserted into a novel written in the third person a long passage in the first person, into a fictitious narrative a large bloc of personal confession. In *The Kreutzer Sonata*, he adopted Turgenev's method, putting a first-person narrative in the thin frame of third-person setting. Just as, in many of Turgenev's novels, a party of gentlemen converse at dinner until one of them begins to recount an episode of his youth, which thereupon becomes the novel, so, in *The Kreutzer Sonata*, the

28 To the French reader, therefore, the English novel and the Russian appear equally to use the method of "superfluous detail." See E.-M. de Vogüé's Introduction to *Le Roman Russe* (Paris, 1886), where the French reader is introduced to the Russian novel by way of George Eliot.

29 Cf. Tolstoy's diary, *op. cit.*, p. 42: "I do not like Arago's travels at all. He is filled with French self-confidence both as to scientific and moral matters."

general conversation in a railway-carriage resolves itself into a personal confession. Turgenev's innovation was epoch-making. Out of it evolved James's *Golden Bowl* and Conrad's *Chance*, novels which do for the third-person narrative what Proust did for the first-person narrative. As Proust reconstructs a train of past events out of the more or less corrupt and sometimes conflicting testimonies of recollection, so Conrad and James reconstruct a train of events out of the more or less corrupt and sometimes conflicting testimonies of different witnesses. But neither Conrad nor James attempted to portray a whole society and the whole of an age. Turgenev tried, in *Virgin Soil* for example, and failed. Turgenev's example could be of no use, therefore, when Tolstoy proposed, in *The Death of Ivan Ilyich*,[30] in *The Decembrists*, in "Two Hussars," in *War and Peace*, in *Anna Karenina*, to portray the whole of a society in one age, or to trace its development through several. He proposed to do this, while effacing himself from his own composition and while applying to his characters the psychological analysis he had learned from the French. And he contrived in the main to do what he proposed. But the false naïveté of the passages that Merezhkovsky noticed are instances in which the strain proved too great and the three demands were not reconciled.

We may return to one of these passages:

How would the Count have borne the illness of his beloved daughter if he had not known that if she did get better he would not grudge thousands more to take her abroad? What would Sonia have done if she had not had the pleasant consciousness of this that she had not undressed for three nights in order to be ready precisely to carry out all the directions of the doctor, and that she now did not get a night's sleep, in order not to let the time pass at which the pills ought to be given. And she was also pleased at this, that she, by neglecting to carry out the instructions, could show that she did not believe in doctors.

The clumsiness, I now suggest, is caused by Tolstoy the omniscient author attempting to disguise the fact of his omniscience.

[30] It may be objected that if *The Death of Ivan Ilyich* portrays a whole society, so does *The Kreutzer Sonata*. The one portrays the Russian bourgeoisie in the face of death, as the other portrays the Russian gentry in the face of sex. But on the other hand we have admitted that *The Kreutzer Sonata* falls into two halves. By the time of the murder *The Kreutzer Sonata* is a triangle melodrama, a pure closet drama.

The neat fall of Rousseau's sentence, as of Stendhal's, of Constant's, of Tolstoy's in the "Sevastopol" sketches and in *Childhood*, advertised the knowledgeability of the author. By clumsy roughening, Tolstoy hopes not to appear knowledgeable, not, indeed, to appear at all. The writing is made clumsy so that the reader shall feel that not Tolstoy, but he himself, has thus seen the baseness of motive in Natasha's father and her cousin. And of course Tolstoy fails. Like Pushkin, though far more grossly, Tolstoy is conspicuous by his absence. The absence of practiced elegance advertises the fact that the practiced hand has left the page. And this in its turn reminds us (what Tolstoy wished forgotten) that the hand is never far away, that without it we should not be reading at all. As it is, we are not grateful for the information given. The discomfort we feel was neatly caught in Leontiev's phrase, "psychological eavesdropping."

It would be relatiely easy to proceed from this toward an analysis of what was wrong with all of Tolstoy's attitude to experience. He wanted to eat his cake and have it, to be an enlightened rationalist and not to be an enlightened rationalist, to appreciate Uncle Yeroshka and also to *be* Uncle Yeroshka, to be as powerful as the teacher and as innocent as the taught.

Instead we shall return to *The Kreutzer Sonata*.

"MAKING STRANGE"

We return to Pozdnishchev's description of the murder:

". . . I was aware that I was striking her below the ribs, and that the blade would penetrate. The moment I was doing this, I knew that I was doing something terrible, a thing I had never done before, an action that would be fraught with frightful consequences. But that consciousness was instantaneous like a flash of lightning, and the deed followed so close upon it as to be almost simultaneous with it. My consciousness of the deed and of its nature was painfully distinct. I felt and still remember the momentary resistance of the corset, and of something else, and then the passage of the knife cutting its way through the soft parts of her body. She seized the dagger with both her hands, wounding them, but without staying its progress."

This is murder in slow motion. Even now the deed is only half-completed. The power of the passage derives from extreme slowing-down of what is normally a rapid event. Murder is normally rapid, not only in life but in literature; more rapid, perhaps, in literature than in life. It is rarely in life that one witnesses murder by stabbing. In literature one does so frequently; and the reader's experience of it is dulled and blunted because in other books he has experienced it so often. Tolstoy's slow motion restores the edge to our sense of outrage. And the slow motion is achieved by analyzing a coherent movement into its constituent moments. This the Russians recognize as a characteristic of Tolstoy's method in all his works:

> The essence of Tolstoy's early art was to push analysis to its furthest limit: hence it is that the details he offers are not complex cultural facts, but, as it were, *atoms* of experience, the indivisible units of immediate perception. An important form of this dissecting and atomizing method (and one which survived all the changes of his style) is what Victor Shklovsky has called "making it strange" (ostrannenie). It consists in never calling complex things by their accepted name, but always disintegrating a complex action or object into its indivisible components; in describing, not naming it. The method strips the world of the labels attached to it by habit and by social convention and gives it a "dis-civilized" appearance, as it might have appeared to Adam on the day of creation, or to one blind from birth who has received his sight. It is easy to see that the method, while it gives unusual freshness to imaginative representation, is in essence hostile to all culture and all social form, and is psychologically akin to anarchism.[31]

The anarchical function of the device is particularly clear in *The Kreutzer Sonata*. In the passage quoted, Tolstoy "dis-civilizes" the act of murder; and most readers would agree with him that murder is uncivilized and requires to be presented as such. On the other hand, chapters v–ix "dis-civilize," in the same way, the institution of courtship; and few readers, perhaps, would agree that this institution is uncivilized and requires to be so presented. Any of the habits or customs of mankind can be subjected to this process and made to look ridiculous and even obscene. And Tolstoy is prepared to do this.

For this device in Tolstoy I do not propose a "source." Indeed it would be ridiculous to attempt to do so. In our day, schoolboys are invited to see themselves as men from Mars,

[31] D. S. Mirsky, *History of Russian Literature to 1881* (London: Routledge, 1927), pp. 326–27.

for the sake of a labored whimsicality in their weekly essay. The device is common currency and has been so at least since the eighteenth century. *Gulliver's Travels* and Kafka's *Investigations of a Dog* are random examples of a deliberate distortion of vision to produce a dis-civilized air in what is described. Tolstoy is remarkable only in that he uses the device so thoroughly, and without warning. Pozdnishchev is not made a man from Mars, nor a Rip van Winkle, nor an abnormally intelligent and articulate dog. He is a man like any other, except that he sees the world as Rip van Winkle would see it.

Percy Lubbock remarked:

> Tolstoy seems to look squarely at the same world as other people, and only to make so much more of it than other people by the direct force of his genius, not because he holds a different position in regard to it. His experience comes from the same quarter as ours; it is because he absorbs so much more of it, and because it all passes into his great plastic imagination, that it seems so new.[32]

To a great extent, I submit, Tolstoy's "looking squarely at the same world as other people" is no more than his habit of using no conventions other than the most familiar and most worn. His device for "making it strange" is something that all readers might have attempted themselves in their bungling attempts to write. It is common currency, a convention so familiar that we no longer see it as conventional. There was perhaps never an artist of such power who was so little of an innovator as Tolstoy. All his originality consisted in pushing to the limit the discoveries made by others.

LERMONTOV

In this respect, there is, among all Russian novelists, no more pregnant contrast to Tolstoy than Lermontov. Lermontov's novel appears in Tolstoy's list of influences, but in his diary the reading of it is recorded without comment. And in general one feels, reading *A Hero of Our Time* with Tolstoy in mind, how little Tolstoy learned from Lermontov and how much he could have learned. For Lermontov's undertaking touches upon Tolstoy's at many points. Lermontov, before Tolstoy, had read Stendhal and sought to incorporate into fiction psychological analysis on the French model. Lermontov, before Tolstoy, had

[32] Percy Lubbock, *The Craft of Fiction* (London: Cape, 1921), p. 48.

subscribed to the ideal of "transparent" prose, and had thus frowned upon that intrusion of the omniscient author which seemed inseparable from the French method of analysis. Lermontov, before Tolstoy, had sought to portray and criticize a whole society and a whole age; to do so, moreover, at no detriment to narrative pace and interest. And Lermontov, before Tolstoy, had seen moral life in his age as a matter of balancing against one another the rights of the will to lead to action and the rights of self-consciousness to introspect. What is more, Lermontov successfully reconciled all these artistic necessities. Lermontov used Stendhal's psychological probe, yet deleted the omniscient author altogether and created to that end the classic Russian style for narrative, the language at its most impersonal and least idiosyncratic. Lermontov created and criticized a whole society and a whole age, but without losing narrative pace and interest from the first page to the last. And Lermontov presented, in the character of Pechorin, the difficulty and moral necessity of reconciling will and consciousness, and agreed that excess of the latter can lame the will.

But Lermontov does not therefore fulminate against all disinterested art, because it does not lead to action, as Tolstoy fulminates in Pozdnishchev's account of the Beethoven sonata:

"It is a different thing if a military march is played, then the soldiers move forward, keeping time to the music, and the end is attained; if dance music is played people dance to it, and the object is accomplished; if a Mass is sung I receive Holy Communion, and here, too, the music is not in vain; but in other cases there is nothing but irritation, and no light how to act during this irritation."

And Tolstoy shows plainly in this novel that he wishes to move the reader to drastic action; so that there are some grounds for supposing that what Pozdnishchev disliked in the art of music Tolstoy disliked in the art of literature.

Now the art of literature as practiced by Lermontov certainly does not lead to action. On the contrary, *A Hero of Our Time* is profoundly ambiguous:

Some readers will probably want to know what I think of Pechorin's character. My reply may be found in the title of this book. "But that is bitter irony!" they will say. I do not know.[33]

[33] Lermontov, *op. cit.*, Foreword to the section "Princess Mary," p. 82.

And the reader does not know either. Hence the profound ambiguity of the book. Lermontov does not even pose the question in person. For the words above are spoken, not by the author, but by a fictional narrator. For Lermontov has anticipated by fifty years or more the experiments of Henry James and Joseph Conrad in stories written from several different points of view. It is a most astonishing innovation, by means of which Lermontov used the psychological analysis he had learned from the French without once assuming omniscience or intruding with personal and direct comment into the course of the novel. Hence, again, the ultimate ambiguity. Lermontov's novel does not move to action. The Russian critics pretended that it did. They pretended that Lermontov, in presenting Pechorin, like Goncharov in presenting Oblomov, made a case for the rooting-out of such socially superfluous types. But in neither case is this true. Lermontov's attitude to Pechorin, like Goncharov's attitude to Oblomov, like Turgenev's attitude to Bazarov, no comment can determine. At no point can it be said that Lermontov speaks through the mouth of Pechorin, or through the mouth of any other character. As a result we cannot say whether Lermontov, in making Pechorin the hero of the age, was or was not ironical. It is Lermontov's distinction that in him this ambiguity was clearly deliberate. For this reason he carried to the limit the self-effacement of the author from the world which he created. His achievement has never been fully appreciated in the West, where it was Turgenev who was applauded for self-effacement and presented as the creator of "the dramatic novel." In fact self-effacement in Turgenev is never so expert, and in some of his novels it is not even attempted.

To the Tolstoy of *The Kreutzer Sonata*, this ambiguity would seem worthless and even vicious. For the purposes of that novel, Tolstoy, it is clear, was too closely wedded to tendentiousness to be able to make use of Lermontov. But a book can be tendentious even though it does not move to action. On its first appearance, Lermontov's novel was taken literally by some readers and some magazines. And Lermontov thereupon composed a Foreword in which he admitted that of course the title was to be taken as ironical. He proceeded to maintain that the book was morally instructive:

You say that morality will gain nothing by it. I beg to differ. People have been fed enough sweetmeats to upset their stomachs; now bitter remedies, acid truths, are needed. Yet you should not think that the author of this book was ever ambitious enough to aspire to reform human vices. May God preserve him from such boorishness! It simply pleased him to portray the modern man as he sees him and as he so often, to his own and your misfortune, has found him to be. Suffice it that the disease has been diagnosed; how to cure it the Lord alone knows![34]

Perhaps to call any work which is morally instructive "tendentious" is to force the sense of tendentiousness. But in the fifties, at any rate, Tolstoy was committed to tendentiousness in no other way than that outlined thus by Lermontov. In this period he was so outspoken against coarser forms of tendentiousness that some critics have defined his attitude (erroneously, of course) as "art for art's sake." There was, then, no reason why Tolstoy, when he was working on *War and Peace* and *The Decembrists*, should not have drawn for a model upon the formal innovations of *A Hero of Our Time*. He did not do so. If he had done so, then each major character would in turn have been given the stage to record his or her view of as much of the train of events as they had seen. Tolstoy would never have intruded at all. The truth about any of the characters or any of the situations would have been deduced by the reader out of a series of conflicting testimonies. And the style would have been purer, more classical, Lermontov's style; for there would have been no occasions such as we have noticed, when Tolstoy intrudes to comment out of his omniscience, at the same time attempting, by deliberate roughening, to conceal the fact of his intrusion. The style and the form go together. Lermontov's style would not have been so impersonal, so transparent, if he had chosen a form into which he had to intrude with direct comment. And the form would not have been so impersonal, if Lermontov had written in any style which drew more attention to itself.

And yet the method of conflicting testimonies of several fictional narrators *is* used. War is seen through the eyes of Volkonski, Bezukhov, the two Rostov brothers, Denisov, and others, each of whom holds the stage in turn. In the same way, Princess Mary and Natasha Rostov are presented in different

[34] *Ibid.*, p. 9.

lights, as Tolstoy presents them through the eyes of one after
another of the principal male characters. The narration is maintained in the third person. But this does not matter in the case
of Volkonski and Bezukhov, nor in general in the case of characters who are keenly self-conscious. In the case of characters
who are less self-conscious than Tolstoy is, Tolstoy succumbs
to temptation and points out inner psychological movements of
which they are unaware. In these cases Tolstoy tries to intrude
without being noticed. And hence arise the impurities of style
which we have noted, and the discomfort we feel about psychological eavesdropping. When Lermontov has to use the
testimony of a comparatively unself-conscious character
(Maxim Maximich, who tells the portion of the novel called
"Bela"), he fills out his testimony not by his own personal intrusion, but by interposing yet another fictional narrator (the
traveling officer to whom Maxim Maximich tells his tale).
Both narrators are limited, but in different ways; and so the
events in question, filtered, as it were, through both sensibili-
ties, appear to the reader more completely and truthfully than
if recorded only by one. Conrad used the same device in
Chance, when Powell, the unself-conscious observer, narrates a
course of events to Marlow, who is more self-conscious, who
narrates them to the reader, Conrad himself having never intervened.

These are complications into which the reader may not care
to penetrate. Tolstoy did not care to do so either. But they are
involved in the search for transparent writing, for the elimina-
tion of the author, as an ideal. And because Tolstoy did not
follow Lermontov into these ramifications of his formal innovation, Tolstoy's prose is less pure than Lermontov's prose and
the omniscient author is less fully obliterated from his work.
In the end, therefore, it must seem that Tolstoy could have
learned more from Lermontov than he did. Lermontov was an
innovator. Tolstoy was not. It was his destiny to push to the
limits the technical resources of the novel as he found it. He
was abreast of his age. Lermontov was in advance of it, too far
in advance for Tolsoy fully to realize the value of his innovations.

As for Lermontov's style, Vladimir Nabokov, who has translated *A Hero of Our Time*, declares:

The English reader should be aware that Lermontov's prose style in Russian is inelegant; it is dry and drab; it is the tool of an energetic, incredibly gifted, bitterly honest, but definitely inexperienced young man. His Russian is, at times, almost as crude as Stendhal's French; his similes and metaphors are utterly commonplace; his hackneyed epithets are only redeemed by occasionally being incorrectly used. Repetition of words in descriptive sentences irritates the purist.[35]

And so, when he acknowledges how "Russian school teachers used to see in it the perfection of Russian prose," Nabokov declares:

This is a ridiculous opinion . . . and can only be held if and when a moral quality or a social virtue is confused with literary art, or when an ascetic critic regards the rich and ornate with such suspicion that, in contrast, the awkward and frequently commonplace style of Lermontov seems delightfully chaste and simple. But genuine art is neither chaste nor simple, and it is sufficient to glance at the prodigiously elaborate and magically artistic style of Tolstoy (who, by some, is considered to be a literary descendant of Lermontov) to realise the depressing flaws of Lermontov's prose.[36]

Some things here—for instance the painstakingly outrageous assertion, "genuine art is neither chaste nor simple"—tell us more about Nabokov, the author of *Lolita* and (particularly) *The Gift*, than they tell us about either Lermontov or Tolstoy. But generally what Nabokov says chimes in well enough with the conclusions reached in this essay. For a prose that is to be impersonal and transparent cannot afford to be elegant; and by the same token a model of Russian prose is likely to be very different from "the perfection of Russian prose." A style that is to be a model for others cannot be impregnated by the distinctive force of savor of the writer who creates it. Precisely to the degree that Lermontov's style is faded, hackneyed and casual (as Nabokov shows it to be), it is more impersonal and more transparent than Tolstoy's could ever be; and to just that degree the shadow of the omniscient narrator falls over Tolstoy's page as it never falls on a page of *A Hero of Our Time*.

[35] Lermontov, *A Hero of Our Time*, translated by Vladimir Nabokov in collaboration with Dmitri Nabokov (New York: Doubleday Anchor Book, 1958), p. xiii.

[36] *Ibid.*, p. xix.

Chekhov

XIV

D. S. MIRSKY

Chekhov and the English

They were not aggressive creatures; it was that that made them so terrible to Helen. They merely observed in passing that there was no such thing as splendour or heroism in the world.

Howards End

The cult paid by the English intelligentsia to Chekhov, at a time when the Russians (reader and writer) have lost touch with the essential aspects of his work and shelved him as a (probably minor) classic, has few parallels in the past of international literary relations, but a close one in the almost simultaneous taking-up of Meredith by the French, also at a time when his own countrymen have given him up as jarringly unreadable. Strong revulsion in the latter, semi-oblivious indifference in the former case are respectively adequate the-morning-after reactions, to the flamboyant colourfulness of the English, and to the smoother greyness of the Russian novelist. As for their fortune abroad, it is the natural consequence of their responding to the states of mind prevalent in post-war England and France better and more exactly than any native writer. The two states are exactly opposed, and may with a degree of simplification, be defined as, in France, an unusually vigorous assertion, in England, an unusually complete rejection of what we may call the heroic values. It is significant that the ascension of Meredith coincides with the eclipse of the most thorough of the French anti-heroists, Anatole France; while in England Chekhov comes as something like the fulfilment of that forerunning apostle of the unheroical, Samuel Butler.

Two features attract the English intellectual in Chekhov, the one ethical, the other aesthetical, but both converging towards what may appear a classical *mediocritas*. The first is his attitude to civilization as a system of purely negative values. It is re-

From the *Monthly Criterion*, Vol. VI, No. 4 (October 1927).

flected chiefly in his letters (which the orthodox Chekhovite almost prefers to the plays and stories), and is best summed up in a letter to his brother Nicholas, where the character of the educated (or rather, well-bred) man, is defined in a succession of eight Don'ts. (The most characteristic is perhaps the eighth: 'They develop the aesthetic feeling in themselves. They cannot go to sleep in their clothes, nor see cracks full of bugs on the walls, nor breathe bad air, nor walk on a floor that has been spat on, nor cook their food over a kerosene cooker.') The other attraction of Chekhov is his style, free from everything sharp and glaring, and all bathed in a perfect and uniform haze, and, closely linked with it, his narrative method which allows nothing to 'happen,' but only smoothly and imperceptibly to 'become.' A technique that is the ripest and latest fruit of the Russian realistic school of the 19th century.

If the ethics of Chekhov are largely a less English form of the negative gentlemanism of Butler (and thus ultimately an extreme and cosmopolitan expression of an originally English upper middle-class ideal), it is clear that as a matter of literary art, Chekhov has no one to compare with in England, where the virtues he excels in have never been cultivated. The English literary tradition had no germs to rear a Chekhov from—and it is curious how indestructible the Elizabethan Adam is, even in the most faithful of English Chekhovites. *Nihil ex nihilo fit,* and without Turgenev and Goncharov before him, Russia herself could never have produced a Chekhov.

In Russian memory Chekhov is connected with a very definite 'context of situation,' with what we call the Eighties. The period (which extends further than 1890) is, in the history of the nation, the gloomy slump before the First Revolution; in the history of Literature, the Indian Summer of the great realistic school of the 19th century. In life, Chekhov's 'message' came as one of resignation and abdication, a despairing abdication of the heroic effort of the Revolutionaries of the Seventies —and a complacent and wistful subsidence into the rut of unheroic life. In literature his work was the fulfilment of the mellifluous realism of Turgenev (for, in Russia, realism is primarily a 'middle style,' avoiding everything salient whether in choice or treatment of subject, and the epithet 'realistic' has an overtone similar to that of the English 'Victorian'). Towards 1900, Chekhov was thus synonymous with national despair and literary *mediocritas*. A reaction against both these aspects became the rallying-point of all that was young and strong. A new revolutionary effort was started in the Nineties, and a wave of national optimism began to rise, and (paradoxically enough, for the alien observer) has ever since been rising ever higher; it has by now washed away the last trace of 'Chekhovian moods,' which have become indissolubly identified with the least attractive section of Russia's past, the years 1881–1900. In Literature at the same time, everything strong and authentic that has come forward since 1900 has been an ever-growing negation of the middle virtues, an assertion of the fundamental anomaly and asperity of art.

The English 'context of situation' to which Chekhov has been so good a response, is very different from the Russian. And before going any further, it is necessary to note that at least in one respect the English are likely to remain imperfect Chekhovites. The Master's purely negative attitude to culture (not the negation of culture, but its acceptance as a system of none but negative values), the attitude outlined in the letter to Nicholas Chekhov, is an attitude that may be admired but is incapable of being assimilated by the cultured Englishman. Chekhov lived at a time and in a country where this negative attitude was the rule, where other than utilitarian values were ignored, and where ethically justified knowledge and altruistic sentiment were regarded as the only aspects of civilisation. The difference of his attitude (if we may generalise it) from that of the Terrorists before him and of Lenin after him, was only that he rejected the heroical *compelle intrare* (into the utilitarian Paradise) of the Revolutionaries. Its difference from Tolstoy's is again only the absence of Tolstoy's heroical puritanity (and of his religious belief). In both cases a greater (and more consistent) 'mediocrity.' It is only after the Nineties that the Russian intelligentsia began that rapid accumulation of positive cultural valuables (which had existed but lain fallow before that time) that has so radically transformed the Russian mind. But the English intellectual, whether he will or not, cannot get rid of the heredity of Coleridge, Arnold and Pater—and the English Chekhovite remains what Chekhov never was, an epicure of Culture. Chekhov's place in the Pantheon of highbrow divinities is what cannot but seem incongruous even to the sophisticated Russian.

The English intellectual's thirst for the unheroic, of which Butler was the forerunner and Chekhov the fulfilment, has come into particular prominence since the late war. The nervous reaction that necessarily came after it was no doubt of great importance in strengthening this attitude, but its roots are much deeper in the past. They are connected with a reaction against the constraint of the 'Victorian Compromise,' against secular traditions of responsible individualism and individualistic discipline, and against centuries of immense creative expenditure. Like the Victorian, the Chekhovian compromise is a middle way, a harmony, a balance. But while Victorianism, that last equipoise of the English mind, was a balance of strong forces strongly suppressed, and consequently all abristle with rough edges of that highly Victorian thing, 'character'—the new Butler-Chekhov harmony is a natural balance of unsuppressed, but naturally inactive forces—an ideal state of maximum entropy.

Chekhov thus appears to possess qualities that must appeal to Classicist and Romanticist alike: the former will admire the balance and measure in his art and mind; the latter the naturalness of the balance, which in its very harmony remains true to self, and imposes no constraint on spontaneous experience.

The most apparent quasi-classical feature in Chekhov is his style. It is a middle style. But for a middle style to rise above mediocrity (in the plain English sense of the word) as Dryden's and La Bruyère's do rise, two things are necessary: a sense of language, and distinctness of diction. In a middle prose that possesses these qualities, that which it is not is as important as what it is. This 'presence of the rejected alternative," gives it a positive sense of rightness, not a negative sense of unwrittenness. Chekhov's middle style is negative. His Russian is not 'distinctive.' He had no sense of words—he did not feel them either as symbols (as the logical writer does), or as entities (as the poet does). Nor has his prose distinctness, for its rhythm is such as to blur and mix. Language in his hands becomes an homogeneous and undifferentiated paste.

This undistinguished and undistinguishing style is, however, admirably suited to express the writer's vision of things. Its grey and even smoothness faithfully reflects the essential sameness and homogeneity of Chekhov's world, that monotonous and undifferentiated mass of existence where what forces there are have shrunk to their last level and are running their last lease of energy, evenly, without jolt or jerk. The forces are so slight, that the merest nothing can deflect a line of human action—unnoticed at first but gradually curving off in a totally different direction—totally different, yet in this world of essential sameness, difference is hardly different from indifference—one direction is very much like its opposite—and all the dimensions are perfectly isotropic. The deflection of human lives by infinitesimal pinpricks, and the resulting curves, are the skeleton (if anything so elusive may be called a skeleton) of Chekhov's stories, and his skill in tracing these curves is truly great. They are marked out by a few points, the initial ones hardly diverging from the pre-pinprick direction, but gradually widening away. Each new point further emphasising the new direction. Chekhov's skill in tracing these curves is all the more marvellous as it must have required an unusually keen eye to single out and follow anything in the immense ocean of his world's sameness.[1]

These pinprick-begotten forces deflect human action, but no human action can deflect them. Unqualified determinism reigns in Chekhov's world, and submission to it is the standard of behaviour (a perfectly disinterested and autonomous morality, for the only reward that crowns the good man's goodness is to be ultimately undone). That man is good and lovable who makes no attempt (or only obviously absurd attempts) to counteract necessity, and the more sensitive and thin-skinned he is, the more he suffers in the act of submitting, the more he is lovable and good. He may writhe and wriggle, he may even struggle ineffectively—but fixity of purpose and steady resolution to act is the unpardonable sin. The man who does not succumb to pinpricks is an insensible brute. The man who knows his mind and works his own way through the world, may still be redeemed by failure and defeat, and if he at last succumbs,

[1] A striking illustration of this isotropy (which is largely conveyed by means of the rhythm of which I will speak presently) is the story *The Lady with a Dog* which unlike most of Chekhov's stories, is, as far as the actual narrative is concerned, a 'rising' story, in the 'major key.' The ultimate direction of the deflected curve of action is more positive and joyous than its pre-deflected direction: it is a change from indifference to passion. In spite of this the effect of the story is the same as that of stories with an opposite narrative development, from positive to negative (from hope to dejection, from passion to indifference).

he may even become doubly worthy of the smilingly indulgent and contemptuous pity that is Chekhov's substitute for sympathy. But if he goes on succeeding and not minding the conquering Pinprick, he becomes the Evil one, the detestable one, the Vulgar one, and is doomed to end his days in loathsome content.

As there is no distinctiveness in Chekhov's style and no colour in the greyness of his world (beyond some slight shadings into a greyish-blue or yellow), so is there no personality in his mankind. But while this mankind is utterly devoid of all that which constitutes the positive value of individuality (difference and uniqueness) it exhibits in an eminent degree all the negative aspects of that phenomenon: the mutual impenetrability of human beings. The absolute watertightness of the compartments into which the homogeneous stuff of Chekhov's humanity is cut out and the consequent impossibility of sympathy, is one of the most constant and characteristic of Chekhov's themes. It finds a technical expression in that favourite device of his plays—the disconnected dialogue where the characters go on exchanging mutually unrelated remarks (a device that gives his plays their peculiar air of unreality). The same impossibility of sympathy gives rise to his peculiar 'dramatic irony'; when sympathy is wanted it is never at hand, and when it is at hand it is not wanted, and only irritates the one sympathized with. (A striking example of this Chekhovian irony is the story entitled *The Post*.) But these isolated beings are not in any positive sense different. The matter that goes to their formation is always the same, and the form does not matter. One set of human cells is like another. The infinite unsurmountable identity of existence.

This on the surface; underlying it is a deeper and more hideous experience. It is an experience more than once revealed by the great Russians, the experience almost clinically described by Tolstoy in that extraordinary fragment of *Memoirs of a Madman*, and voiced with all his tragic strength by Dostoevsky in *Memoirs from Underground*, and, more epigrammatically, in that dreadful flash of grey gloom—Svidrigaylov's vision of 'eternity as a Russian bath-house with cobwebs in the corners.' In English literature it is evoked with a power worthy of the great Russians by Mr. Forster, in the last experience of Mrs. Moore in *A Passage to India*. It is not merely pessimism or despair—it is ultimate and absolute, but at the same time unspeakably mean and devoid of vastness and tragic grandeur. It robs existence of all value. It is, in Mr. Forster's words, 'something snub-nosed, incapable of all generosity—the undying worm itself.' It is a hard psychological fact, but naturally enough it is particularly tempting for a religious interpretation. It may be similar to the experience familiar to the Mystics, which St. John of the Cross symbolized in the image of *la noche escura* and which seems to be the unavoidable penalty and environment of the mystic's absolute bliss. (All the work of Leo Shestov, one of contemporary Russia's profoundest minds, has been an attempt to interpret it in this religious and mystical light.) Tolstoy fought it with the arms of religion, and his accounts of it (besides *Memoirs of a Madman, Ivan Ilyich,* and *Master and Man*) are 'historical' accounts of something overcome in the past, when the triumph of the worm recedes before the ultimate victory of the mystic light. Dostoevsky's religious weapons were of a less authentic and effective cast—gigantic makeshifts—but in *Memoirs from Underground,* and in isolated characters of the big novels, he came near achieving a genuine imaginative catharsis of it.

Chekhov, being fundamentally irreligious, could not follow Tolstoy. His one recourse was to art. But here again the levelness of his nature makes him different from Dostoevsky. Dostoevsky's disease was acute, Chekhov's chronic—the undying worm lay quiet and comfortable and fairly inactive in the middle hollow of his globe. The entropic levelness of Chekhov's creative self precluded the possibility of his wrestling with the worm as Dostoevsky wrestled. His only way out was to submit, and to make himself comfortable with it, by keeping it as far as possible lulled. Hence in all his mature work he steadily distils a sweet and comforting decoction of despair, which will produce a happy and 'drowsy numbness.' This is attained by a rhythm which may be described in exactly the words Mr. I. A. Richards uses to describe the rhythm of Mr. de la Mare; it is 'a lulling rhythm, an anodyne, an opiate, it gives sleep and visions, but it does not give *vision*, it does not awaken.'

There is, of course, a vast difference between the dreamlands of Chekhov and of Mr. de la Mare—and Chekhov's way of reaching it is certainly the more remarkable. To decoct a soothing opiate from fairies and fantoms is a simpler matter than to decoct it from the joyless reality of Chekhov's world. But that is not what he really does: his anodyne is made out of nothing (*Creation out of the Void* is the title of Shestov's remarkable essay on Chekhov, though the words are given a different application). The reality remains where it is, as joyless as ever and untransformed by any imaginative process. It is only veiled by an opiate mist in which it bathes but which does not adhere to it. The mist is the rhythm, the lulling, sweetly soothing keen of Chekhov's prose. It lulls the mind, blunts its hideous pain, dims the vision and brings immaterial, unsymbolical, drowsy visions which may be the very ripples of the river that flows down to Nirvana. Like the reality its office is to blur, the rhythm is negative, 'entropic,' and monotonous. Only its value is different. It is not coloured with the joyless greyness of life, but the sweetly restful greyness of falling to sleep. This is why for all the gloom of Chekhov's world his action on the reader is comforting, and comfortable. A triumph, certainly, of art over knowledge. But an art that is nearer kin to the technique of the hypnotizer than to the human art that begets positive values.

It is not possible, of course, to give the exact formula of Chekhov's rhythm, but like every lullaby it is a simple one. In the stories it is achieved largely by a certain monotonous parallelism of sentences, and a certain drooping becomes always more marked towards the end of the story, which always vaguely and droopingly dissolves into the void like a track losing itself in a plain. This indefinite ending seems to be a necessary condition of the effect. In the plays, the same effect is produced by different means. The disconnected dialogue plays a main part, as well as the recurrence of verbal and symbolic leitmotives. The indefinite ending, always removed a certain distance from (what may be by courtesy called) the climax, is as necessary a condition in the plays as in the stories, and purely physical effects, like the bursting of a string, are not shunned. Like every opiate, Chekhov's works in a purely physical way, on the nerves. The acquiescence of the mind is by no means requested. The spell works of itself, and determinism triumphs once more. Though, as a rule, the faithful reader is only too ready to succumb to it.

The obscuring, dimming, quality of his rhythm prevents us from ascribing any tragical quality to Chekhov, for tragedy, above all, requires clear vision, and the confrontation of the conflicting forces in the clear and even light (not in an even haze) of suspended judgment. (Besides, the forces in presence must be of a certain level of tension—greater than the differences of level to be discovered in Chekhov's world.) There are, however, in the work of Chekhov, two stories where the lulling rhythm is absent, and is replaced by a clearer and sharper one. Where, consequently, there is no sweet and drowsy numbness, but the clear light of real vision. These are *My Life* and *In the Ravine*, which stand so strangely out from the rest of his work. The two stories would no doubt profit from the anonymity advocated for poetry by Mr. Forster, and not having to connect them with the other work of Chekhov. Perhaps they are a truer expression of the essential Chekhov, but in that case the essential Chekhov is most certainly absent not only from the plays and other stories, but also from the letters he wrote and from the face he showed his contemporaries. For in the letters and in the face there was that same soothing and comforting quality, as in his imaginative work. But *My Life* and *In the Ravine* refuse comfort, and no haze is allowed to blur the sharp outlines of reality.

There is, I know, a 'heroic' interpretation of Chekhov, and with certain qualifications and assumptions, it may be the right one. Not that his acceptance of life with all its hopelessness (the attitude revealed in his stories—except those two—plays or letters) may be recognized as heroical. It is not heroical because Chekhov had neither the will nor the strength to be a rebel. He had no undauntable desire to curb. He regarded Revolt as, if frustrated, piteously and lovably absurd, if for the time victorious, vulgar like all success. But what may be heroical in Chekhov is that he profited nothing by the comfort his opiate wand dispensed to others. To himself his rhythm was no anodyne. In the ultimate hopelessness of his hell he used the little force he had to comfort with his incantations his fellow-sufferers down there and the unknowing infants above. If this be so, Chekhov is a hero, something of a Grand Inquisitor, who keeps his knowledge and his pain to himself, while doing his best to keep the human herd in blessed and drowsy ignorance. But the Chekhovite who accepts the comfort is anything but a hero. He abdicates his greatest duty, the duty shared to-day by all men who are to remain individuals, and who do not thirst

for Nirvana—the duty of refusing to be comforted. To the
stripped and cast-out mankind of to-day, Chekhov is the arch-
seducer. To succumb to him is as sweet as it is for the worn-
out wayfarer struggling with the blizzard to go to sleep in the
snow—it is the sweetest of spiritual deaths.

There are, probably, people in England insensitive enough to
be proof against the lulling music of Chekhov, and they, if
they are Chekhovites, concentrate either on his mastery as a
short-story writer, or on his ethical doctrine of negative perfection. The first of these approaches is, from the literary point
of view, perfectly legitimate, and the quality of Chekhov, being
a quality opposite to all qualities peculiarly English, a certain
infusion of it into English Literature may not be amiss, for if it
is poison, there are in the English organism quite enough anti-
toxins to counteract it. His narrative technique may have and
has had a useful influence on English, as the opposite technique
of O. Henry may have and is having a useful influence on
Russian fiction. In a catholic hierarchy of literary values,
Chekhov has his place, though it is nowhere near the top of the
pyramid, but somewhere near the middle of one of its sides. In
any purely aesthetic acceptance of Chekhov, it is above all
necessary to keep him in his right place. Fortunately (and this is
the redressing irony of the case) extreme Chekhovism carries
in itself its own antidote: the grotesque sense of disproportion
that will compare Chekhov to Shakespeare, is so exceedingly
inconsistent with the middle ways of Chekhov that one who is
guilty of it is for that very reason a bad Chekhovite. A principal safeguard of English literature against Chekhov is its indestructible sense of the individual, of character and personality, in which Russian literature itself was so strong in the great
days of Dostoevsky, Tolstoy and Leskov, but which it has
since lost. Chekhov marks the nadir—and to-day it is once again
laboriously being built up by some of the younger men (especially Fedin, whose work might be inscribed *À la recherche de
la personnalité perdue*), though the great majority are still without it. But the sense of the individual is only one of the aspects
of the sense of the Different, and in other forms of the latter
Russian literature since 1900 has been rich. It is precisely the
development of this sense that has helped us out of the quag-
mire of Chekhov.

As for Chekhov's ethics, Russia is safely free and in no danger of reverting to them in any near future. But for intellectual England with her disillusionment in all active and all group-values, and her violent relaxation after centuries of individual-istic discipline—Chekhov's is the most attractive creed, especial-ly if one is sound or shallow enough not to realise the worm beneath it, and unreflecting enough to submit to his siren-rhythm unconsciously. In one respect, as I have already said, the English intellectual will not follow Chekhov—he will not contemn the positive cultural values—Poetry and Art—but on the contrary utilize them as a parallel and perhaps even more potent opiate. The modified Anglo-Chekhovian type is likely to spread among the (imaginatively) middle strata of the intel-ligentsia of this country, and is already prominent among some of its most successful writers. But the more creative levels of the English mind as well as its strongest critical intellects are free from the debilitating influence, and with them the real tra-dition (if it is a tradition) of Shakespeare is more alive than it has been for many generations—a subject, however, too impor-tant to be discussed in the concluding paragraph of what is merely an essay on Chekhov.

XV

THOMAS MANN

Chekhov

When Anton Chekhov died of tuberculosis of the lungs in Badenweiler in July 1904, I was a young man who had entered the literary field with a few stories and one novel which owed a good deal to the narrative art of nineteenth-century Russia. Yet I have tried in vain today to recall the impression made upon me at the time by the death of the Russian writer only fifteen years older than myself. I can remember nothing. The announcement in the German press must have left me rather unmoved. And no doubt whatever was written about Chekhov on that occasion had failed to deepen my awareness of this man who had died too early for Russia, too early for the world. Very likely these obituaries testified to the same ignorance that determined my own attitude to the life and work of this author, an attitude that was to change but slowly with the years.

What were the reasons for this ignorance? In my case it may be partly explained by my admiration for the "great work," the "long wind," the monumental epic sustained and completed by the power of unyielding patience, by my worship of the mighty creators like Balzac, Tolstoy, Wagner, whom it was my dream to emulate if I could. And Chekhov, like Maupassant, whose work incidentally I knew much better, expressed himself in the more restricted form, in the short story, which did not require years or a decade of heroic perseverance but could be tossed off by literary lightweights in a matter of days or weeks. For this medium I felt a certain scorn, little realizing what inner depth the short and concise can acquire in the hands of genius; how brevity, by embracing the whole fullness of life, can rise to a positively epic level, can even surpass in artistic intensity works of monumental stature, which are bound occasionally to flag, to lapse into a venerable dullness. If in later life I understood this fact better than in my youth, it was due mainly to my preoccupation with Chekhov's narrative art, which is unsurpassed in European literature.

To speak in more general terms, I feel that Chekhov was underestimated for so many years in western Europe, and even in Russia, on account of his extremely sober, critical, and doubting attitude toward himself, above all toward his own work—in a word, on account of his *modesty*, which, however endearing a virtue, was not conducive to making the world consider him great and important; indeed, it could be said that by this modesty he set the world a bad example. For the opinion we have of ourselves is not without influence on the picture other men paint of us; it colors their ideas, sometimes even distorts them. This short-story writer remained too long convinced of the insignificance of his talent, of his artistic unworthiness. He acquired some faith in himself, the faith that is essential if others are to believe in us, only by degrees and very painfully. To the end he had nothing of the literary *grand seigneur* about him, still less of the sage or prophet of Tolstoy, who looked benignly down on him and, according to Gorky, saw in him "an excellent, quiet, *modest* fellow."

Coming from a man whose immodesty was no less colossal than Wagner's, such praise is a trifle surprising. No doubt Chekhov would have accepted it with a polite, ironical smile; for politeness, dutiful veneration tinged with irony, set the tone of his relations with the giant from Yasnaya Polyana. Occasionally, not of course face to face with the overwhelming personality but in letters to a third person, this irony broke into open rebellion. On his return from his "descent into hell," his trying journey to the penal island of Sakhalin, Chekhov wrote: "What a dull, sour fellow I should be today had I remained between my four walls! Before this journey, for instance, I considered Tolstoy's *Kreutzer Sonata* an important event; now it strikes me as comical and absurd." Tolstoy's imperial—as well as questionable—prophetic airs irritated him. "To the devil with the philosophy of the mighty ones of this world!" he wrote. "All great sages are as despotic as generals, and as rude as generals, convinced as they are of impunity." This gibe was provoked by Tolstoy's denunciation of doctors as useless scoundrels. For Chekhov himself was a doctor, a man dedicated to his profession, and he believed science to be one of the forces making for progress, to be an enemy of disgraceful human conditions, since it enlightened both heads and hearts. The wisdom of "oppose no evil," of "passive resistance," the contempt for culture and progress in which the great man indulged, appeared to Chekhov as so much reactionary twaddle. However great a man may be, he has no business laying down the law on topics of which he is totally ignorant; it was for this that Chekhov reproached Tolstoy. "Tolstoy's morality has ceased to affect me," he wrote. "At heart I don't approve of it. I myself have peasant blood, and no one can impress me with peasant virtues. I have believed in progress since my childhood. Sober reflection and a sense of justice tell me there is more love for mankind in electricity and steam than in chastity and fasting."

In short, he was a positivist—from modesty; a simple servant of enlightening truth who never for a moment claimed any of the liberties usually taken by the great. Once, when commenting on Bourget's *Disciple*, he inveighed vehemently against the disparagement of scientific materialism masquerading as idealism. "Such crusades are incomprehensible to me. To forbid a man the materialistic conception is to forbid him to seek the truth. Outside matter there is neither experience nor knowledge, and therefore no truth."

Chekhov's persistent self-doubts as an artist extended, if I am not mistaken, beyond his own self; they embraced art, above all literature. He found it repugnant to live alone "between my four walls"; he considered that the pursuit of art should always be complemented by practical, social activity in the world, among men, in the midst of life. Literature, to use his own words, was his mistress, while medicine was his lawful wife, toward whom he felt guilty of the infidelity committed with the other. Hence the harassing journey to Sakhalin, endangering his already precarious health, followed by his sensational report on the island's unspeakable conditions, a report that actually led to some reforms. Hence, too, his unremitting activity as a country doctor which went hand in hand with his literary work; the administration of the district hospital in Svenigorod near Moscow; the battle against cholera fought on his own small property in Melikhovo, where he succeeded in having isolation wards erected. It was here, too, that he acted as trustee to the village school. Meanwhile, his literary reputation continued to grow; but he eyed this growth with skepticism and a stricken conscience. "Am I not fooling the reader," he asked, "since I cannot answer the most important questions?"

These words had a profound effect upon me; it was thanks to them that I decided to delve deeper into Chekhov's life, one of the most moving and captivating biographies that I know. He came from Taganrog on the Sea of Azov in south Russia, a small provincial town where his father, a lower-middle-class bigot (whose own father had been a serf), kept a grocery store and bullied his wife and children. The old man also dabbled in ikon-painting, strummed amateurishly on the violin, had a passion for liturgical music, and organized a church choir in which his sons had to sing. These stray hobbies were probably responsible for the business going bankrupt while Anton Pavlovich was still at school, and for the father having to flee from his creditors to Moscow. Yet in the heart of this narrow, lower-middle-class bigot there evidently lurked some dim artistic seed, destined to germinate and unfold in only one of the offspring. True, one of the elder brothers became a "publicist," the other a painter—an insignificant publicist, and a painter who, like the former, drowned what talent he may have had in vodka: weak, decrepit characters whom the only stable member of the family tried in vain to support.

For the time being the boys had to help their father with the selling of his wares, run errands, and on holidays get up at three o'clock in the morning to rehearse with the choir for the religious services. In addition there was the Taganrog Latin school, a soul-destroying drill-ground in which both teachers and pupils were instructed from above to stifle the least sign of independent thought. Life was akin to hard labor, monotonous, vapid, oppressive. But one son, Anton, the secretly chosen, had his own strange ways of compensating for this dismal atmosphere. He possessed a natural bent for gaiety and the poking of fun, for clowning and mimicry, a talent which fed on observation and was translated into hilarious caricature. The boy could take off a simple-minded deacon, a local official shaking his leg at a dance, a dentist, a police sergeant's behavior in church. He could copy them all so supremely well, in a manner so true to life, that the whole school marveled. "Do that again!" they cried. "That's really something! We saw it too, and it didn't seem funny. But when this little devil does it, we burst out laughing. He makes it seem more like life than life itself. This is something new. Ha, ha, ha! What fun! Now then, enough of this irreverent horseplay! But listen, before you stop, do again the police sergeant setting off to church! Just once more!"

What makes its appearance here is the primitive origin of all art, the inclination to ape, the jester's desire and talent to entertain, a gift that was to employ very different means in the future, was to pour itself into very different forms; it was to ally itself with spiritual principles, to undergo moral ennoblement, and to rise from merely amusing trifles to soul-stirring achievements. Yet even in his bitterest, most serious moments Chekhov was never entirely to lose his sense of the farcical, his work was always to retain much of the brilliant aping of the police sergeant and the dancing official. . . .

After the father had been obliged to close his shop and flee to Moscow, Anton Pavlovich, then sixteen, spent three more years in Taganrog to finish his education. For if his most cherished desire, to study medicine, were to be fulfilled, he had to graduate from Latin school. And graduate he did. Having passed through the three upper forms on a tiny scholarship supplemented by miserably paid lessons to younger students, he obtained his graduation certificate and followed his parents to Moscow, where he entered the university.

Did the young man who had escaped from the narrow, provincial existence feel happier in the great city? Did he breathe more freely? Alas, no one could breathe freely in Russia then. It was a stifling, gloomy life in which men, intimidated by brutal authority, slunk about in hypocritical submissiveness, censored, bullied, and bellowed at by the state. The country groaned under the ultra-autocratic regime of Alexander III and his ghastly minister Pobedonoszev—a regime of hopelessness. And among Chekhov's acquaintances many a fine mind, delicately balanced and gasping for the air of freedom, literally succumbed to hopelessness. Gleb Ouspenski, an honest portrayer of Russian peasant life, went out of his mind. Garshin, whose melancholic fiction Chekhov highly respected, committed suicide. The painter Levitan, with whom Anton Pavlovich was on friendly terms, also attempted to take his life. Vodka exerted an increasingly strong attraction among intellectuals. They drank from despair. Both of Chekhov's brothers drank, and rapidly came down in the world despite Anton's fervent pleadings to pull themselves together. They probably would have been drunkards had there been no Pobedonoszev, and they could, alas, have referred among others to dear, good Palmin the poet, another friend of Anton's, who also drank.

Anton Pavlovich did not take to drink, neither did he grow melancholy or lose his mind. In the first place, he eagerly pursued the study of medicine, which was beyond the control of M. Pobedonoszev; as for the general despair, he armed himself against it as he had against the dreariness of Taganrog: he made fun, he caricatured the police sergeant, the stupid deacon, and the official at the ball. But he no longer took them off by mimicry, he aped them in writing. He sat in the noise and chaos of his parents' apartment, which he shared, and wrote for any comic paper that liked to indulge in a little cautious satire. He tossed off all kinds of odd things, very short, hastily jotted down: anecdotes, dialogues, humorous gossip, thumbnail sketches of provincial weddings, drunken tradesmen, bickering wives or those gone astray, an ex-sergeant who kept shouting at everybody—and all this with such zest that people would exclaim, just as they had at Taganrog: "This is really something! The knack he has! Do it again!"

And he did it again and again, exuberantly, inexhaustible in small observations and comical imitations of daily life, although to combine the exacting study of medicine with this public clowning must have put a considerable strain on the young man. For these sketches, after all, had to be shaped, given a point, something that required a mental effort, and considerable numbers of them had to be produced if the miserly fees were to accumulate sufficiently to pay not only for his studies but also to contribute substantially to the support of his parents, his younger brothers and sisters, for the father earned next to nothing and at nineteen Anton was the mainstay of the family. The name he used as provider for comic papers was Antosha Chekhonte. . . .

And then something strange occurred, something characteristic of the willful spirit of literature and proof of the unexpected consequences that can occur once this art is embarked upon at all, no matter how expedient, casual, or frivolous the reason may be. This spirit "knocks at the conscience"—as Antosha Chekhonte, the jester, said himself. He has described in a letter how—amidst the comings and goings in his parents' apartment, surrounded by screaming children, the sound of a music box and his father reading aloud next door—he was sitting at an unprotected table, his literary work before him *"knocking mercilessly at my conscience."* This seemed hardly fair, considering the work was intended merely as a joke to amuse the bourgeois world. But what a moment ago I referred to as strange, characteristic, unexpected, is that gradually, without his knowledge or conscious consent, there had crept into his sketches something originally not meant for them, something springing from the conscience of literature as well as from his own personal conscience: something which, while still gay and entertaining, contained a sad, bitter note, exposing and accusing life and society, compassionate yet critical—in a word, literature. For this note that had crept in was directly connected with writing itself, with form and language. This critical sadness, this rebelliousness expresses the longing for a better reality, for a purer, truer, nobler, more beautiful life, a worthier human society. And this longing was reflected in the language, in the obligation to treat it as a work of art, a "merciless" obligation that was undoubtedly part of the change that had crept into Antosha's formless scribbling. Fifteen years were to pass before Gorky pronounced judgment on this same Antosha: "As a stylist Chekhov has no equal, and future literary historians, reflecting on the development of the Russian language, will maintain that this language has been created by Pushkin, Turgenev, and Chekhov."

These words were uttered in 1900. Just now we are concerned with the years 1884–5. Having completed his studies, Anton Pavlovich, then twenty-four, took a job as an intern at the district hospital of Voskressensk, where he performed autopsies on the corpses of suicides and others who had died under suspicious circumstances. He continued, nevertheless, to write comic sketches, for this had become a habit. Among these stories a few slipped in—"The Death of an Official," "The Fat and the Lean," "A Delinquent"—whose composition had given him particular pleasure. Because their humor was tinged with bitterness, it is possible that they did not altogether please the general public, but they caused readers here and there to raise an eyebrow. One of these was D. W. Grigorovich. Who knows Dmitri Vasilievich Grigorovich? Not I. Frankly, I had never heard of him until I began to study Chekhov's life. And yet at that time he was a widely respected author, a distinguished man of letters who had earned a considerable reputation with his novels on the life of serfs. It was this famous, already elderly man, once a friend of Belinsky, later of Turgenev and Dostoevsky, who one day wrote a letter from St. Petersburg to the young Dr. Chekhov in Voskressensk near Moscow. It was a very serious letter, marking perhaps the most moving, surprising, and epoch-making event in Chekhov's life. "You possess, dear sir," he wrote, "a very exceptional talent which, I am convinced, has no need to recoil from the most difficult tasks. It would be a tragedy were you to squander your gifts on literary trifles. I feel the urge to implore you not to do this, but to concentrate on work of genuine artistic merit."

Anton Pavlovich read these lines in black and white, and under them the signature of the celebrated man. Probably never again in his life was he to feel so bewildered, so thrilled, so overwhelmed. "I almost broke into tears," he wrote in answer, "and feel that your letter has left a deep mark on my soul. I feel dazed and quite incapable of judging whether I deserve this high praise or not. . . . If I do possess a talent worthy of esteem, let me confess to the purity of your heart that I have not until now respected this gift of mine. . . . *There is always sufficient reason to be unfair to oneself, highly suspicious, and morbidly sensitive.* . . . Hitherto I have adopted an extremely frivolous, careless, and superficial attitude toward my literary activities. . . . I just wrote, taking care at all costs *not to waste on my stories those images and characters that are precious to me.* These, God knows why, I have protected and kept carefully hidden." This is what Chekhov wrote to the old Grigorovich in his letter of thanks which later became famous. Having written it, he went off to perform an autopsy or perhaps to visit a typhus case in the district hospital—let us say to a typhus case in memory of Lieutenant Klimov's spotted fever, the story of an illness written somewhat later with masterly skill from the patient's point of view by Anton Chekhov, who, after receiving that letter, never again signed himself Antosha Chekhonte.

Anton Pavlovich was granted but a short life. He was only

twenty-nine when the first symptoms of tuberculosis appeared. As a doctor he recognized them for what they were and certainly harbored no illusions that his vitality could carry him to the patriarchal age of a Tolstoy. One wonders whether his awareness of his brief stay on earth did not largely contribute to his strange, skeptical, and infinitely endearing modesty, which continued to characterize his artistic and intellectual attitude, including even the instinct to make this modesty a special feature of his art, elevating it to a specific magic of his existence. Roughly twenty-five years—this was the time allowed him for the developing and perfecting of his creative talent, and he certainly made full use of the years. Some six hundred stories bear his name, not a few of which are "long short stories," among them masterpieces such as "Ward Number Six," in which a doctor, disgusted by the stupidity and misery of the world of normal men, forms such a close relationship with an interesting lunatic that this world declares him a lunatic, too, and locks him up. Although this eighty-seven-page story, written in 1892, avoids any direct accusation, it is so devastatingly symbolic of the corruption and hopelessness in Russia, of the degradation of mankind toward the end of the autocracy, that it prompted the young Lenin to say to his sister: "Last night after finishing that story I felt very uneasy. I couldn't sit still in my room. I had to get up and go out. I felt as though I myself were locked up in Ward Number Six."

But while in the midst of quoting and praising I must certainly not forget to mention "A Tedious Tale," my favorite among Chekhov's narrative works, a truly extraordinary, fascinating story whose atmosphere of strange, gentle sadness is unlike anything else in world literature. Not the least surprising feature of this overwhelming tale, announcing itself as "tedious," is that it has been put into the mouth of an old man by a man of thirty with infinite understanding. The old man is a world-famous scholar, a general by rank, an Excellency, a term by which he frequently refers to himself in his confessions. "My Excellency!" he says in a tone suggesting: "Good Lord!" For, although high up in the official hierarchy, he has enough intelligence, self-criticism, and criticism in general to look upon the fame and respect paid to him as absurd. In the depths of his soul he is a desperate man because he realizes that, despite all its rewards, his life has always lacked a spiritual center, a "central idea," that basically it has been a meaningless life. "Every feeling, every thought," he says, "lives isolated within me, and no analytical observer, however experienced, could find in my judgments on science, the theater, literature, etc., etc., what is called a central idea or the spirit of God in man. *And if this is lacking, then there is nothing.* . . . It is therefore not at all surprising that the last months of my life have been clouded by thoughts and feelings worthy of a slave and a barbarian, and that now I am indifferent to everything. If there is nothing in a human being's life stronger and more important than outer circumstances, then indeed a common cold is sufficient to upset his equilibrium, and all his pessimism as well as his great and trivial thoughts have no more significance than symptoms—nothing else. I am defeated. This being the case, there is no point in continuing to think, no point in arguing. I shall just sit and wait in silence for what is to come."

"And my ending is despair"—Prospero's last line keeps recurring to the mind while reading the confessions of the famous old Nikolai Stepanytsch. "Quite frankly," he says, "I just don't like the popularity of my name. I feel it has deceived me." When Anton Chekhov made the old man say this and what has been quoted above, he was a young man. Yet he had not long to live, and perhaps this was why he managed to anticipate with such uncanny insight the mood of old age. To the dying scholar he gave much of himself—above all, this: "I just don't like the popularity of my name." For Chekhov himself did not like his growing fame; "for some reason [he] felt uneasy about it." Was he not deceiving his readers by dazzling them with his talent, since he could not "answer the most important questions"? Why did he write? What was his aim, his faith? Where was the "spirit of God in man"? Where was the "central idea" of his life and writing, "without which there is nothing"?

"A conscious life without a definite philosophy," he wrote to a friend, "is no life, rather a burden and a nightmare." Katya, a shipwrecked actress, the famous scholar's ward and the only human being to whom he is still attached, for whom he feels an aging man's secret tenderness, asks him out of profound confusion and despair: "What shall I do? Just one word, Nikolai Stepanytsch, I implore you. What shall I do?" And he is obliged to answer: "I don't know. Upon my honor and conscience, Katya, I don't know." Whereupon she leaves him.

The question "What's to be done?" keeps cropping up in a deliberately confused manner throughout Chekhov's work; the strange, helpless, stilted way in which his characters hold forth on the problem of existence almost borders on the ludicrous. I can no longer remember in which story, but somewhere a lady appears and says: "Life should be observed as through a prism —that's to say, it should be seen in refractions, should be divided into its simplest elements, and then each element studied separately." His short stories and plays seethe with this kind of dialogue. In part it may be just a satirical description of the Russian love for the interminable and fruitless philosophical discussion—a kind of persiflage that can also be found in other Russian writers. But in Chekhov's case it has a very special background, a specific, disconcertingly comical artistic function. For example, "My Life," a story told in the first person, is filled with arguments of this sort. The "I," with the nickname of "Better-than-Nothing," is a utopian socialist in revolt against the existing order; he believes in the necessity of manual labor for all, deserts his own, the educated class, and dedicates himself to a dismal, hard, ugly proletarian existence whose brutal reality exposes him to many painful disappointments. Sorrow over his son's eccentricity brings the father, a man devoted to tradition, to the grave, and it is also the young man's fault that his sister goes astray and comes to grief. One character, Doctor Blagovo, says to the narrator: "I respect you, you are a noble soul, a true idealist. But don't you think that if instead of spending all this will-power, intensity, and energy on changing your life you had spent it on gradually becoming, say, a great scientist or an artist, your life would have been both wider and deeper, in every respect more productive?" No, answers "Better-than-Nothing," what is of vital necessity is that the strong should not enslave the weak, the minority should not become a parasite of the majority; that everyone, the strong no less than the weak, the rich no less than the poor, should share equally in the struggle for existence, and in this respect there is no better means of leveling than manual labor and compulsory service for all. "But don't you think that if everyone, including the best men, the great philosophers and scientists, were to take part in the struggle for existence and spend their time breaking stones and painting roofs, it would mean a serious menace to progress?" This is a good question; but not good enough to prevent an even better or at least equally good answer. And from the subject of progress, the conversation moves on to its aims. Aims and limits of universal progress, in Doctor Blagovo's opinion, lie in infinity, and to contemplate progress as limited by man's needs and temporary theories he finds positively strange, to say the least.

What an argument! If the limits of progress lie in infinity, then its aims must be indefinite. *"How can man live without knowing what he is living for?"* "Granted. But this 'not knowing' is less boring than your 'knowing.' I am climbing a ladder which is called progress, civilization, culture. I keep on climbing higher and higher without knowing definitely where I am going, but for me this wonderful ladder alone makes life worth living. You, on the other hand, know what you are living for: you live so that some people should not enslave others, so that the painter and the man who grinds his paints for him should eat the same food. But surely this is the dull, humdrum, kitchen side of life! To live for that alone strikes me as nauseating. . . . We must keep in mind the great Unknown which awaits mankind in the distant future. . . ."

Blagovo is arguing with great fervor, yet it is clear that his mind is occupied with thoughts of another nature. "I suppose your sister is not coming?" he says, consulting his watch. "She mentioned yesterday that she might call on you this afternoon." So he has come simply to meet the sister with whom he is in love, has been talking just to while away the time! By this human motive underlying his words and clearly written in his face, anything he says turns to irony and is smilingly devalued. "Better-than-Nothing's" attempt radically to change his life is devalued, or at least rendered problematical by the degrading disappointments he encounters and the guilt he is taking upon himself in the process; the visitor's dialectic turns to irony by being used to kill time. The truth about life, to which the writer should be in duty bound, devalues his ideas and opinions. *This truth is by nature ironical,* and it can easily happen that a writer who puts the truth above everything else is reproached by the world with lack of conviction, indifference to good and evil, lack of ideals and ideas. Chekhov objected to reproaches of this kind. He trusted the reader, he said, to fill in the suppressed "subjective"—that is, the critical—elements lacking in the story, to supply for himself the ethical point of view. Why, then, his "uneasiness," the dislike for his fame, this feeling of misleading his readers with his talent because he could not answer the most important questions? What is the source of this uncanny ability to put himself into the position of the despairing old man who realized that his life had lacked the "central idea . . . without which there is nothing," and who, to the bewildered girl's question: "What shall I do?" was obliged to answer: "Upon my honor and conscience, I don't know"?

If the truth about life is by nature ironical, then must not art itself be by nature nihilistic? And yet art is so industrious! Art is, so to speak, the very essence of work in its highest abstract form, the paradigm of all work, it is work itself, and for its own sake. Chekhov believed in work as few others ever have. Gorky said of him that he had "never known anyone feel so deeply that work is the basis of all culture as Chekhov did." And indeed he worked incessantly, indefatigably, regardless of his delicate constitution and the debilitating nature of his disease, worked every day to the end. What is more, he persisted in this heroic labor while continuously doubting its value, despite the guilty awareness that it lacked the "central idea," that he had no answer to the question "What can be done?" and that he was shirking the issue by mere descriptions of life. "We just depict life as it is," he said, "without taking one step further." Or: "As things stand, the life of an artist has no point, and the more talented he is, the stranger and more incomprehensible his role becomes, because he is obviously working to amuse a foul beast of prey, and by so doing helping to support the existing order." By existing order is meant the unbearable conditions under which Chekhov lived in the Russia of the 1890's. But his distress, his doubts about the value of his own work, his feeling for the strangeness and incomprehensibility of his role as an artist, such doubts are timeless and not confined to conditions prevailing in Russia at the end of the nineteenth century. By "conditions" is meant bad conditions, showing an unbridgeable gulf separating truth from reality, which always exists. Chekhov has fellow sufferers today, too, writers who do not feel at ease with their fame because they are "amusing a forlorn world without offering it a scrap of saving truth"—so we are told, at least—and who, like him, can identify themselves with the aged hero of "A Tedious Tale" who has no answer to the question "What shall I do?" These writers, too, are unable to say what the value of their own work is; nevertheless, they go on working, working to the end.

There must be something in this strange "nevertheless," it must have a meaning, and so give a meaning to work as well. Does work itself perhaps, however much it may look like amusement, contain something ethical, something of service to the human cause, leading in the end even to the "saving truth" toward which a bewildered world is stretching out its hands? Earlier in this essay I spoke of literature's spirit of willfulness, of its unexpected consequences, and tried to describe how this spirit, quite unintentionally on his part, entered the young Chekhov's scribblings, automatically raising their moral level. This process, continuing throughout his whole literary career, can be recognized at every phase. One biographer says of him: "What seems remarkable in Chekhov's development is the *close connection between his rise to the mastery of form* and the change in attitude toward his time. It was this attitude that determined his choice of subject matter, his characterization and control of action, and can be recognized in all of them. Indeed, here and there this new attitude is expressed through his protagonists as conscious reflection revealing an unerring instinct and a subtle power to distinguish between those forces which are soon to belong to the past and those of a new era pointing to the future." What I find interesting about this comment is the discovery of a connection between Chekhov's rise toward mastery of *form* and his growing sensitivity toward the social evils of his time—in other words, his deepening awareness of what is condemned by society and dying as well as of that which is to come; in short, the connection between the aesthetic and the ethical. It is surely this connection which gives to the industriousness of art its dignity, its meaning, its usefulness; it also explains Chekhov's immense respect for work itself, his disapproval of all idle parasitism, his increasingly outspoken condemnation of a life which, as he said, "is based on slavery."

This is a harsh verdict to pass on a bourgeois capitalist society proud of its humanitarianism and deaf to the notion of slavery. But our story-teller displayed a remarkably acute eye for the doubtfulness of human progress in general, and for the social and moral conditions following the liberation of the peasants in his native Russia—conditions which nevertheless do have a certain general validity. "Side by side with the gradual development of humane ideas," Chekhov made his "Better-than-Nothing" say, "the gradual growth of ideas of a very different order can be observed. Serfdom has been abolished, but [he could also have said: just because] capitalism is on the increase. Even now, in the very heyday of liberal ideas, the majority as usual has to feed, clothe, and defend the minority while itself remaining hungry, inadequately clothed, and defenseless. Such a state of affairs can easily be made to fit in with any ideological currents of thought you like, for *the art of enslaving is also gradually being refined*. We no longer flog our servants, but we practice slavery in more subtle ways; at least we know how to justify each particular case. Of course we hold humane ideals in high esteem, but if now, at the close of the nineteenth century, it were possible to shift the burden of our most unpleasant physiological functions onto the working class, we should certainly do so, and afterward justify ourselves by saying that if the best men, the great philosophers and scientists, were to waste their precious time on these functions, progress would seriously suffer."

This is but one sample of Chekhov's way of ridiculing the self-righteousness of the "progressivists." As a doctor he had a pronounced contempt for the palliatives with which these people treated the social sickness. He is extremely funny in the story "A Doctor's Visit," where he makes the governess of a wealthy manufacturer's family extol over sterlet and Madeira the blessings of these palliatives. "Our workers are very contented," she says. "Every winter in the factory we have theatrical performances in which the workers themselves take part. They also have lectures with a magic lantern, a splendid tearoom, and several other amenities. The workers are very devoted to us, and when they heard that my young lady had taken a turn for the worse, they ordered special prayers to be said. They may not be educated, but they do have feelings."

Yet the man from whose practice this story is told, head physician Korolyov, whose real name is Anton Chekhov, can only shake his head at her words. "While looking at the factory buildings and the barracks where the workers were asleep," we read, "he was reminded once more of what he always thought when he saw factories. Even though the men had theatrical performances, magic lanterns, factory doctors, and all manner of improvements, the workers he had met that day on his way from the station did not look in any way different from the men he had seen in his childhood before the existence of improvements and performances in factories. As a doctor with a sure judgment of chronic ailments whose prime cause was unknown and incurable, he also looked upon factories as an anomalous phenomenon whose cause could likewise be neither detected nor removed; and although he did not consider all improvements in the lives of factory hands to be superfluous, he nevertheless compared them with the patching up of incurable diseases." If cure at all, one can hear him say, then not the diseases, but their causes. "Infirmaries, schools, reading-rooms, and pharmacies are also nothing but tools of slavery under the given circumstances—that's my conviction." A conviction that must not allow us to forget that Chekhov himself founded schools and hospitals in his district. But this did not set his mind at rest. "What matters most," runs the sentence into which he increasingly condensed his thought, "is to break out of the rut; everything else is unimportant."

But, taking into account the all too "given" circumstances and the fact that everything has its incurable necessity, how was this to be done? What was the answer to the question: "What can we do?" The uneasiness caused by this question haunts numerous characters in Chekhov's stories. In "A Doctor's Visit" he coined the phrase "honorable sleeplessness." In this story Doctor Korolyov has been summoned to the intelligent, unhappy young lady, heiress to a million rubles and some factories, because she suffers from nervous fits and insomnia. "It's not that I feel ill," she says herself, "I am just uneasy and filled with anxiety, because it has to be like this and cannot be otherwise." It is quite clear to the doctor what he ought to tell her: Give up the five factories and the million as soon as possible and cast that devil out! And it is equally clear to him that she thinks the same, but is simply waiting to have it confirmed by someone she trusts. But how can he put it to her? One shrinks from asking a condemned man why he has been condemned, and it is also painful to ask the wealthy why they need so much money, why they make such poor use of their wealth, why they don't give it away, even when they realize it is the cause of their unhappiness. And once this kind of conversation is begun it invariably becomes embarrassing, painful, and boring. This is why he answers her frankly but in a consolatory tone: "It's in your role as factory-owner and wealthy heiress that you are dissatisfied; you don't feel entitled to wealth, so you cannot sleep. This is preferable, of course, to your being satisfied, to sleeping well and believing that all is as it should be. *You are suffering from an honorable sleeplessness.* Whatever else it may be, this is a good sign. The notion that our parents could have had a conversation like this is unthinkable; they did not discuss things at night, they slept soundly. But we of our generation sleep badly, torment ourselves, talk a great deal, and are all the time trying to decide whether we are right or not. For our children and grandchildren this question of being in the right or not will already have been decided. They will have a clearer vision. Fifty years from now life will be beautiful. . . ."

Will it? One has to face the fact that man is a failure. His conscience, which belongs to the spirit, will probably never be brought into harmony with his nature, his reality, his social condition, and there will always be "honorable sleeplessness" for those who for some unfathomable reason feel responsible for human fate and life. If anyone ever suffered from this, it was Chekhov the artist. All his work was honorable sleeplessness, a search for the right, redeeming word in answer to the question: "What are we to do?" The word was difficult, if not impossible, to find. The only thing he knew for certain was that idleness is the worst, that man has to work because idleness means letting others work for him, means exploitation and oppression. In his last story, "Betrothed," Sasha—who, like Chekhov, is consumptive and soon to die—says to Nadya, another girl unable to sleep: "Please understand that if your mother and grandmother do nothing, it means that others are working for them, that they are usurping someone else's life. Do you think this is decent? Isn't there something wrong? . . . Dear, sweet Nadya, go away! Show them that you are sick of this stagnant, gray, sinful life! Prove it to yourself! I swear you won't regret it. You will go away; you will study and let yourself be guided by your fate. As soon as you have taken your life into your own hands, everything will be different. What matters most is to break out of the rut; everything else is unimportant. Now, shall we leave tomorrow?" And Nadya really does go. She leaves her family, her ineffectual fiancé, renounces marriage, and escapes. It is a flight from the shackles of class, from a way of life felt to be out of date, false, and "sinful," which keeps recurring in Chekhov's work, the same flight on which the aged Tolstoy embarked at the last moment.

Some time later when Nadya, the escaped bride, pays a visit to her old home, it seems to her "that everything in the town had grown old and out of date, and was just waiting either for the end or for the beginning of a bright, new life." Sooner or later this new life was bound to come. "The time will come when not a trace will remain of Grandmother's house, where things were arranged in such a way that the four servants had to live in one room in the basement, in filth—one day all this will be forgotten, no one will even remember the house." Indeed, poor Sasha himself has told her: "Not a stone of your town will be left standing, everything will be blown up from its foundations, everything will be changed as though by magic, and huge, magnificent houses . . . with beautiful gardens and fountains will stand here, a new kind of people will live here, and every man will know what he is living for. . . ." This is one of the euphoric visions of the future which Chekhov, who in his heart knew that "life is an insoluble problem," occasionally permitted either himself or one of his characters. These visions have a somewhat feverish quality, suggesting the tender reveries of a consumptive, as when he speaks of the "perhaps imminent day when life will be as bright and joyful as a peaceful Sunday morning." The outlines of his vision of human perfection in the future are vague. It is the picture of a union between beauty and truth based on work. But in his dream of the "huge magnificent houses . . . with beautiful gardens and fountains" that are to rise in place of the dying, outdated town, is there not something of the socialist passion for building with which modern Russia, despite all the horror and the hostility it provokes, impresses the Western world?

Chekhov had no contact whatever with the working class, nor had he studied Marx. Although he wrote about work, he was not, like Gorky, a workers' poet. Yet he expressed his grief over social injustice in sounds that moved the hearts of his people, as in that tragic, magnificent social panorama "Peasants." Here at a religious festival the ikon of the Holy Virgin, "The Giver of Life," is carried round from village to village in a procession. In the midst of the dust and noise a vast crowd of villagers and strangers surges forward to meet the ikon; the people stretch out their hands to it, gaze at it eagerly, weeping: "Patroness! Mother!" "It was as though everyone suddenly realized that there was no void between heaven and earth, that the rich and powerful had not taken possession of everything, that there still existed a refuge from injury, from slavish bondage, from crushing unendurable poverty, from the terrible vodka. . . . Patroness! Mother! But hardly had the thanksgiving service ended and the ikon been carried off, when everything went on in the same old way, and the sounds of coarse drunken voices could be heard again from the tavern."

The compassion and bitterness about everything going on as before is authentic Chekhov, and I would not be surprised if this author's popularity, so spontaneously manifested at his death and funeral in Moscow, were based on such descriptions. This demonstration caused a government newspaper to remark that Anton Pavlovich had probably belonged to the "stormy petrels of the Revolution."

He did not look like a stormy petrel, nor like the moujik-turned-genius Tolstoy, nor like Nietzsche's pale criminal. The photographs show a slender man dressed in the fashion prevailing at the end of the nineteenth century: a starched collar, a pince-nez on a ribbon, short goatee, regular features marked by suffering and friendly melancholy. These features suggest intelligent attention, unassumingness, skepticism, and kindness. It is the face, the deportment of a man who does not make much fuss about himself. And if he already looked upon Tolstoy's teaching as "despotic" and described Dostoevsky's work as "good, but immodest, pretentious," it is easy to imagine how grotesque the arrogance of an empty mind must have appeared to him. Whenever he portrays this type, he is extremely funny. Many decades ago I saw his play *Uncle Vanya* performed in Munich. It is one of his quiet, light-stepping plays that spring entirely from the feeling for a dying, outdated, all but fictitious existence, the world of the landowning class; a play that replaces all dramatic, spectacular effects by the most subtle intensity of lyrical mood—a mood of end and farewell. In it appears a senile celebrity, a caricature of the hero of "A Tedious Tale," an emeritus professor and privy councillor who writes about art without the slightest knowledge of the subject, and who, moreover, tyrannizes the whole house with his sniveling old-age self-pity, his imagined importance, and his gout: a nonentity convinced of his dignity. It is to him that a lady says when kissing him good-by: *"Do get yourself photographed again,* Alexander Vladimirovich!" Throughout my life whenever I've thought of: "Do get yourself photographed again, Alexander Vladimirovich!" I've had to laugh. And when I sometimes feel like saying to this person or that: "Get yourself photographed!" it is Chekhov's doing.

As for him, he did let himself be photographed—when he had to. The portraits do not betray any signs of a tempestuous emotional life; it is as though this man had been too modest even for passion. The story of his life mentions no great infatuation for a woman, and his biographers believe that he, who wrote so brilliantly about love, never experienced erotic ecstasy. In the country at Melikhovo a beautiful, impulsive girl called Lydia Mesinova was a frequent guest; she fell desperately in love with him, and he went so far as to exchange letters with her. But his *lettres d'amour* are said to have been written in an ironical vein and to show a reluctance to express any deep emotion, a result perhaps of his illness. The pretty Lydia herself admitted that he twice turned her down, whereupon she consoled herself with the writer Potapenko, another visitor to Melikhovo and, incidentally, a married man. But if Lydia could make nothing of Chekhov, he knew what to make of the episode, which he wove into his most frequently produced play, *The Seagull.*

Only three years before his death, however, he did marry; a marriage that took place thanks to his happy relationship with the Moscow Art Theatre and his friendship with Stanislavsky, for his bride was the talented actress Olga Knipper. Letters to her in his own hand have survived, and they, too, are most reticent and confined to a playful, ironical tone.

Owing to his marriage, his friendship with Gorky, and his cordial relations with Tolstoy, who spent some time convalescing in a castle near Yalta, these last years in the Crimea, where his consumption obliged him to live, were perhaps the happiest of Chekhov's life. It was also at Yalta that he was visited by the whole cast of the Moscow Art Theatre, which had come there in order to act his plays before him. His election to honorary membership in the literary section of the St. Petersburg Academy of Science gave the sick man a childish pleasure. But two years later, when Gorky's election was annulled on account of his radical opinions, Chekhov, like Korolenko, resigned in protest.

His last story was "Betrothed" (1903), his last play *The Cherry Orchard*. In both works a spirit, facing dissolution with composure and making no fuss even about illness and death, sowed a seed of hope on the very brink of the grave. His life's work, although it laid no claim to the monumental proportions of the epic, nevertheless encompassed the whole of Russia, that vast country's natural landscape forming the background to the appallingly unnatural conditions of its pre-revolutionary era. "The impudence and idleness of the strong, the ignorance and animal submission of the weak, everywhere unbelievable poverty, oppression, degeneracy, alcoholism, hypocrisy, and dishonesty. . . ." Yet the nearer his end approached, the more movingly an inner light of faith in the future flowed round the dark picture, the more fervently the poet's loving eye looked forward to a coming community of human beings, proud, free, and active, to "a new, dignified, and sensible way of life on whose threshold we may already be standing, of whose appearance we occasionally get a glimpse."

"Good-by, my dear, dear Sasha," says Nadya, the "Betrothed," to the dead man who has persuaded her to flee from a false existence. "And before her mind there rose a vision of a new life, wide and free, and this new life, still obscure and full of mystery, called to her and beckoned her." A dying man wrote those lines shortly before his end—and perhaps it was nothing but the mystery of death that was calling and beckoning. Or may we believe that the passionate longing of a poet can actually alter life?

Let me admit that I have written these pages with deep sympathy, stirred by the poetry of my theme. Chekhov's ironical attitude toward fame, the doubts he felt concerning the sense and value of his work, his disbelief in his own greatness contain in themselves the elements of a quiet, modest greatness. "Dissatisfaction with oneself," he said, "is one of the foundation stones of every real talent." Here his very modesty becomes self-affirmative. Rejoice in your dissatisfaction, he is implying, for it proves that you are more worthy than the self-satisfied—possibly even great. None of which diminishes the sincerity of his doubt and self-dissatisfaction. For him work, pursued relentlessly to the end with the awareness that one has no answers to the final questions, while one's conscience pricks one for throwing dust in the eye of the reader, remains a strange obligation in spite of all. It comes to this: One "entertains a forlorn world by telling stories without ever being able to offer it the trace of a saving truth." To poor Katya's question: "What am I to do?" one can but answer: "Upon my honor and conscience, I don't know." Nevertheless, one goes on working, telling stories, giving form to truth, hoping darkly, sometimes almost confidently, that truth and serene form will avail to set free the human spirit and prepare mankind for a better, lovelier, worthier life.

Gogol

XVI

PHILIP RAHV

Gogol as a Modern Instance

In reflecting about Gogol while preparing my remarks for this commemorative occasion I found myself thinking of him first of all as a peculiarly modern instance of the literary artist. This may surprise those who see him entirely in terms of the Russian background, placing him all too securely within a nearly self-sufficient national tradition. There is no denying, to be sure, that the Russian background is of primary importance for the understanding of Gogol's creative course. He crosses the frontiers of language far less easily than writers like Turgenev and Dostoevsky and Tolstoy and Chekhov, whose creations exercise an appeal unconfined by differences of nationality and cultural setting. Gogol's work, with the possible exception of his story "The Overcoat," cannot be said to have become an intimate possession of the Western world; only in the Russian milieu is it an indispensable part of a literary education. But the reason for that is quite simple. Gogol's characters, like Chichikov and Khlestakov, are no less universal than the characters of Tolstoy and Dostoevsky. What hinders us in our appropriation of them is the fact that Gogol is so great a master of style and verbal orchestration that his power to move us is virtually indissoluble from his language.

Another approach to Gogol is by way of his creative psychology, in which one recognises certain traits that recall us to the fate of modern literature. It is above all our sense of the deeply problematic character of this literature that impels us to conceive of Gogol as our contemporary. His creative psychology is so tortuous and obsessive, so given over to moods of self-estrangement and self-loathing, so marked by abrupt turns from levity to despair, that one cannot but see it as a tissue of

From *Image and Idea* by Philip Rahv. Copyright 1949 by Philip Rahv. Reprinted by permission of the publishers, New Directions.

contradictions from top to bottom. These contradictions are at once the secret of his poetic power and the cause of his ruin as a man—his tragic renunciation of the creative life in mid-career and the frightful end that came to him under the stress of a spiritual crisis of a surpassingly primitive and even savage nature. It is easy enough to expatiate on the neurotic components in his make-up, or, to put it more precisely, on the unmistakable pathology of his life-experience. Let us keep in mind, however, that in the case of great artists neuroticism is never in itself a sufficient explanation. For the neuroticism of such artists tends to assume a symbolic meaning, taking on the supra-personal significance of a general state of mind or of a radical change in consciousness. In this sense it becomes possible to relate the discontinuities and discords in Gogol to the problematical character of the modern artist as a type. Gogol's dilemma was that he was incapable of reconciling the meaning of his art with the meaning of his life. This discord, to which the artists of the modern epoch are peculiarly open, was scarcely operative in the classic ages of literature when life and art were not at war with each other but were integrated by common presuppositions and a common faith.

The problem of the separation of art and life has an objective historical import that is not to be grasped if analyzed solely from the standpoint of the artist's personal character and disposition. It is exactly from this point of view that Arnold Hauser discusses the struggles and sufferings of Flaubert. Hauser attributes Flaubert's lack of a direct relationship to life, his dogmatic aestheticism and his turning away with disdain from human existence as a symptom of "the gulf that has opened up in the modern artistic career between the possession of life and the expression of it." Gogol, too, wanted to possess his life in a manner quite incompatible with his expression of it; and there is still another way in which we might link these two novelists in spite of the obvious differences between them. Both are leading protagonists in the extremely complex and perilous passage of European literature from romanticism to realism. Like Flaubert, Gogol is an inverted Romantic trying to resolve the tension between actuality and romance, between the deflation and inflation of life's vital illusions, by the most rigorous application of rhetorical and stylistic force, by exploiting the necromantic properties of language so as to establish some kind of psychic control and a measure of moral poise, however precarious. In wholly different ways both of these literary artists used language as a shield against chaos and as a therapeutic resource; and both were compelled to create prodigious images of negation even as they inwardly yearned to utter the saving, the positive, the loving word. Thus Flaubert, who began as a Romantic, was inclined from the outset to idealize love; yet what he actually wrote is novels about the destructive effects of love and its power to entangle us in fatal illusions. The theme of love was of course closed to Gogol by his prohibitive fear of sexuality, but in his own chosen themes he too was compulsively driven to expose precisely that which he would have liked to portray in glowing colours. Starting from the invulnerably naive premise that it was his task to idealize the feudal-bureaucratic order of imperial Russia and to paint an idyllic picture of the rural squires, what he in fact produced is a picture so grotesquely satiric that it could easily be made to serve as an instrument of social disruption. Flaubert found his ideal enemy in the bourgeois, whom he tirelessly berated, while Gogol, inasmuch as in his time the Russian bourgeois existed as no more than an embryo in the body politic, seized on the government official and on the parasitic landlord as types whom he could paralyze with his satiric virus and then fix forever in the monstrous tableau his imagination constructed. Even Flaubert's statement, *Madame Bovary, c'est moi* has its parallel in Gogol's remark that in laughing at his characters the reader was really laughing at their author, for he had impregnated them with his own looseness and "nastiness."

It is not difficult to recognize in Gogol some of the features of Dostoevsky's underground man, in particular the split between sickly, spiteful vanity on the one hand and aspirations toward truth and goodness on the other. Some Russian scholars have surmised that Dostoevsky had Gogol in mind in his portrayal of Foma Fomich, the buffoon-like protagonist of his long story "The Friend of the Family." Whether this surmise is correct or not, there is indeed something in Foma Fomich's insufferably didactic tone, in his outrageous preaching of virtue and uplift that reminds us irresistibly of Gogol's vainglorious and clownish bombast in that incredible book, *Selected Passages from the Correspondence with Friends,* probably the most implausible work ever produced by a writer of genius.

The truth is that Gogol was quite aware of his own "underground" traits, and he spoke more than once of "the terrible mixture of contradictions" of which his nature was composed. This master of language, the first truly important artist of Russian prose, strove with might and main to overcome what he regarded as the morbid negativism of his relationship to life, a striving pitiful in its futility; for as he himself admitted in "The Author's Confession," his real predilection was "for bringing out the trivialities of life, describing the vulgarity of mediocrity . . . and all those small things which generally remain unobserved." What is missing, however, in this self-analysis of Gogol's is any hint of the astonishing comic sense that enabled him to invest mediocrity and smallness of soul with a superreal quality that ultimately acts to liberate us and restore us to our humanity. The one thing that Gogol failed to believe in is that laughter cures. His conviction of guilt and unworthiness forced him to hold out obstinately against that catharsis of laughter for which his readers are immensely grateful to him.

Gogol was in no sense a cultivated man of letters. He appeared on the literary scene like an utterly unexpected and rude guest after whose departure life at home could never again be the same. It does not matter that the rude guest's performance was not quite understood for what it was, that a critic like Belinsky, for instance, could cite this performance as an overriding example of the writer's assumption of responsibility to society, of his civic consciousness and fidelity to the factually real. What was then chiefly overlooked in Gogol was the fantastic gratuity of his humour and his transcendence of the limited social motive through the unearthly and well-nigh metaphysical pathos of a supreme creation like "The Overcoat." For in truth Baschmatskin, the little copying clerk who is the hero of that story, attains a stature far greater than that of any mere victim of an unjust social system. He is a timeless apparition of humanity *in extremis*, of man homeless not only in his society but in the universe. There is one story in American literature, Melville's "Bartleby the Scrivener," which has a spiritual affinity with "The Overcoat." But it is no more than affinity. Melville's story, for all its profound overtones, lacks the inner coherence, the resonance, and marvellous stylization of Gogol's masterpiece.

But having allowed for the period prejudices of a critic like

Belinsky and discounted the narrowly sociological approach to Gogol, I still cannot accept the aesthetic-modernist reading of his work that we get in Vladimir Nabokov's critical study of him. Brilliantly appreciative as Nabokov is of the grotesque side of Gogol and, indeed, of all that side of him relating to the poetry of the irrational and the spirit of incongruity and mystification, he has no eye whatever for his subject's place in literary history and social and national peculiarities. Nabokov seems to suffer from something like a phobic fear of all interpretive techniques not strictly literary in reference—a fear driving him toward the extremely one-sided emphasis which takes the literary act to be a phenomenon solely "of language and not of ideas." And Nabokov reduces his formalist bias to sheer absurdity when he goes so far as to state that "Gogol's heroes happen to be Russian squires and officials; their imagined surroundings and social conditions are perfectly unimportant." He is equally vehement in denying that Gogol can in any way be characterized as a realist. It is true, of course, that Gogol never deliberately set out to describe his social environment; but the fact is that his subjective method of exaggeration, of caricature and farce, produced an imagery of sloth, ugliness, and self-satisfied inferiority which, if not directly reflective, is none the less fully expressive of the realities of life in Czarist Russia. Moreover, Nabokov ignores the dynamic plebeianism of Gogol's genius. For that is what enabled him to make a radically new selection of material and to assimilate to his medium elements of everyday existence, with their lowlife and vulgar details, heretofore excluded by the aristocratic conventions of literature in Russia as elsewhere. Even if the creatures of his imagination are not so much "real people" as caricatures, he none the less contributed greatly to the development of realism by opening up the lower reaches and underside of life to literary portraiture.

It is impossible to abstract Gogol from his historical moment and to dissociate the necessary and contingent elements of his creative personality so as to arrive at the pure substance of Gogolism. Nabokov's rite of purification converts Gogol into the ghost of his own work. I do not object to Nabokov's Gogol because he bears so little resemblance to the Gogol of Belinsky and Dobroliubov but rather because Nabokov's Gogol is too pure to be true, too literary and abstract to be genuine. The poet who inserted into *Dead Souls* epic apostrophes to Holy Russia—apostrophes infused with messianic hope in which love and despair are inextricably mingled—was not a purist writing in a vein of exclusive subjectivity and dedicated to the tormenting refinements of his solitary dreams. He too, like all of Russia's great writers, suffered with his country and its people.

About the Editor . . .

DONALD DAVIE, sometime Fellow of Trinity College, Dublin, and of Gonville and Caius College, Cambridge, is Professor of Literature at the University of Essex, Colchester, England. He is the author of *Purity of Diction in English Verse, Articulate Energy, The Heyday of Sir Walter Scott,* and *Ezra Pound: Poet as Sculptor,* as well as of several collections of poems.

DATE DUE

AUG 12 '68			
DEC 18 '68			
JAN 25 '71			
MAY 22 '73 FEB 2 5 1981			
GAYLORD			PRINTED IN U.S.A.